Hollywood Through My Eyes

HOLLYWOOD THROUGH MY EYES

The Lives & Loves of a Golden Age Siren

MONICA LEWIS

with Dean Lamanna

CABLE PUBLISHING

HOLLYWOOD THROUGH MY EYES
   The Lives & Loves of a Golden Age Siren

First Edition

Published by:
   Cable Publishing
   14090 E Keinenen Rd
   Brule, WI 54820

   Website: www.cablepublishing.com
   E-mail: nan@cablepublishing.com

Hardcover: ISBN 13: 978-1-934980-88-0
            ISBN 10: 1-934980-88-9

Soft cover: ISBN 13: 978-1-934980-89-7
             ISBN 10: 1-934980-89-7

Library of Congress Control Number: 2010943397

Cover design by Norm Dodge www.nightshore.com

All photos and graphics in this book are from the Monica Lewis Lang Collection
unless otherwise noted.

Research for "Selected Appearances and Works" by Alan Eichler
Permission is given by Chiquita Brands, LLC for use of their trademarked Chiquita Banana images.

Printed in the United States of America

To my family, past and present.
I am, because of you.

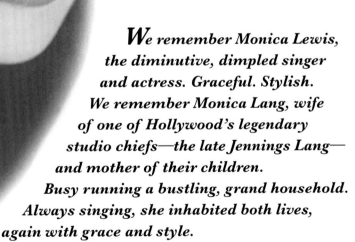

We remember Monica Lewis,
the diminutive, dimpled singer
and actress. Graceful. Stylish.
We remember Monica Lang, wife
of one of Hollywood's legendary
studio chiefs—the late Jennings Lang—
and mother of their children.
Busy running a bustling, grand household.
Always singing, she inhabited both lives,
again with grace and style.
Monica Lewis Lang, still diminutive, still dimpled.
As devoted a grandmother as she is a mother.
As she was a wife. Still a wonderful singer.
And now, an author. Still living life with grace and style.

—Alan & Marilyn Bergman,
award-winning songwriters, *The Way We Were, Yentl*

CONTENTS

Growing up in Chicago with a family of
musicians determined to take the high road,
even when the Great Depression forces us
to follow our dreams east.

Singing on the 1940s New York nightclub
circuit en route to national broadcast and
recording stardom—and helping Ed
Sullivan become a legend along the way.

Hollywood here I come! Romancing Ronald
Reagan and making new celebrity friends
while hustling as a 1950s contract player
for Metro-Goldwyn-Mayer studios.

FOREWORD

The rhythm of life carries many people in and out of one's existence—yet it less commonly introduces us to souls who prove enduringly harmonious. Monica Lewis is, for me, one of those rare individuals. With her, I share not only a close and long-lived friendship but a deep love for the art of making music.

Although Monica and I were born and raised on different continents, our growth into musical professionals—she as a pop singer, I as a pianist and composer—was influenced similarly by American jazz and the mid-20th century Big Band sound. And we both got our most important breaks from virtuoso musician-bandleaders of the time: Benny Goodman and Dizzy Gillespie, respectively. Stateside and abroad, it was an era of great creative inspiration and experimentation clear across the entertainment spectrum, and we immersed ourselves in it, found nourishment in it.

By 1958, when I moved to the United States from my native Buenos Aires, Argentina, Monica was an established nightclub vocalist, recording artist, radio personality, and film and television performer. An unflagging, highly visible patriot, she was respected for her continuous promotional and volunteer work for the military during World War II and the Korean War, and for weekly recorded broadcasts she made for the troops who remained stationed overseas thereafter. She truly symbolized the country at its best.

Monica and I first met through her husband, Jennings Lang, MCA/Universal Studios executive, when I resettled in Los Angeles in the early 1960s. It was my childhood dream to create music for cinema; Monica and Jennings gave me that opportunity. Their belief in me paved the way for my eventual scoring of more than 100 television and film productions—including the themes for popular shows like *Mission: Impossible*, *Mannix*, and *Medical Center*, and hit movies such as *Cool Hand Luke*, *Bullitt*, and one of my personal favorites (conceived by Jennings himself), *Rollercoaster*. If not for the social grace and networking ease of this highly approachable power couple, I never would have enjoyed an extended collaboration with Clint Eastwood, with whom I worked on four of the *Dirty Harry* films.

Beyond her timeless voice and strong mothering instinct, Monica Lewis embodies the extraordinary qualities of loyalty and philanthropy. For decades, she has been passionately involved in the promotion and preservation of all forms of music, supporting such entities as the Los Angeles Philharmonic, L.A. Opera, Young Musicians Foundation, Henry Mancini Institute, and Los Angeles Jazz Society.

My wife Donna and I love Monica dearly. And we are delighted that her fans, old and new, can now enjoy the music of her words. For everyone else, the discovery of an earthy, ever-vibrant Golden Age player—and an adventuresome witness to history—follows.

Photo: Joel Lipton

Lalo Schifrin
Los Angeles, California
Spring 2011

INTRODUCTION

Iwas called "America's Singing Sweetheart"...

Contrary to Hollywood norm, I have never been confined to an institution, nor have I required the services of a detoxification program. I never snorted cocaine, injected heroin, abused prescription drugs, or smiled drunkenly with my crotch exposed while exiting a limousine. Nor have I suffered a nervous breakdown.

A dull, mundane life? No way—not even by today's scandal-ridden, shame-as-fame celebrity standards. Indeed, beyond my poor-yet-loving and musically rich upbringing in Chicago, I have had the great good fortune of having lived several wonderful lives. And as I complete this photographic memoir in my 89th year, I can assert that, despite a few jarring bumps along the road, my journey has been a rollicking one. (Forgive me the chutzpah of wanting it to continue for another 89.)

My career course was set after my family resettled in New York in the 1930s. I became the vocalist for the "King of Swing," Benny Goodman—the greatest band leader of all time—and quickly established myself as one of the country's top pop singers in those days of radio and regal nightclubs.

Along an illustrious route that took me to venues and broadcast programs from New York to Los Angeles (and back again), I welcomed (or cautiously avoided) romances with Ronald Reagan, Frank Sinatra, Kirk Douglas, Ed Sullivan, Herman Wouk, and other exceptionally talented, larger-than-life, history-making men.

I will recall them intimately in these pages.

Like other star-gazing aspirants, I made the most of being busty, leggy, cute, and—especially—melodious. Deploying my God-given attributes as an MGM contract player, the oh-so-a-peeling voice of Chiquita Banana, the "Miss Leg-O-Genic" spokesmodel for Burlington Mills hosiery, and an American pie cover girl for magazines from coast to coast (and beyond), I also delighted the masses and our troops in Korea with uncommon ardor. I pushed as hard as I could in television and the movies, too—knowing that if the going got tough, I could always return to song.

From an insecure kid who could sing her heart out, and did, I matured into a woman of the world—ready to begin yet another adventurous life as Mrs. Jennings Lang. When I married this colorful and innovative (and sometimes controversial) MCA/Universal Studios

executive in 1956, I not only became his partner, but the mother of his children, a supporting player in many of his films, and an indefatigable hostess who, during the alternately tumultuous and terrific 1960s and 1970s, turned her Beverly Hills mansion into a philanthropic playground for the Washington and Hollywood elite.

Tragedy derailed our fabulous lifestyle in the 1980s, forcing me to rally my earliest survival skills and my singing talent in order to hold my family together.

Instilled in me before birth, lyricism has always trumped hardship and cynicism to fuel triumph. And now that many of my performing contemporaries have documented their ups, downs, and run-arounds in show business—or have, sadly, passed on—it's time for perhaps a final, fresh perspective on the Golden Age and subsequent evolution of entertainment. Through *my* eyes.

With Love,

Monica Lewis
Los Angeles, May 2011

Me at age five. It's obvious why Mama always called me her "darling dimple doll."

1 WHEN THE WORLD WAS YOUNG

*F*rom the beginning there was music.

In the spring of 1922, a sweet, promising breeze swirled through the windows of an austere Chicago maternity ward overlooking Lake Michigan.

Jessica Lewis, a lovely woman with a porcelain complexion and huge eyes the hue of heavenly amber, smiled and unfurled her arms to accept her May blossom baby. *"My darling dimple doll—to think I didn't want you,"* she whispered to the infant, hugging her tight to her bosom. *"To think that my family was already complete. I promise, little one, that you will get my best for the rest of my life. You will be my greatest aria."*

Music: We lived it, breathed it and spoke it. My mother Jessie was an opera singer, and my father Leon was a pianist, conductor, and composer. By the time I was born, my sister Bobbe, at age eight, had earned her seat at the family's Steinway grand piano. And my seven-year-old brother Marlo was well on his way to mastering the violin. Our family was about love and music; together they were our bond, our spiritual sustenance.

As a small child in Chicago gathering awareness during the Jazz Age of flappers, bootleg hooch, Charleston dancers, and the Great Depression, I could not have foreseen the wealth of experience, and the experience of wealth, that would characterize my adult years. My family's apartment often went dark because we could not afford the electric bill, and that terrified me to tears. My mother would rush about lighting candles; my father leapt to the piano and segued from Chopin to "Happy Birthday." Bobbe and Marlo would hum and sing. Fear gradually gave way to festivity and, cradled securely in my mother's lap, I saw life as a safe place, a warm place.

My parents called me their favorite lawn ornament.

Our home on Pratt Boulevard in Rogers Park—then an upper-middle-class neighborhood—was the narrow second floor of a three-story, three-family walk-up. Each apartment extended from the front of the building to the back and had a rear porch with stairs leading to the back yard, where there was a fabulous lilac tree and plenty of grass on which to play. In the frigid Midwestern winters, my father would flood the ground to convert it to a skating rink. At the rear alley, I always got excited and waved when the milkman and the iceman arrived in their horse-drawn wagons to deliver their goods.

But I'm getting ahead of myself....

Jessica Lewis was gorgeous, and so indeed was her voice—which was akin to Kiri Te Kanawa's but a bit lighter. Born in 1890 to a tri-lingual schoolteacher mother and a father who was a prominent orator and lawyer in Chicago, she was very artistic and always strived for excellence. She met the acclaimed Italian tenor Enrico Caruso, who was under contract with the Metropolitan Opera in New York, and she became a protégé of Mary Garden, the era's greatest opera star. Before she turned nineteen, she had successfully auditioned for the Chicago Opera Company, whose cast until then had always been Italian. She made her debut in the company's presentation of *La Bohème* and went on to become an opera star herself, performing at the Met in 1920—two years before my birth.

My father, born in Kansas City, was a *wunderkind* who launched his concert career at age five with the help of special booster pedals on the piano.

Chosen as a scholarship pupil at seventeen by the Leschetizky Foundation, created by the Polish piano virtuoso Theodor Leschetizky, Leon relocated to Vienna for three years to study under this maestro.

The Leschetizky Method of piano is evident in the positioning of the musician's hands at a classical concert or jazz performance. The pianist keeps the wrists completely straight, letting the fingers do the movement and thereby getting the most

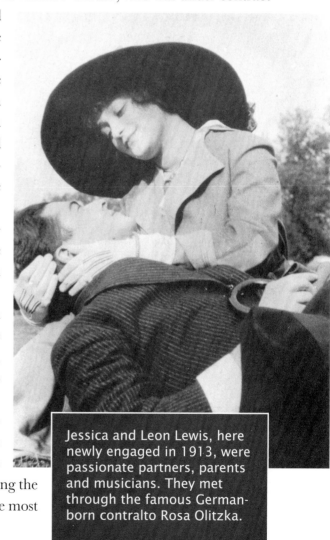

Jessica and Leon Lewis, here newly engaged in 1913, were passionate partners, parents and musicians. They met through the famous German-born contralto Rosa Olitzka.

out of the keyboard, especially through trills and pianissimos. Daddy could tap an ivory so sharply in this way that he could shatter a sugar cube with the same motion. Notwithstanding Vladimir Horowitz, the greatest pianist of the twentieth century, nobody played Chopin better than my father.

My parents were introduced through another great opera singer, Rosa Olitzka, who was also a coach. For weeks, Jessie had seen a photograph of Leon Lewis on Rosa's piano and kept asking her, "Who is he?" Rosa finally explained, "He just got back from Vienna and I'm using him as my accompanist while he's trying to sort out his life."

Who really maneuvered it remains a mystery, but one evening Jessie and Leon ended up appearing for lessons with Rosa at the same time. Rosa said, "Why don't you both go out for tea? I don't want to see either of you tonight. It's my fault—I didn't schedule you right." So out they went, and they fell in love. They were both twenty-three when they got married. Bobbe was born well short of nine months later. And Marlo arrived within twenty-two months of the wedding.

Motherhood clearly interfered with Jessie's career. She believed that once the kids were eight and seven, she would return to work because the Chicago Opera Company wanted her back. Whenever she wasn't with the children, she was at the opera house. Then she got pregnant with me. She was displeased by this development, but it wasn't because she didn't want me. She didn't want *any* baby at that time.

Mama's beauty was matched by her voice. She was a shining star of the Chicago opera world.

To expel her frustration—or, more accurately, the source of it—Jessie took up basketball and engaged in all sorts of strenuous physical things that pregnant women typically avoid. She was warned to halt such activities or risk a miscarriage which, of course, is what she wanted.

When nothing happened, she and Leon somehow found a doctor to perform an abortion—a highly illegal service in those days. They were instructed not to eat and to be at the office at 7:30 in the morning. After sitting there for three hours, Leon, who wasn't completely sold on this course of action, asked the secretary when the doctor was coming. She said, "I don't know, he's in court." With that, he turned to his wife and announced, "We're out of here." They went straight to a Chinese restaurant.

It was while sating their delayed appetites with ginseng tea, pork-fried rice, and egg rolls that they decided to have this third child.

My mother waited until my teens to make this revelation.

My desire to entertain emerged early. By 1925, I was already on a roll.

I was neither shocked nor horrified; I just felt sorry that she had endured such extreme emotions. She bore the guilt because she loved me so much, and she was so grateful that I was okay.

From then on, I always wished her guilt would go away so that she wouldn't be so consumed with my welfare.

Decades later, a friend of mine who's a staunch anti-abortionist said, "Look what you've done in your life, and what you've given to people. You could not have done that if you weren't here." But I'm not of the same philosophy. I understood my mother's hesitance; I did not resent her for wanting to forsake another addition to the family to pursue her career. I've never felt that I was on borrowed time or that my existence is something fortuitous.

If nothing else, it calls to mind that old aphorism, "With two, you get egg roll." In this case, with a couple egg rolls, I got life.

My pre-adolescent years were blissful simplicity. I had Mama, Daddy, my big sister, my older brother, and my best friend Ellen, who lived downstairs.

We never had dogs or cats—just smaller pets, including a bird, aquarium fish, and chameleons in a cage. Bobbe and I shared a cramped room filled with dolls. I loved my dolls, and I loved dressing and naming them, but I absolutely worshipped my sister. As most little ones do when night shadows menace, I would crawl from my safety-sided youth bed into Bobbe's bed, and she would embrace me like a doll of her own.

Marlo had his own room and, aside from his violin and assorted musical instruments, it was a decidedly male space. There was the typical sports paraphernalia—a baseball bat, tennis racket, several footballs, and a prized putter our father had given him. By the time he was fourteen, Marlo would follow Daddy, a certified golf nut, onto the greens.

As the youngest, I had to go to bed much earlier than my siblings. It was, like having to attend a different school, something that kept me apart from my brother and sister, with whom I was anxious to catch up. But there was no way I could get there.

As difficult as the disparity between our ages and life experience was during childhood, time eventually would become a great leveler and place the three of us on equal social footing.

Always bordering on anemic, I was not a robust child, but I was a happy one. I loved everyone and everything (except the liver extracts, cod-liver oil, and iron Mama obliged me to take). I dove into tap and acrobatic lessons, and I began reading very early.

Radio dominated the era. While Sundays were devoted to broadcasts of opera and the New York Philharmonic, other evenings we'd listen to the likes of Ella Fitzgerald and

Frolicking on the shore of Lake Michigan with my big sister Bobbe, 11, and brother Marlo, 10. I so wanted to catch up with them socially.

Big Band music. I absorbed it all while playing with my dolls under the dining room table, and before long I was mimicking Ella, Mama, and whoever else I heard.

At age five I attempted the piano. My fingers were too short to make the full octave, so I usually wound up humming and fidgeting. My father beseeched my mother, "Forget it, Jessica. Just let her sing!"

Yet it was evident even then, in my most nascent warbling, that I was not blessed with Mama's voice, nor was I ever going to have her operatic power and range. Musically, my family considered me hopeless.

Upon returning to America and marrying Jessie, Leon became president of the Chicago Music College. And that, combined with his talent, ultimately led to his becoming a top dog in Chicago's musical scene. From the late 1920s through the early '30s, he was head of CBS Radio's music department—originating from WBBM in the famous Wrigley Building downtown, by the Chicago River. Daddy often would walk the few blocks from our home to Lake Michigan, where he'd pick up a speedboat that took him directly to work.

Daddy made waves beyond broadcast. In those pioneer days of cinema, superstars Mary Pickford, Charles Chaplin, and Douglas Fairbanks created United Artists Motion Picture Company and owned movie theaters all over the country. They appointed my father creative director of the huge United Artists Theatre in Chicago. In those days, there was vaudeville between the film showings, and many great acts performed there. Daddy wrote scores that

Daddy, a student of the Polish piano maestro Theodor Leschetizky, also was a highly accomplished conductor and composer.

were performed live by musicians to accompany the silent movies. I was always so thrilled watching the vaudeville portions: my father's orchestra rose dramatically from the pit, Daddy bowed to the audience, and then he conducted the overture.

Reflecting on Daddy's natural showmanship, it isn't hard to see how his kids would get caught up in the evolution of a business on the brink of introducing variety shows, "talking pictures," and television. It was our destiny.

On a purely social level, Jessie and Leon Lewis brimmed with charisma. They were colorful, charming, and hip as hell for people of their age and time. They were terrific role models for us. I think the greatest job in the world is child-rearing, and if you don't do that right, you may as well do nothing. My parents did it right.

The rules of our household were unique. Sure, the Good Book stuff was there, but our home life wasn't preoccupied with a traditional religious background; foremost, it was about being fair and honest. It was a much freer upbringing than that of other people I knew and would come to know—including my future husband, Jennings Lang, who emerged from a very orthodox home environment.

The Lewis family modus operandi was based upon music—and cleanliness. We were a very immaculate clan. Germs, to my mother, were the devil. Everything got cleaned in scalding water. *Everything.* We were allowed to play in the dirt and to garden and, of course, were expected to wash our hands thoroughly afterward.

But those activities didn't invoke the same sanitary panic as moving through public places. You opened doors with your elbows. If you took public transportation, you had to wash your hands at your destination because you had used coins and turnstiles. You did not place a hand on banisters in public without a handkerchief. And that cloth would be boiled promptly at home.

While most parents of young daughters were wary of would-be suitors, I wasn't allowed to touch an unprotected doorknob until I was of legal age.

Despite Mama's bacterial obsession, we had more than our share of fun. It wasn't like we'd all go on picnics; family recreation tended to vary due to the age spread. On weekends, if he wasn't conducting a band concert, Daddy would treat us to lunch in a nice hotel and then maybe a movie. Or we would go to a museum and then get ice cream. He did special things with my brother. Marlo got to listen to all the bands, and he attended all the rehearsals and learned to play all the instruments from the musicians. My sister and brother were driving when they were fourteen. (Licensing laws were not as restrictive as they are today.)

Like Daddy, Mama was very generous. She had what we used to call "a hole in her pocketbook," because when there was no other money available, she'd reach in there and manage to find a few bucks. She loved presenting gifts, and she always maintained a hospitable home. Even if it was just cream cheese on a piece of bread, everyone was served—and with the most radiantly welcoming smile you can imagine.

Outside the house, my mother never looked less than terrific. Gloves were a necessity, even when going to the grocery store. Her sense of style, of how to design jewelry—there was not anything she attempted that she didn't do super well.

At no time, not even on the leanest days, did we ever live as if we were without funds. Appearances mattered, and whether it was something as simple as displaying two fresh-cut flowers in a vase just inside the front door, beauty, or at least some token of it, was essential.

Lewis family membership had its requirements. You had to be musical, you had to be clean and—above all—you had to look marvelous.

Partly because I was a little kid, and partly because of my parents' over-protectiveness, I wasn't fully aware of current events in those early years of the twentieth century. But some bad news did filter through.

I remember hearing about Leopold and Loeb, two wealthy teenage University of Chicago students who schemed to pull off "the perfect crime" by kidnapping and murdering a fourteen-year-old boy. It was the Jon-Benet Ramsey case of its day, and it would become the grist for many dramatic works.

Me at 11, just before we left the Windy City for New York in 1933. My unflappable exuberance in the face of adversity—in this case, the Great Depression—would serve me well as an adult.

Leon and Jessie Lewis

I also heard my elders talk a lot about the Charles Lindbergh baby kidnapping. But no one sat down and explained that situation to me.

When 1929 rolled in, the crash was unmistakable. People hurled themselves from windows after losing their life savings, and bread lines snaked down the street as the Great Depression tightened its national grip. Although everything around him was falling into shambles, Daddy remained unruffled and pleasant. Sporting an English walking suit adorned with a pearl stick pin and ascot tie, he would hold my little hand confidently as we strolled through the park.

Mama dealt with the crisis in practical ways. She had taught herself how to sew, and she devised a way to recycle the pants cuffs of a man's suit into a lady's waistband. And since men's suits were always of good quality back then, she took some of my father's clothes and made them into tailored suits for my sister and me. I wore mine to school with a sweater or a shirt and felt positively stylish.

The economic climate didn't get panicky until I began to overhear the crying, the arguments, and the fear in my parents' voices as their finances shrank. By 1933, Daddy was losing money dangerously fast. Marlo, then eighteen, was employed as a typesetter after school at a Chicago newspaper; when he returned from a long shift, my mother would shake her head as she soaked his battered fingers and mutter, "No violin hands should be subjected to this work."

And then the worst: CBS had a shakeup and canceled all of its live music programs, leaving Daddy with no job. Because his family always came first, Daddy had to make peace with himself as a consummate artist, supplementing his income to support his growing brood by playing in restaurants and all kinds of commercial venues. His non-judgmental and easy, laid-back manner was an inspiration to me and to others.

Many musicians resorted to selling ties door-to-door. My mother started hocking her jewelry and, at Thanksgiving, she flirted with the butcher to get us a free turkey. Finally, my parents decided they had to move to New York, where Daddy had a brother.

Daddy's last Chicago gig that summer was at the World's Fair, where he was appointed head of the Hollywood Pavilion. Our family spent a lot of time there. I got to meet many movie people and was terribly impressed by Tyrone Power.

Daddy earned a lot of money for that—half of which he used to pay off debts. Afterward, we piled as much as we could into the family's last major possession, our Pierce-Arrow town car (it was the Lincoln Continental of its day), which would carry us to New York City.

Yanking up our roots was hard. Bobbe and Marlo had to leave Northwestern and Chicago universities, where each had a musical scholarship. My mother had to bid farewell to the Chicago opera world as well as her friends. And I had to do whatever I was told. For me, it was the beginning of developing pointer-dog characteristics: I would go on to spend most of my life saying, "Where do I have to be?" and "What time do I have to be there?"

Prior to our departure, Bobbe, by then nineteen, had met a friend of Vladimir Horowitz. The fellow was part of a very rich, respectable family in Toronto, and he had asked her to marry him. At the invitation of his family, we rerouted our trip east through Canada and spent a weekend at their lavish home.

My sister had it in her mind that she was going to save the Lewises by getting hitched to this privileged twentysomething. After our visit, my sister confessed to my parents that she wasn't in love and that there was no way she could do it. They were appalled that she'd even consider wedding a man for whom she had no deep feelings, but they viewed it as a life lesson.

Bobbe's decision was honest and, although we didn't know it then, would prove right for everyone. She felt in her heart that there was still time for us to get back on our feet.

I didn't understand everything that was happening. As we resumed our journey to New York, all I knew and cared about as a wide-eyed eleven-year-old was that my favorite doll was in my lap and the doll buggy was stowed in the trunk. In that moment, my comfort, my childhood world—even in a state of upheaval—was complete.

The Big Apple had bigger plans.

By 1947, after taking Manhattan as a top vocal talent, I was filled with aspiration and expectation— and ready for the world.

2 A KISS TO BUILD A DREAM ON

Rolling into New York in September 1933 was like entering a wonderland. I was totally overwhelmed by Manhattan's lights, sights, heights, and dynamic mix of clamor and glamour. The flashy marquees lining Broadway and Times Square masked any sign of the Great Depression. And I was relieved to see that the two-year-old Empire State Building, stretching skyward boldly and gleaming with promise, bore no ill effects from the cinematic onslaught of King Kong (still images of which had frightened me in a newspaper a few months earlier).

To my young eyes, the city was so dense it resembled one big hotel—only there would be no valet parking, attentive bellhop, or luxury suite awaiting the Lewis family after our wearying trek from the Midwest.

Shortly after we arrived, my father had to sell our car and then borrow money from his brother, who had rented a dark, spare brownstone apartment for us. Mama brightened the space with her magically feminine touch while Dad remained upbeat, but without money, there was no hiding that it was a very unsettled time. Putting college on hold, my sister and brother sought and found work quickly, and I picked up where I had left off in Chicago and enrolled at a New York City public school.

Within a year we moved to a nicer yet still-cramped apartment on West End Avenue. There I shared a room with Bobbe, and Marlo slept on the living room couch. Our family's utilitarian living arrangements were necessary because of the tough economic times, but we stayed close-knit and idealistic.

I wanted to learn as much as I could about the world. Beyond classical, jazz, and Big Band music, our radio was the main conduit for current events. We followed the horrific Dust Bowl conditions in America's Midwest. The desperation of the 1930s gave rise to the gangster era, with reports of daring heists committed by the Ma Barker Gang, Bonnie and Clyde, and John Dillinger followed by news of their demise in dramatic FBI shoot-outs. We also heard about Germany's new leader—a man named Adolph Hitler, who was the only person I ever grew to hate with all my heart.

I was fascinated by it all. But for a small girl, navigating this exciting new city was my primary lesson in worldliness.

My entrance into the huge, public, all-girls Julia Richman High School on the Upper East Side was a big social boost. There, I made friends with the help of five-cent lyric sheets, which were sheet music of each week's top songs nationally. My classmates often didn't know the music, so at lunchtime I would impress them by singing "I've Got You Under My Skin," "Pennies from Heaven," "Sing, Sing, Sing," and the other hits of the time. I became especially popular with the rich kids, who invited me to perform at their parties.

Instinctively, I knew that song would be my path to a better life.

Although my main "job" was to finish high school and grow up, I envied Bobbe and Marlo's ability to contribute to the household income. In 1938, at the age of sixteen, I started looking for employment after school. I visited ad agencies and told them that I was an artist, and I even ventured into the garment district to see if I could model shoes. But I was considered jail bait, and it didn't help that my birth name, May, sounded so youthful and plain.

Enter Arthur Sheekman, the former show business columnist for the *Chicago Sunday Times*. Arthur had moved to Hollywood to write for legendary funnyman Groucho Marx (*Monkey Business*, *Duck Soup*); there, he married actress Gloria Stuart, a Santa Monica, California, native who achieved her greatest fame at age 87 as the elder Rose DeWitt Bukater in the smash 1997 movie *Titanic*. Arthur and my father had a mutual friend—a theater manager in Manhattan, who would admit me to his venue free to watch plays from the standing-room-only section. One evening, Arthur was back there with the manager enjoying the show when he saw me behind a pillar. The three of us chatted briefly at intermission.

Arthur was sweet. "I've never seen a girl who looked like a 'Monica' more than she!" he remarked to the manager, chuckling.

I loved the name. My parents did, too, and they did what had to be done to make it legal. I officially became "Monica Lewis."

About six months before finishing high school, I accelerated my courses because I could not wait to enter the real world. After graduating, to assuage my family, I attended night school at Hunter Women's College, where I took any course that didn't involve working with numbers.

While at Hunter I heard that auditions were being held for the part of the cigarette girl in a Broadway musical called *Johnny Two-by-Four*. To everyone's delight, I successfully auditioned for the $50-a-week gig. There were several very beautiful girls hired as background, one of whom was Betty Joan Perske—later to become very famous on stage, in fashion modeling, and on the silver screen as Lauren Bacall. (Betty married actor Humphrey Bogart just a few years later, in 1945.) She was total dynamite, and with her husky voice, she didn't sound like anyone else. In addition to having a great sense of fun, she loved to dance, so we always jitterbugged between rehearsals. Unfortunately, Betty had the measles for most of the short-lived production.

My own part in the show was brief. But I was finally a working member of the Lewis clan. At the end of each week we all happily pooled our earnings on the dining room table. Our sense of shared responsibility for the family bills and debts was part of the love that held us together in the waning years of the Depression.

Not long after my Broadway mini-debut, during a stroll with my father one afternoon, we ran into an agent he knew—Sol Tepper, a nightclub booker. Dad introduced us and told Sol that I danced and sang. "If you say she sings," Sol said with a big smile, "I bet she sings!" He asked me to audition at his office.

My father helped me obtain a work permit—I was only seventeen—and get some photos. My sister had a boyfriend in the fashion industry who loaned me a black velvet dress adorned with delicate pearls. Bobbe also assisted with my hair, makeup, and false eyelashes. I was a kid trying to pass for thirty-five.

I cinched the audition.

Sol booked me in Baltimore, Philadelphia, and Chicago. Mama accompanied me on all of the dates, knowing that I'd be working some dingy spaces with even dingier characters. I earned $75 a week, from which I had to pay my own transportation.

Between performance dates, I both escaped and fed my show business ambition by catching up with the latest big movies from Hollywood. My turn-of-the-decade favorites included *The Wizard of Oz*, with Judy Garland's to-die-for talent; *Gone with the Wind*, with a swoon-inducing Clark Gable; and *The Grapes of Wrath*, based on John Steinbeck's Depression-set novel and starring a young, ruggedly handsome Henry Fonda. The rapid advances in sound and image, particularly in the use of Technicolor, were breathtaking. And I couldn't resist New York's ornate theaters, which were like giant jewel boxes filled with dreams and magic.

Sharing a happy tune with Mama at our family's Manhattan apartment. It was my way of relaxing as my career moved into high gear.

At home, listening to one of my favorite musical programs, *Your Hit Parade*—a Saturday night countdown of the week's most popular tunes—helped balance the news of ominous things occurring overseas. But the din of World War II soon rose above the music. The surprise attack by Japan at Pearl Harbor on December 7, 1941, shook the country to its very foundation. Until that point, the United States had avoided embroiling itself in the conflict, but the "date that would live in infamy"—as President Franklin Delano Roosevelt indelibly described it—pulled us right in. It was that era's 9/11. Suddenly, boys that I knew were off to war and, much too often, their subsequent deaths.

Against the surreal backdrop of global conflict, I somehow continued to aspire and my budding career began to bloom. I secured a radio job in New York on *The Gloom Dodgers*— a cheerier-than-Cheerios weekday wake-up program that aired five days a week at 6 a.m. on WHN. It was a very popular show with news clips, quips, songs, and a live orchestra. I also appeared Saturdays on WMCA radio, where for five dollars I sang for fifteen minutes accompanied by an elderly church organist who thought he could play jazz. Some pretty strange music wound up on the air.

Despite pulling together odd jobs, I didn't feel legitimate until I snared a ten-week engagement at the most famous and elite of venues, the Stork Club, on East 53rd Street just east of Fifth Avenue. The very symbol of café society, it was the glamorous haunt of numerous celebrities, aristocrats, and nationally syndicated *New York Daily Mirror* gossip columnist Walter Winchell—a one-man TMZ—who fancied the place his personal fiefdom.

At the Stork Club I sang with a Latin band led by Fausto Curbelo, who had worked with Xavier Cugat, a Spanish-born bandleader who helped to popularize Latin music in America. I played claves and stood before a barely-on microphone. Sherman Billingsley, the club's crass former-bootlegger boss, only wanted me for window

A hit with the nightclub set, my early-1940s dimples-and-daisies look helped me land a lucrative run at New York's famed Stork Club.

dressing and felt that if I could be heard above the table chatter, people would pay too much attention to my voice instead of his high-profile clientele.

Sherman's true designs became apparent one night when he asked me into his office. "The only friend you got here is me," he said. He then gestured me to a corner, where there was a laundry basket filled with money. "Look at all this green stuff, honey. Come closer and I'll give you some of it. There's plenty for people I like. And one thing I like for sure is pretty little Jew girls."

Appalled, I fled. But I didn't tell my family about it for fear of losing the work. For the toil and the club owner's torment I earned just $50 a week—but the job was very close to home. So from 7 p.m. until midnight for the rest of my run, I continued to sing. And I avoided being alone with Sherman Billingsley.

The war and our awareness of it were constant. Hitler's forces were taking one country after another in Europe, and news about the atrocities against the Jews was beginning to surface. I could not comprehend the horror of man's inhumanity to man. In New York, there were blackout curtains on the windows and frequent air-raid tests. As I left a rehearsal one day, the air-raid sirens began blaring. I ran for blocks screaming "Mama!" until I reached our home.

During this period, in 1943, I befriended Leonard Feather, one of the world's foremost jazz critics. A total music buff and himself a musician, Leonard wrote for *Metronome* and *DownBeat*—the *Rolling Stone* magazines of the day—and later authored the revered *Encyclopedia of Jazz* before settling in as jazz critic for the *Los Angeles Times*. He was one of my earliest supporters.

Through Leonard I met many people who impacted my life and career. Being embedded in Harlem jazz culture, he introduced me to the elite black musicians in New York, including the legendary Duke Ellington, Billy Strayhorn, and Ellis Larkin. They liked him because he wrote so eloquently of their work. Jazz, after all, was founded on African-American talent— originating in the Southern Blues and New Orleans before going "hot" in Chicago and then spreading to New York and across the country. While racism existed, great music—not skin color—was the unifying force among performers. The jazz community did more for integration than most, even though later civil unrest would show that much, much more needed to be done.

Leonard was always aware of opportunities. When one came up involving the King of Swing, Benny Goodman, he

Benny Goodman, the "King of Swing," did much to help jump-start my career in New York. Here he is pictured in the hit 1943 wartime romantic musical *Stage Door Canteen*.

thought of me immediately. Benny, I knew, was a key figure in both musical and racial integration. A lifelong jazz enthusiast, accomplished arranger, and stellar clarinetist, he broke color barriers by bringing African-American musicians into his band and taking jazz mainstream—rendering it accessible to young white audiences by making it danceable and incorporating song. His innovation was called "swing." And he was known for making careers.

The Benny Goodman Orchestra was at that point not only the most famous band in the world, but in history. Between tours, Benny played Manhattan's Astor Hotel Roof—in the early 1940s, *the* place to see and hear the Big Bands. It had a great dance floor, terrific food, and a huge bandstand. The venue had remote hook-ups for radio, so Benny's performances were heard all over the country.

Leonard called to tell me that Benny's vocalist, Peggy Lee, had eloped with the guitarist, and that the bandleader was scrambling to fill the two-week slot. "Can you be at the Astor Roof at 3 p.m.?" he said. It was a cattle call.

I was very frightened. This was the big time!

The hotel was a madhouse when I arrived. About 300 girls were there to audition—some in bobby socks and saddle shoes, some in stiletto heels and borrowed sexy dresses. Desperation was in the air. Finally it was my turn to hand my audition piece, "It Don't Mean a Thing (If It Ain't Got that Swing,)" to the pianist. My knees were shaking, but I sang.

Clarinet in hand, Benny looked me up and down and said, "Okay, kid. Come back at 7 p.m. You're hired."

I ran home, screaming, "We gotta find something for me to wear!" Everyone flipped and started tearing through closets and drawers. My sister called her best friend, Irene Wouk, who rushed over with a red and white flower-print dress with short puffed sleeves and a tight bodice. For good luck, I added Mama's red velvet cape—the same one she wore to her debut with the Chicago Opera Company.

That evening on the Astor Roof, Benny gave me a song called "Mexico Joe." He played it for me on his clarinet during the break, and ten minutes later all of listening America heard me sing it. It was not one of Benny's better tunes. But that ditty made me Benny Goodman's "girl singer"—the lingo for a female vocalist.

I was in shock. There wasn't time for nerves; I just *did* it.

It helped that Benny thought I was darling, in an avuncular way. He hardly talked to me, except, "Hi, kid. You're doing really well. Keep up the good work." He told my mother, "She sings well and she's cute. You got a winner." At $75 a week, I felt like one!

Amusingly, I think Chicago-born Benny was more interested in my father's depth of music experience and knowledge than in me. Benny wasn't one for chatting casually about jazz or pop songs; he wanted to discuss Schubert and quintet music with someone who knew the history and language. Dad filled that need to a tee.

I was thrilled when Benny asked me to go on tour. But my parents, knowing the pressures and pitfalls of the road, felt I wasn't ready and nixed the idea. I was deeply disappointed.

My remaining an appendage to Benny's orchestra, in hindsight, would have sidetracked my soloist goals. Big Bands were a species on the verge of extinction; except for Doris Day, Helen O'Connell, Dinah Shore, and a few others, most band singers didn't have much visibility after that. In terms of both sound and image, musicians became increasingly rebellious through the next decade, and—with the "King of Rock," Elvis Presley, at the vanguard of those delivering African-American musical influences to ever-widening audiences—rock-and-roll got a foothold. The death knell for the Big Bands was sounded by the British Invasion and its amalgam of rock, beat, and pop music in the early 1960s.

Had my parents not intervened and I was permitted to tour with Benny, I would have become a has-been a'borning.

Behind the music, my tender romantic tendrils had begun to unfurl. My first boyfriends were the bestselling-authors-to-be Herman Wouk and Sidney Sheldon. Since I never finished college, my attraction to creative, intelligent men would suffice as higher education for much of my life.

Through Bobbe's friendship with Irene Wouk, the Lewis clan got to know the entire Wouk family—including younger brother Victor and big brother Herman. After graduating from Columbia University in 1934, Herman wrote for comedian Fred Allen and his radio troupe, the Mighty Allen Art Players, and also scripted radio spots selling United States war bonds. His talent was undeniable. Older by seven years, he first noticed me at sixteen but waited until I was nineteen before beginning an extended courtship.

One evening Herman took me to dinner with his mentor at Columbia, the noted philosopher Irwin Edman, to whom he would later dedicate his debut novel *Aurora Dawn*. It was, at best, an awkward social call as I struggled to hold my own between these two formidable intellects. During the conversation I asked basic questions: "Where is that?" "What does that mean?" "Can you explain that again?" I wanted to learn and thought I was being polite.

The fact was that I still had the inquisitiveness of a little girl. In performance, I was practiced at *playing* an adult; I looked sophisticated in a fancy gown and hairdo, striking a provocative pose. But following my act I would put my hair in pigtails, get back into flats, and my father or brother would take me home.

After leaving the restaurant, Herman blasted me for not having just sat quietly and posed as an Edman disciple. "How dare you try to voice your views!" he said, his hands white on the steering wheel as he branded my behavior an effrontery.

I steamed. As we crossed the George Washington Bridge, I plucked from my purse a collectible silver dollar he had given me. I said, "Herman, watch."

I pitched the coin into the Hudson River.

Future bestselling author Herman Wouk was my first suitor. Our families were close, but he and I were miles apart in terms of education and ideas of fun.

18

Whether appearing as sweet-and-fizzy as soda pop or as an adult flirtatiously sipping it, I transformed myself into whatever my work demanded. In August 1944, "America's Favorite Nickel's Worth," Pepsi-Cola, paid me $200 to perform half of a promotional jingle duet called "Make it Pepsi-Cola for Two," plus pose for some print publicity (opposite). My effervescent stint as the summer replacement for the famously elegant supper-club chanteuse (and early Liberace inspiration) Hildegarde on NBC Radio's hit musical quiz show *Beat the Band* helped land me the ad job.

PRESSING DISCS FOR VICTORY

Victory Discs, known popularly as "V-Discs," were oversized phonograph records of unbreakable vinyl distributed to thousands of U.S. military personnel throughout the world between 1943 and 1949. Destined to become collectibles, the bulky records delivered America's best musical voices, movie soundtracks, radio broadcasts, and bands.

I made V-Disc recordings in my spare time during my run on the hit national radio program *Music that Satisfies* and continued to do them for several years.

Not surprisingly, this risqué V-Disc promotional image devised by CBS publicity was a big hit with servicemen. It also infuriated my ex-boyfriend Herman Wouk, who was a Navy man at sea when it appeared widely in *Stars and Stripes*, the independent daily newspaper for the U.S. Armed Forces. Herman wrote me the most scathing letter—as only a writer could write—stating that he was "shocked" and "appalled" that I had "sunk to this level." (For the "record," I was in a strapless bathing suit behind the big circular prop.)

His eyes flared. "Why did you do that?!"

"Because I want you to understand," I said, closing my purse with a snap. "I'm not afraid of being poor because I know I will always make a dollar. I'm not afraid of asking questions because I have no illusions that I will ever have a Ph.D. or teach at Columbia, or be that philosopher, or you. I will not be intimidated."

Herman dropped me off at home, livid. I'm not sure how he ultimately felt about what I had said. After a while we talked and I saw him again—casually.

We were never intimate. But after Herman joined the Navy and began writing books, our relationship did make its way into his Pulitzer Prize-winning 1951 novel *The Caine Mutiny*. He used my early music business experience to flesh out the character of a nightclub singer, stage-named May Wynn, who was the protagonist's love interest. (In an ironic, only-in-Hollywood twist, Donna Lee Hickey, who played "my" role in the 1954 film adaptation, legally adopted "May Wynn" as her own stage name—unknowingly taking my birth name full circle!) Herman's own military service, of course, also was the foundation of his blockbuster 1970s World War II novels *The Winds of War* and *War and Remembrance*.

Unlike Herman Wouk, Sidney Sheldon, whom I met while he was writing training films for the Armed Forces in New York, would become a comfortable lifelong friend. While Herman was serious and searching for greater meaning, Sidney was funny and always analyzing behavior. Sidney's powerful gift for observation led to his mastery of every genre, from Oscar-winning screenplays (*The Bachelor and the Bobby-Soxer*) and Tony Award-winning musicals (*Redhead*) to Emmy-winning sitcoms (*I Dream of Jeannie*) and bestselling novels (*The Other Side of Midnight*, *Master of the Game*). He loved my determination—a trait displayed by most of his female characters.

I do not know which man was more passionate; I wasn't ready for either of them. (It didn't help that Mama always reminded, "Don't get pregnant, for God's sake!") I was, however, sure that both men would succeed professionally. With optimism resurgent in the Depression's wake, all of us felt we would flourish.

The prestige of my Benny Goodman experience added a new gloss to my radio jobs, and I used it to score other gigs. I found myself singing on programs featuring orchestral maestros of swing like Morton Gould, Raymond Scott, and Ray Bloch.

In September 1944, I made a guest appearance with Guy Lombardo and His Royal Canadians on Guy's Saturday evening radio show *Musical Autographs*—broadcast with a live audience from the Roosevelt Hotel, where the band enjoyed a long-term residency. You'd think it would have been a kick for me, since I had grown up hearing the Ontario native's band play "Good Night, Sweetheart" every New Year's Eve and watching my parents dance to it. Not to mention that most of America had come to embrace Guy for his rendition of "Auld Lang Syne"—a Times Square broadcast tradition every January 1st.

The problem was, Guy was so square. His beat was too accurate; it just didn't swing.

Guy Lombardo and I became acquainted on his radio show in 1944, and together at Decca Records a few years later we recorded several songs, including "Let's Be Sweethearts Again" and "Don't Call It Love." Personally, he was gracious; musically, I thought this New Year's Eve fixture was the ultimate Times "Square."

Older people liked it a lot, but for my taste it was too simplistic.

Guy, along with other major talents like the Andrews Sisters and Bing Crosby, was a mainstay at the Decca record label—one of the biggest music producers of the era. He and his brother Carmen, who ran the band, were very nice as well as generous in their promotion of me. But I'll never forget the hideous headache I got when I first walked in and heard the opening bars of Guy's music.

A few weeks later I got a surprise call from CBS. It was planning a new radio program called *Music that Satisfies*, to be sponsored by Chesterfield Cigarettes and broadcast nationally. My friend (and future Radio Hall of Fame inductee) Martin Block, New York's top disc jockey with a closed-studio show called *Make Believe Ballroom*, would be emcee. Martin took an air-check tape from one of my five-buck WMCA radio broadcasts to Chesterfield's advertising honchos. They decided I was the perfect co-host and handed me a thirty-nine week contract. I was elated! It was my big national break.

Music that Satisfies and CBS gave me enormous publicity. My petite, five-foot, newly red-haired visage traveled from coast to coast on magazines, newspapers, songbooks, and Sunday supplements. In the middle of it all, I happily participated in special benefits for charities and orphanages as well as the on-going war-bond drive. Every performer was asked to volunteer for the latter; among many appearances for the cause, I sang at a rally on Governor's Island and stood tirelessly in the center of Times Square, directing people to the sales booth.

And then in April 1945, while we were rehearsing *Music that Satisfies*, the news broke that President Roosevelt had died from a cerebral hemorrhage. Nobody really knew how sick Roosevelt had been; most didn't know that he could not even stand. It was a big shock, and our broadcast was preempted by the coverage. The band and I hung out in the studio and cried.

It was an incredibly sad time. But for me it also was an awesomely busy, exciting one. I was becoming a household word.

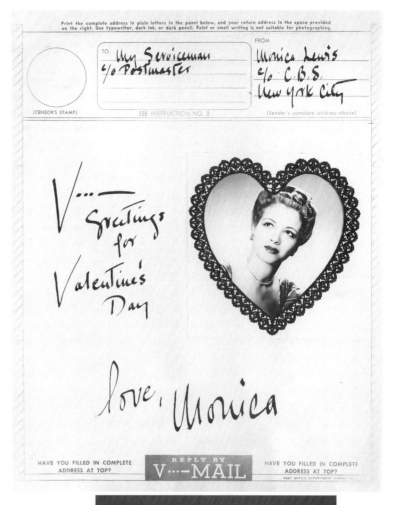

In February 1945, CBS publicity generated morale-boosting Valentine's Day greetings for Americans serving in World War II by displaying my image on a military-regulation Victory Mail form. Known simply as "V-Mail," these messages were transferred to microfilm to help expedite mail delivery to troops overseas.

Harry S. Truman had been the U.S. Vice-president for less than three months when the passing of FDR forced him to occupy the White House. In early August 1945, he decided to move World War II toward a close by dropping atomic bombs on the Japanese cities of Hiroshima and Nagasaki. The resulting toll and images were devastating, and I found it

Making MUSIC THAT SATISFIES

Launched by CBS Radio in October 1944 and sponsored by Chesterfield Cigarettes, *Music that Satisfies* was my first regular job with a major network. The live program featured new musical numbers voted upon by a panel of judges, plus special singing guests like Frank Sinatra, Perry Como, and Eddie Cantor as well as great bandleaders such as Tommy Dorsey.

A 27-year-old baritone named Johnnie Johnston and I co-hosted Tuesdays through Thursdays, doing one show at 7:15 p.m. and the same show again exactly three hours later for the West Coast. Paul Baron conducted the CBS Orchestra and we'd roll out the songs and predict the hits. It was one of radio's most popular broadcasts.

Along with this success came my first competitive challenge from a male colleague. Johnnie, who had seven years of on-air seniority, often hogged the microphone when we'd do a duet. One time, when we were to perform a Chesterfield promotional jingle called "A Story of Two Cigarettes," he was, in keeping with the theme, a complete butthead and an utter pain in the "ash"—whining that he wanted to sing it solo. He always tried to get his way.

But I got something better: a national-level career boost. And at a then-whopping $250 weekly, I was to that point probably the best-paid singing "cigarette girl" ever!

With CBS Orchestra conductor Paul Baron at the keys, I predated Michelle Pfeiffer's famous piano-top moves in *The Fabulous Baker Boys* by forty-five years. Paul was great, but my co-host, Johnnie Johnston (center), was less than fabulous.

Sharing a menu between broadcasts with film actor Michael O'Shea (*Lady of Burlesque*, *Jack London*) and singer Perry Como. While Frank Sinatra was the master at turning song into story, Perry was the best at singing purely for song.

JUNE 1945

Frank and I during his co-hosting stint on *Music that Satisfies*. I will always remember him as he was in the 1940s—a cute, skinny guy with wavy hair, a killer grin, truly blue eyes...and *that voice*.

FRANK SINATRA

I first met the beloved entertainer alternately known as "Ol' Blue Eyes" and "Chairman of the Board" in early 1945, when he stood in as my co-host on *Music that Satisfies*. Frank, who had gone solo in 1942 after getting his break with Big Band leader Tommy Dorsey, was a consummate musician, and his appreciation of a lyric was unlike anything before or since in American music. Of course, he also was young, fun, and hot. But Frank developed his lifelong, worldwide following with his *talent*. And virtually to the end of the century, from popular songs ("In the Wee Small Hours," "My Way") to powerful movie roles (*From Here to Eternity*, *Suddenly*), he redefined the word.

Between my two coastal radio broadcasts of *Music that Satisfies* one evening, I was relaxing by myself at Lindy's—a deli on Broadway that catered to the show business crowd—when my server alerted me to a call in the restaurant's phone booth. I went to the booth and picked up the handset.

"Hello?"

"Hi, it's Frank Sinatra."

I figured that Frank had a spy in the restaurant. "Well, hi," I said.

"Are you going to have dinner? What about afterward?"

With Frank's wife and his womanizing reputation in mind, I remained unspecific. "I won't be staying here long."

"Will you have dinner with me?"

"I can't," I said curtly. "I have other plans."

"What about tomorrow night? I'll send a car for you."

I decided to stop it right there. "Frank," I said, "I love you and think you're just about the best thing in the world. I'm very flattered. But I can't go out with you."

"And pray tell why not?" he said, stunned.

"It's real simple," I explained. "You're married. You're just plain, old-fashioned Catholic married."

It was quiet on his end. Then: "You're serious."

"Yes."

"Well," he said, after another lengthy silence. "I can't fight that."

"No, you can't," I said, taking a deep breath. "I wish your marriage well. If it is ever a different situation, we'll be sure to have dinner. I know we'll always be friends."

"Okay, kiddo," he said. "Sing pretty tonight."

Was this conversation significant? Perhaps not. But I was impressed that Frank, with his colossal ego, didn't get nasty. Some have called him beneficent; others, ruthless. I can speak only from my experience: Frank was complex and, like anyone, capable of mood swings. But in whatever stage of life we found ourselves, he was always interested in what I was doing. He was generous, kind, and respectful to me whenever and wherever I encountered him.

The protective role Frank assumed in my life freed us to be friends. And while that may not have been *his* way, I am glad it was *our* way. It was a relationship more valuable to me than any short-lived liaison could have been.

28

Thanks to the aggressive public relations department at CBS, I graced the covers of many trade magazines and song-books (which contained hit song lyrics) during the first half of 1945. The estimable jazz critic Leonard Feather, a good friend, wrote for *DownBeat*.

hard to accept that this was the only way we could save the rest of the planet. It was a reality-altering chain of events.

Just a few weeks earlier, my personal world had been rocked as well.

Leonard Feather introduced me to a young man named Bob Thiele, an heir to the Baker's Chocolate fortune. Bob was in the National Guard at the time but wanted to become a record producer. He had been a jazz buff since a kid, following swing players like other boys chased fire trucks. By his late teens he was making records in his parents' Forest Hills, Long Island, home. He also worked as a disc jockey at WHN in New York.

Bob was boyishly cute, with ashy-blond hair, a square jaw, and blue-gray eyes. We were both twenty-three, and being young and foolish, we both very much wanted to get married. On July 27, 1945, we tied the knot at the Waldorf-Astoria Hotel. It was quite a summer; I was working like crazy, and film and radio star Bob Hope had just taken notice of me, requesting a set of my photos.

Almost from the beginning, my new husband's possessiveness created tension in our marriage. But we managed to make a beautiful "baby"—an independent jazz record label called Signature. We earned a healthy respect within an industry dominated by four wax pressers: Columbia, Victor, Decca, and Capitol.

Signature recorded talent both new and established, including my dear friend Hazel Scott, a marvelous African-American singer, pianist, and Carnegie Hall semi-regular who did an album of classics and jazz for us. In addition to bankable voices like Hazel's and my own, the label benefited from my ability to identify songs with mainstream potential. My rendition of "Put the Blame on Mame" was a national hit. And a little-known piece I had introduced through the label, "I Have But One Heart," not only was a smash for Signature but went through the roof when Vic Damone and Frank Sinatra each recorded it a year later. My performances of "Day by Day" and "The Christmas Song" were among those that had disc jockeys naming me one of the top ten girl singers in nationwide polls.

Although my marriage was imperfect, Signature was an unqualified success—and I had achieved recording stardom.

With my publicity increasing apace, I continued to push myself professionally. I joined a radio program called *Milkman's Matinee* on WNEW, the New York City area's leading station. It ran from midnight to 6 a.m. with disc jockey Art Ford. I'd sing a corny opening theme song: "When the world should all be sleeping, and the memory comes creeping, it's

THE MONICA LEWIS FAN CLUB

Almost everyone who was anyone had a fan club. I established my own—replete with membership card, official photo, and member deeds—in the summer of 1945. It was comprised mainly of servicemen and teenage girls.

MONICA LEWIS
FAN CLUB
MEMBERSHIP CARD
1945

John Doe
MEMBER

Monica Lewis

Member Deeds...

1. Because Monica is always dressed neatly, fresh, and clean, I will follow her example.

2. Because Monica is always courteous, kind, thoughtful, and helpful to others, I will do likewise.

3. Because Monica is always on time for work, I will go to school or work on time.

4. Because Monica is all out for victory, I will do more for the war effort so that America may have a victory.

5. Because Monica is all out for racial and religious tolerance, I, too, will be truly American, having no prejudices.

no cabaret; it's the *Milkman's Matinee.*" Then I'd say, "Okay, Art Ford, take it away!" And Art would respond, "Thank you, Monica Lewis—and good morning world!" The gig was great because Art played the heck out of my Signature records.

I enjoyed further promotion, with backing from my recording partner Ray Bloch and his orchestra, on my own weekly radio show: *Monica Makes Music.* I turned on the chat, charm, and cheer for this short-lived program, which was sponsored by Signature and featured a string of talented musicians.

All of this work and attention culminated in September 1946, when I made my headline solo debut at the Blue Angel—Manhattan's "*chic*est" club. The great jazz pianist Ellis Larkin, who had become a close friend, was my accompanist. Frank Sinatra and the crème de la crème of New York society packed the intimate space on opening night. I sang my damnedest in a suitably angelic white lace blouse and black skirt, with a ribbon in my hair.

This 1946 Signature Records photograph taken by James J. Kriegsmann adorned the cover of *Band Leader and Record Review.* Kriegsmann, whose studio was in Times Square, was my favorite portraitist. Besides his fantastic eye, he was also noted for welcoming African-American performers as clientele in an era when many studios did not—and being of the jazz world, I admired that.

The crowd loved me, and Frank's presence guaranteed widespread, enthusiastic press exposure. The Blue Angel held me over five weeks beyond my originally scheduled two.

In early January 1947, I decided that my marriage to Bob Thiele wasn't working. Bob, jealous of virtually any man that came near me, spent his time drinking and spying. And I spent mine thinking and crying. We just weren't ready for the adult commitment called marriage.

Since I couldn't get a divorce in New York, where you had to prove adultery, my parents called my uncle, Sidney Lewis—a tenacious Chicago lawyer who had done bond work for

Signature's success cemented my status as a trade publication cover girl.

John Dillinger. He said, "Fly Monica over. I'll help her get out of it."

Per Chicago law at the time, if somebody hit you on two different occasions in front of a witness, it was grounds for divorce. So my uncle coached me and two "witnesses" whom I had never seen in my life—and never would again. I got Bob to agree to this fiction by telling him I'd go on to Las Vegas to dissolve our marriage if he resisted.

The divorce proceeding unfolded like a little drama, and it was hysterical. The first "witness" who took the

BOB HOPE

During my sensational fall 1946 solo run at the Blue Angel nightclub in Manhattan, I received a surprise telegram from Bob Hope—the comic genius who had risen to fame through vaudeville, Broadway, radio, and movies (and would continue to soar in television). Bob, whose radio show normally originated from Los Angeles, invited me to appear on a one-shot live October broadcast from New York. As a major fan, I was hugely flattered, and he was just lovely toward me.

After I met with Bob to discuss what he wanted musically, he told me to report to his music director, Desi Arnaz. Desi, who by this time had been married to Lucille Ball for six years, was fabulously talented and a real innovator. At the start of the next decade, he and Lucy would pioneer the television situation comedy with *I Love Lucy* and form Desilu, one of the medium's biggest production entities. It was a privilege to witness the easy rapport between Bob and Desi, and how they laughed at each other's jokes—enjoying their success yet unaware that they were legends in the making.

Bob Hope, of course, was more than an indefatigable showman. He was a real humanitarian who, from World War II through the Persian Gulf War forty-five years later, entertained the troops overseas by way of the United Service Organizations (USO). (The U.S. Congress declared him an honorary armed forces veteran in 1996.) Bob confided to me that he kept busy constantly because—despite his evident love of golf—he was uncomfortable with leisure and silence. He was most at home in the spotlight, where he brought boundless joy and laughter to the world.

Me with the "King of Comedy" and his zany sidekick, Jerry Colonna, just before airtime in New York. Bob's talent radar had picked up my "Put the Blame on Mame" rendition and performance publicity shot.

GENERATING BUZZ FOR GENERAL ELECTRIC

Since mid-1944, I had done print and radio advertising campaigns for several major national advertisers. I scored one of my biggest promotional contracts in 1946. My then-husband Bob Thiele, the founder of Signature Records, inked a distribution deal for the label with General Electric, which in turn hired me to front its radio products. It was a mutually beneficial arrangement, and I did my best to bring sex appeal to self-charging portable radios and radio tubes. GE kept me at it for a year—and my face inspired the company to produce some fun and classy ads for magazines including *Collier's*, *Life*, *Look* and *The Saturday Evening Post*.

MONICA LEWIS,
popular star of radio and
Signature Records.

I appeared for GE at the Radio Parts Show in my hometown of Chicago in early 1947. Company sales manager Russell Metzner provided an assist as I signed promotional posters for the conventioneers.

New 3-way Personal Radio

You'd never dream any 3-way portable could be so light, so compact, and still have such full tone, such ample power. You'll want this new G-E Personal Radio with you everywhere. At home, you play it on house current—either a-c or d-c. Away, you use its thrifty, long-life batteries. Handy as a wrist-watch—smart as a Hollywood fashion—remarkably low-priced. An ideal gift—a wonderful radio to own.

GENERAL ELECTRIC

LEADER IN RADIO, TELEVISION AND ELECTRONICS
General Electric Company, Bridgeport, Conn.

natural color tone radios

Lovely automatic radio-phonograph. Mahogany veneered 18th Century period cabinet. Natural color tone from radio, and from records played by the amazing G-E Electronic Reproducer. Model 326.

General Electric's finest table radio-phonograph—with automatic record changer. Glorious natural color tone radio. Amazing G-E Electronic Reproducer reveals new beauty even in familiar records. Model 304.

Superb FM-AM automatic radio-phonograph—You enjoy natural color tone from both radio and records. FM, standard, and short-wave radio. G-E Electronic Reproducer. 9 tubes plus rectifier. See Model 417.

chair said he was in a restaurant and saw Bob slap me. The judge asked me if this had occurred. I said, "Yes." Then the other "witness" stepped up and said, "I was walking out of a phone booth and saw them having an argument—and he slapped her!" The judge said, "Did that happen, Miss. Lewis?" I responded solemnly, "Yes, it did."

The judge studied me. "Is everything true?"

I straightened up a bit. "Yes, Your Honor."

Hardly missing a formal beat, the judge leaned forward slightly. "What are you doing January 16th?"

"I don't know," I answered. "Why?"

"We're having a convention, and we'd love you to be our guest artist."

My posture relaxed. "I'll check my calendar," I said, stifling a giggle. "But I'd be honored, Your Honor."

He promptly granted the dissolution. I was free.

My divorce from Bob Thiele was the true beginning of my maturity. I had finally experienced genuine emotional pain. My recognition of the difference between my family, which talked only of music and harmony and humanity, and the realities of the world beyond it thickened my skin.

Fortunately, my professionalism remained intact. Ongoing work included a fifty-two-week contract with *The Jan August Show*, a long-running Saturday evening radio program on the Mutual Network sponsored by the Revere Camera Company. Jan August was hot at the time— "a maestro," as one writer put it, "of the 88 keys." I didn't think he was a bad pianist. But he had no feel for jazz; it was all florid, with lots of arpeggios. The job was a paycheck to me.

Leaving Signature was, of course, part and parcel of the divorce, but the label continued to benefit from sales of my music (to the tune of more than one million of my records sold by the end of 1948!). After *Billboard* magazine named me one of the "10 All-Around Popular Female Vocalists" for the twelve months between June 1946 and June 1947, Decca Records snapped me up and gave me a whole new launch. Over the course of my two years with the company I completed more than seventy-five recordings.

My Decca debut platter, "The Gentleman is a Dope"—my personal swan song to Bob Thiele—sold briskly, and I landed several Top 10 hits for the label. "A Tree in the Meadow," which I performed with the up-and-coming pop quartet, The Ames Brothers, was named the country's number-one jukebox single by *Variety*. Margaret Whiting also did a cover of this English tune, but it was I who discovered and imported it.

Between my work for Decca and a potassium-rich deal I inked with United Fruit Company to pitch its Chiquita Banana brand, the reach and recognition of my name and voice achieved critical mass. A "top banana" never went unnoticed by the talent agencies: Music Corporation of America, better known as MCA—the most powerful agency and the archrival of William Morris—called me and said, "You've got a good act. We think you should

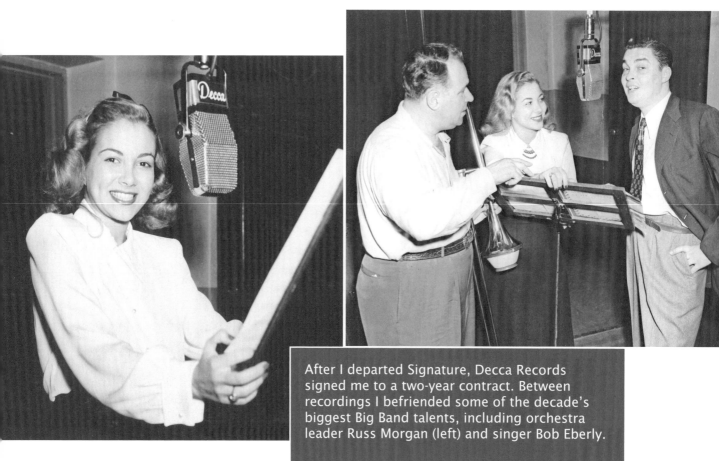

After I departed Signature, Decca Records signed me to a two-year contract. Between recordings I befriended some of the decade's biggest Big Band talents, including orchestra leader Russ Morgan (left) and singer Bob Eberly.

hit the road and hype your records." My father was an early client of the company when he had a band in Chicago; MCA founder Jules Stein himself had signed him. And now the timing for me was perfect. It represented not only my shift from growing up to surviving, but also my new attitude: *Get what you can.*

Unlike today's more managerial-style agencies, MCA allowed hardly a minute of its clients' time wasted—making the absolute most of its ten-percent agent commission. And they kept me working, baby! I was booked in nightclubs and hotel ballrooms across much of America. Working fifty weeks a year, my life consisted of cutting records, going on tour, cutting records, and going on tour. I sang, rehearsed, and garnered headlines wherever I appeared.

As for myself, I was getting a lot of the things I wanted—especially the latest fashions. Entertainers, naturally, were expected to dress to the nines. I kept two sets of wardrobes, including one containing off-the-shoulder décolleté gowns, often trimmed with sequins or bugle beads, for nightclub engagements.

I had the measurements beloved by designers—and the media. In the realm of music, few other top female singers photographed as well. And the cameras always followed. I not only accepted this paparazzi "sentence" with grace, I enjoyed it.

Even as my professional trajectory soared, the emotional contrails of my failed marriage lingered. My realization that every aspect of my career was controlled by men—the bookers, the record producers, the musicians—made me totally distrust the opposite sex. (And don't even get me started on Joseph McCarthy, the Red Scare-baiting Wisconsin Republican senator whose rabid witch hunt for Communist sympathizers ruined many, including friends of mine in the entertainment business.) My behavior with guys became pretty erratic as a result.

Perhaps it wasn't a coincidence that some of my more suggestive tunes, like "I'm Gonna Be a Bad Girl," "Midnight Masquerade," and "A Thousand and One Nights,"

My post-divorce rebound included a fling with progressive jazz bandleader Stan Kenton.

At a *Billboard* magazine-sponsored gathering of top musicians in Chicago (left to right): Stan Kenton, Maria (Mrs. Nat) Cole, Sarah Vaughan, me, and Nat King Cole.

were becoming jukebox standards. At the time I felt that most men only wanted one thing. And I had decided that I wanted it from *them*.

I was using sex for all the wrong reasons. Clearly, I needed reaffirmation, but the men I bedded had to have something else going on. Mostly, they had to make me laugh instead of cry. To ensure I wouldn't be hurt, I was allowing no one to claim my soul.

My higher profile at Decca Records renewed interest in my older hit tunes as well as buoyed my new ones—keeping me prominent on the covers of songbooks and trade magazines.

Still, there were guys who tested me with an old ploy: They'd tell me what was wrong with me so that I would feel vulnerable enough to ask, "Well, how can I do this right?" Stan Kenton, an incredible Big Band leader I had first met when he was a guest on *Monica Makes Music*, was an example.

Tall and imposing, Stan was complicated and interesting as both a musician and a man. Like Glenn Miller, he created a sound that some considered radical. Describing his work as "progressive jazz," his arrangements were sensational—closer to concert orchestrations than to anything danceable—but his cacophony of heavy brass was not an ideal backdrop for my melodic vocals. He could only use singers who sang in a metallic staccato fashion like Anita O'Day and June Christy, the latter of whom performed with Stan the million-selling song "Tampico."

Stan definitely made his mark on music. He had less success with me. He started out by calling, and I agreed to a couple dates. "You get me so mad," he blurted to me after a pause in our conversation over dinner one evening. "You should be dreaming of being the greatest pop singer, but all you want to be is a big star. Forget this nonsense! Come away and marry me—we'll make beautiful music together."

I laughed and said no. I knew the cacophony would kill me.

Now, Stan was a good guy. Charming and dynamic, he had a strong intellect and knew about a lot more than just music. But he had already exceeded my reduced attention span. He was no longer interesting because all he wanted to talk about was me. And I definitely wasn't looking for another husband.

Stan Kenton accompanied me on piano at many benefits, and we became good friends despite my need to shunt his advances. Romantically, it was a waste of time—as were my untold number of other post-divorce dalliances.

It didn't matter to me then. I was sure I would live forever.

"Ladies and gentlemen, we have a reeelly big *shewww....*"

The oft-mocked final word of television host Ed Sullivan's trademark program introduction was, of course, "show." Ed's distinctive intonation made it sound like something you'd lace on your foot—apropos, because he wore the advent of TV historically well.

Without me, he'd never have gotten there.

Although all-electronic television had been around in some form in the U.S. since at least 1939, when FDR talked about the "experimental" technology at the New York World's Fair, it was slow to develop due to the material and technical demands of World War II. By 1948, when the large, squat, heavy box with the small round screen had begun its inexorable march across the land, all three of the major broadcasting networks—the Columbia Broadcasting System (CBS), the National Broadcasting Company (NBC), and the American Broadcasting Company (ABC)—had some kind of TV programming available at different times between 6:00 a.m. and 10:00 p.m.

ED SULLIVAN

Like many of us making a living in the public eye, Ed found himself in an advantageous position as television gained momentum in America in the late 1940s.

Ed Sullivan was a well-known syndicated Manhattan gossip columnist—a rival of Walter Winchell since the mid-1920s, when both were staffers at the tabloid *New York Graphic*. The two writers were a study in opposites: whereas Walter was a slick, flagrantly bullying and nattily dressed talent hound, Ed was an awkward, mildly truculent, and conservatively attired sports editor. Yet Ed lasted well beyond Winchell, Hedda Hopper, Louella Parsons, Earl Wilson and the other gossips. The key to his survival was that he became genuinely star-struck after leaving sports writing for celebrity tattling.

Ed preferred fawning over fomenting. After he caught my solo nightclub debut at the Blue Angel in the fall of 1946, he went out of his way to mention me regularly in "Little Old New York"—his flagship *New York Daily News* column.

One year later, Ed invited me to be the star vocalist for the *Harvest Moon Ball*, the annual variety show he emceed at the Loew's State Theater. The production combined professional acts with the fox-trotting, waltzing, and jitterbugging dance-contest winners. Ventriloquist Paul Winchell (no relation to Walter) and his inimitable "pardner," Jerry Mahoney, filled the comedy slot, and I donned toy guns and a cowboy hat to perform a Western number, "I'm the Howlin'est, Hootin'est Gal in Town." Partly out of gratitude, and partly to help him loosen his straitlaced public image, I folded Ed into my act—dragging him onstage to fasten my fancy beaded holster.

Ed was as gratified as I that the critics were unanimous in their praise of my performance. "Monica Lewis, making her theater [debut]...sold with her rich voice," *Billboard* magazine gushed. "Her encore had the clamoring-for-more audience refusing to accept her beg-off!"

The master of ceremonies, to my surprise, also refused to accept my beg-off. Ed, a married man, was very protective and treated me wonderfully. But he fell in love with me. What I considered an unwanted development would, ironically, lead to his becoming a pioneer in the TV revolution.

Ed was a game accomplice onstage during the 1947 production of the *Harvest Moon Ball*, but I didn't realize he was sweating bullets as he helped me holster-up as the "Howlin'est Hootin'est Gal in Town."

Ed missed being the first big little-screen star by just twelve days: On June 8, 1948, co-median Milton Berle, a buddy of mine who had developed a national following through his own radio show and on the club circuit, introduced NBC's *Texaco Star Theater*. (Eventually renamed *The Milton Berle Show*, its loose TV comedy-variety format was perfected a few years later by Sid Caesar and Imogene Coca's *Your Show of Shows*). But Ed's talent showcase made the biggest impact on the tube by far, launching the world's best acts for a record twenty-three years. There is nothing comparable in the annals of entertainment.

It all began in the fall of 1947. Ed, a *New York Daily News* gossip columnist, tapped me to be the marquee singer for the *Harvest Moon Ball*, his annual variety show at the Loew's State Theater on Broadway. It was a major Manhattan stage appearance and a tremendous score for me, as Ed could have hired Rosemary Clooney, Betty Hutton, Kitty Kallen, or any of the other hot singers. The glitzy venue was also premiering the Anthony Quinn oil-drilling drama *Black Gold*; big-city movie showings in the late 1940s were part of a larger package comprised of a newsreel, a cartoon, the film, and a stage revue. For many singers, including Frank Sinatra, they were a stepping stone from the club set to a general audience—and hopefully to Hollywood.

I earned great reviews and was thrilled with this career boost. Until I realized Ed was putting the make on me.

This was not good. Ed had a reputation in talent circles for having lots of girls. Moreover, he was twice my age, he was an Irish Catholic, and he was married to a Jewish woman named Sylvia with whom he had fathered a daughter.

Oy vey!

Ed was sly, avoiding public overtures. And in private he was cautious. His words changed but the theme never varied: "I'm really drawn to you. We'd make a great pair." He worked every possible angle—sending flowers to my mom, squiring me to chic restaurants "to talk business." The conversation always ran to how his marriage was an "understanding" (read "permissive") one.

For a while Ed's overtures were merely an annoyance outweighed by our professional relationship…until Ed's jealously started to flare. I first witnessed this when my brother picked me up at the Loew's State after the show one night. Ed thought Marlo was a boyfriend and demanded that I identify the handsome guy waving to me from the curb.

"Oh, sure," Ed said, shoving his hands into his pockets after I told him the "stranger" was my brother.

"No, really," I said. "Marlo's in advertising and broadcasting. You ought to talk to him."

Ed sweetened up fast upon hearing this because it was a legitimate suggestion: He was chairing the New York Heart Fund and was seeking help with the campaign. For me, it was an opportunity to deflect Ed's deepening attention, and I seized it. I gave him Marlo's phone number.

I knew my brother had his hands full. By this time he had finished his schooling, held a top advertising position, and was owner-producer of the six-times-weekly celebrity interview radio series *Luncheon at Sardi's*, which was scripted by his wife Mina Bess and was both named for and broadcast from the popular after-premiere eatery in New York's theater district. But

Ed's confidence and enthusiasm—he signed notes to my brother, "Your lovin' cousin..."—were infectious.

Ed knew he couldn't sing, dance, or tell a joke with any flair, so he entrusted himself to Marlo and Mina Bess, who believed polishing Ed's Everyman appeal would enable him to shine—particularly in the new medium of television. They were convinced after helping Ed produce a wildly successfully variety-show fundraiser for the Heart Fund that attracted the biggest names in the business.

"Kiddo," Ed said to my brother, "what's to stop us? If I can deliver the bodies free to every charity that comes along, I can do it for television! We could bring vaudeville back so big nobody will ever remember it died!"

Ed and Marlo's TV brainchild, initially titled *Toast of the Town*, debuted June 20, 1948, at the newly refurbished Maxine Elliot Theatre on West 39th. The live CBS broadcast featured Dean Martin and Jerry Lewis, Richard Rodgers and Oscar Hammerstein...and *me*! Ed's high-profile roster, plus his hiring of Ray Bloch's orchestra as the house band, made headlines. The Emerson Radio & Television Company quickly hitched to the publicity bandwagon as the first sponsor, and the excitement took on a life of its own.

Living up to the hype was a challenge. The broadcast being in black and white (it wasn't until late 1950 that RCA introduced all-electronic color television), I had to have my hair lightened further so that it wouldn't appear too dark. And production techniques were so primitive that there was no such thing as a simple zoom shot. Marlo, never the neophyte, wanted me to sing a ballad in close-up, so he had me kneel on the edge of the stage—the sole camera barely a foot from my nose—and clutch a bouquet to conceal the microphone.

For me, it was an oddly narcissistic stunt. There I was, staring at my own image reflected in a big, unblinking eye as petals brushed my chin and I crooned, "I'm in the Mood for Love." With that kind of intimacy, how could I not be?

Since there was no fade to black, the stage manager had to douse the lights while the crew repositioned the camera for Ed. I almost tripped over the host as I groped my way off stage—not that he would have minded the inadvertent contact. For the guest shot I earned all of $25. But I made it back a thousand times in publicity and in my half dozen or so return appearances.

The show was a smash despite its birdseed budget. Marlo was the program's guiding light because Ed, while hip to dog acts and ventriloquists, was severely culture-challenged. Fortunately, Marlo had the patience of an educator and the ability to make anyone feel better about his or her abilities with a simple embrace. He had an inordinate amount of class and successfully imbued some of that in Ed, who had none.

*M*ARLO *LEWIS AND* THE ED SULLIVAN SHOW

Almost as an afterthought, I introduced my brother Marlo and Ed Sullivan in September 1947 during my appearance in the *Harvest Moon Ball*. Marlo, throughout his twenties, had made the most of his creativity and smarts—rising to the top ranks of Madison Avenue advertising as executive vice president of the Blaine Thompson Agency. He possessed a sweetness and decency that was rare in the media world. Just as remarkable was his devotion to his spouse Mina Bess, an extraordinary copywriter; together they were a powerhouse team.

Ed had just been appointed chairman of the New York Heart Fund and needed the kind of campaign savvy Marlo and his wife offered. Having reluctantly done promotional work for some of gossip columnist Walter Winchell's self-serving causes, both Marlo and Mina Bess were wary of Ed at first. But after meeting with him, they were impressed by his will to accomplish and warmed to him.

The radio campaign Marlo and Mina Bess successfully developed for Ed climaxed with a star-packed three-hour show at New York's Copacabana nightclub featuring Bob Hope, Jack Benny, Jimmy Durante, Martha Raye, Pearl Bailey, Bing Crosby, and Louis Armstrong—the greatest jazz figure of the 20th century. Marlo recognized at once that the vaudeville on the Copa stage that evening would transfer naturally to television. Ed flipped over the idea, urging my brother to become his partner and pitch it to the networks.

In early 1948, Marlo presented the program concept to CBS, which quickly greenlit it—anxious to compete with a show just introduced on NBC by ever-popular comic Milton Berle. CBS offered Marlo the title of producer and $400 a week to deliver six acts and a line of dancing girls every Sunday. The network proposed three titles: *Tops in Town*, *Talk of the Town* and *Toast of the Town*. The last survived a trademark search, and it stuck for seven years until Ed and Marlo earned enough clout to rename the program *The Ed Sullivan Show*.

The series' audience-pleasing variety format helped establish the course of television, and early appearances by the likes of Elvis Presley and The Beatles hugely influenced music and popular culture. Together, Marlo and Ed not only made CBS the number one network, they created a new phenomenon— the mass TV audience.

Marlo directs Elvis Presley on the set of *The Ed Sullivan Show* in 1956. Ed's concerns that the hip-swiveling rock 'n' roller stuffed the crotch of his pants prompted Ed's order that Presley be shot only from the waist up as he performed.

Although Ed was preoccupied with polishing his show and maintaining his newspaper column for most of that landmark summer, he was hot on my tail again at the first cool breath of fall. His pursuit intensified as his confidence grew with the program. And I grew tired of his persistent checking-in. Besides, I was dating other men. I was having a ball with a young disc jockey, William B. Williams, who became a very big star in New York radio as one of Martin Block's successors on *Make Believe Ballroom* and originated the indelible nickname "Chairman of the Board" for Frank Sinatra.

Still, Ed loomed large—his efforts to steal my attention with sweet nothing-filled phone and written messages as overwhelming as they were overbearing. I decided to throw a bucket of ice water on him during lunch at Tavern on the Green. Numb at first, he quickly became agitated.

"Who's gotten to you?" he demanded, paranoia flaring in his big blue eyes. "Who's telling you to do this?"

Glancing over the edge of our banquette, I settled back and stared at him wearily. "I'm sorry," I repeated. "I just don't feel right about it."

"I'm in business with your brother!" he defended. "What could anyone say?"

Ed was turned down very infrequently, and his frustration with me was palpable. He blathered about asking the Cardinal for a dissolution of his marriage. He could have been bluffing, but alarms were sounding. It was getting out of hand.

Louis Sobol, a columnist for the *New York Journal*, kindly took me aside after seeing me with Ed a few times. "People are saying you're Sullivan's girlfriend," he cautioned. "You gotta watch that. Don't get trashed along with Ed's other girls."

My consorting with Ed on any level was risking a scandal. With all his calls and gifts, his attachment had moved well beyond flirting. While I was appearing in Baltimore during a huge storm, a special messenger appeared at my dressing room door with a beautiful umbrella adorned with an expensive beaded evening bag. Inside was a card: "Stay dry, I love you."

I was verging on panic. And I was afraid someone was going to get hurt. So I flat-out told Ed no. He was furious. But at least he could work it out in confession.

The tone of my ongoing association with Ed Sullivan was edgy at best. Ed avoided becoming so attentive again as to renew his status as a gossip target, and he remained cordial because he was a friend of my family. But he held a grudge forever. In 1963, well after I married Jennings Lang, I asked Ed to send his talent scouts to hear our son, jazz pianist Mike Lang, who was playing at the venerable Village Vanguard for winning the Notre Dame Inter-Collegiate Jazz Festival. It was a simple, reasonable favor. Ed failed to follow through.

I never talked to Marlo about my Ed Sullivan crisis, though I suspect he knew. Unfortunately, he was stymied by being in the middle—unable to advise me and unable to tell Ed to get lost. (My brother never seemed bothered by this, but years later I was shocked to find that every one of Ed's shows in which I appeared was missing from the CBS archives. With a bow to Oliver Stone, I say conspiracy.)

The façade Ed developed with Marlo's help served him well. His earlier press-trench pugnacity evolved into a welcoming and gentlemanly persona on the small screen. Still, for his program's duration, Ed suffered withering jabs at his mannerisms, faux paus, and halting

MEETING DEAN AND JERRY AT THE COPA

June 1948 was, for me, a month to remember. In addition to appearing on Ed Sullivan's very first TV broadcast, I was the opening act for comedians Dean Martin and Jerry Lewis at the Copacabana—the "hottest club north of Havana," as it was immortalized three decades later by Barry Manilow in his classic disco tune. This was the big debut for Dean and Jerry, who went on to become two of the 20th century's biggest show business phenomena.

The duo played to sell-out crowds at the Copa and totally slew cosmopolitan New York. The show consisted of the dancing Copa Girls, a singer, and the headline act, in that order, but the audience was so loud in its hankering for Dean and Jerry that they began their verbal volleying during the vocalist's final song. Two previous chanteuses vacated the thankless slot quickly.

THE COPACABANA
presents
THOSE HILARIOUS STARS OF STAGE, SCREAM AND RADAR

DEAN   JERRY

MARTIN LEWIS

in The Copa's Gay New Revue with

MONICA LEWIS

RAY MALONE • BETTY BONNEY • WARDE DONOVAN

AND OF COURSE,
THE LOVELY

Copa Girls

FOR DINNER AT 8 • AFTER THEATRE AT 12
LATE HOWL SHOW AT 2

I received an emergency call from the Copa's Great Dane of a manager, Jack Entratter. He was desperate for a resilient, good-humored singer. "Dean and Jerry want to know if you're interested," he begged.

I had worked with both guys previously. Dean and I first met when I was on WMCA, where he also had a radio show. I found him darling—the rare talented singer who also was funny. And I had known Jerry since he was nineteen, when his repertoire was limited to lip-synching and making funny faces. "I'll take the chance," I told Jack, trying to temper my enthusiasm.

It *was* a difficult job. How do you silence an expectant crowd? I relied on every instinct, pulled out every trick. The first number was always a sacrifice because the women in the audience were judging your weight and fashion sense while the men were making their own evaluations. During the dinner shows, my opening number had to compete with tinkling silverware and shouts of "Pass the rolls!" (Within a few weeks, I was popular enough to demand a no-serving rule during my performance.) My second song was a soft, heart-wrenching piano or guitar ballad with a pin spotlight that shrank slowly until it framed only my face. That always grabbed 'em.

I remained with Dean and Jerry at the Copa for several months through the end of their run. It was prime exposure for all of us.

speech. "Ed Sullivan does absolutely nothing. *But*—he does it better than anyone else," once quipped comedian Alan King.

Yet no one could diminish the fact that the fourteen-year association between Ed and Marlo made them millionaires and saw my brother, by age thirty, named executive producer in charge of comedy and variety programming at CBS. They shared the international George Foster Peabody Award for excellence in radio and television in 1956. Marlo, who also helped launch shows for beloved entertainers Jackie Gleason, Dinah Shore, Phil Silvers, and Red Buttons, went on to help found the Academy of Television Arts and Sciences and was elected to the Television Producers Hall of Fame in 1992.

Finding myself squarely in the midst of the intersection between radio and television, I was, and still am, proud to have linked this momentous creative team. Even if it was just as an excuse to get Ed Sullivan off my back.

"Sultry songlark." "Vocalovely." "Vivacious thrush."

The late 1940s found journalists labeling me in just such overheated ways. Apparently, the common ornithologisms for girl singers—"songbird," "chirp," and "canary"—weren't quite descriptive enough for my combination of sound and stage presence. It was almost a relief when *The Philadelphia Inquirer*, in a fit of alliterative lustiness, dubbed me simply "Luscious Lewis."

Critics, in noting distinctions among the singing sisterhood, increasingly characterized my voice as "torch style." I was a soloist and a stylist: I had the jazz feel for everything, so I never felt I had to interpret the song exactly the way it was written. Lyrically, I didn't have a specific trick or method; it was about my feelings for the material, and what I wanted it to make me feel. More important was how I could make the *audience* feel about the song or about me singing it.

It helped immensely that I had developed a natural affinity for playing to the crowd. I knew I always had the guys on my side, but I also wanted the gals in the audience to see me as their friend. In whichever club I was playing, I would walk partly around the room en route to the stage—greeting some of the women personally with a big smile while complimenting them on their evening wear. Mid-song, I cemented the connection by staring directly into the lights to get teary-eyed. I freely employed the techniques of dramatic acting to enhance the experience. The bottom line: My job, like every performer's, was not to bore the audience.

This seamless, in-the-moment expertise was crucial not only to my work onstage, but in the recording studio. Tape didn't yet exist; there was no splicing on a 78 rpm shellac record. If you made a mistake when cutting a record, you had to start over from the beginning. And live television was *live*, which was part of its appeal. It forced everyone to be disciplined and professional, to be at their best all the time.

Live performing is life itself. There are no do-overs.

Warming up before one of my 1948 appearances on *Toast of the Town*, surrounded onstage by (clockwise from left) director John Wray, producer Marlo Lewis, musical director Ray Bloch, and host Ed Sullivan.

As if it weren't enough to be "America's Singing Sweetheart," as Decca cheerfully publicized me, I was also its *selling* one. My reps—high on endorsement deals I had struck with Chiquita, General Electric, and others—continued inking lucrative promotional contracts. I scrambled to fulfill them. Hardly a national brand-name vice went unsold by my wholesome image between 1948 and 1949. In print ads and radio spots, I pitched—among many other products—Camel Cigarettes, Rheingold Extra Dry Lager Beer, and Piel's Light Beer.

My brother, while happy for my exposure, wasn't thrilled to see me reduced to ground chuck by the same advertising machine he operated. It was typical of him to encourage me not to underestimate—or worse, sell out—my singing talent.

Professional guidance aside, it was rare of Marlo (or my sister Bobbe) to play cupid. So it was a bit startling when he phoned from the *Toast of the Town* set to rave about a twenty-something gentlemen who had just costumed singer Lisa Kirk. "I never saw such beautiful clothes!" he said. "His designs are magnificent—so original. He's a really nice young guy, too. You've got to meet him."

The fellow's name was Burton Miller. I called him and we agreed to meet at a corner coffee shop. I didn't know what to expect, but I felt right at home with him when he walked in and introduced himself as "Burt." He was casual, unaffected, and handsome—a model of conservative elegance in neat slacks and an elbow-patch sports jacket. We bonded quickly as I told him my stage act needed a makeover. I loved his ideas, and we forged a partnership.

Backstage at *Toast of the Town* sharing makeup tips with young film actress Margaret O'Brien (*Jane Eyre*, *Meet Me in St. Louis*) and singer Vic Damone, a pal since my early radio days.

Burt and I planned something special for my second opening at the Paramount Theater. We thought it would be an audience-wower for me to do an on-stage clothes change combined with a tap dance! My outfit was designed so that I could easily sashay behind a screen at stage left, drop my gown to reveal a leotard, and continue tapping with at least one foot while Burt switched my shoes—all while the band sang in unison "Where's Monica?" with a hand-clapping beat. I made a deal with the drummer to cover my taps in case I missed one or two. We had it down pat after two performances. The crowd just loved it.

Burton Miller was a miracle for my career—and for my life in general. I felt completely comfortable with him. We wanted nothing from each other but good company and creative exchange. Then something bizarre happened.

Burt's dad called me long-distance and offered me one million dollars to marry his son.

The elder Miller, who had made his fortune as a Pittsburgh Buick dealer, could not accept that Burt was homosexual. Burt's mother knew and accepted her son's orientation; she also told me her husband couldn't deal with it. It was clear Mr. Miller needed some sort of reaffirmation for the benefit of his own masculinity. I guess he thought that if anyone could set Burt straight, I could—or at least he'd find comfort in knowing that his son was with me.

It would have been hilarious had it not been so pathetic.

Burt fumed after I told him about his father's indecent proposal. When he calmed, he suggested we take the money and run. "We'll fly around the world and buy lots of clothes wherever we land," he enthused. I convinced him that for a global tour taken with our extravagant tastes, the money wouldn't last six months.

I loved Burt and he loved me. But it wasn't my place to tell Mr. Miller that if he could reconcile that his son was a wonderful, vital, and creative person, he wouldn't be making this stupid offer. "I'm just not

You'd never know my big sister and I were eight years apart in this 1948 portrait by ace celebrity photographer James J. Kriegsmann. In addition to being an accomplished classical pianist, Bobbe wrote crossword puzzles for *The New York Times*. Hysterically funny yet practical, she possessed an Auntie Mame demeanor but fancied herself Rita Hayworth. No one has ever been kinder to me.

I rounded the bases with "Pittsburgh's Pride," professional baseball player Ralph Kiner—and had a lot of all-American fun with him between games. (The medallion was from another special man with whom I would indulge in a romance later.)

ready to get married again," I finally told Burt's dad. "But if there was any man in the world I'd marry, he would be your loving, loyal son."

It was a bitter pill for Mr. Miller. Yet for me and Burt, who would become one of Hollywood's top film and TV costumers (*The Front Page, House Calls*), it was the start of something as heavenly as wedded bliss: a life-long friendship.

Another good friend of mine, Jack Eigen, hosted a New York talk radio program called *Meet Me at the Copa* that aired nightly from midnight to four a.m. on WMGM from the lounge of the Copacabana nightclub. The show had a gigantic regional audience of about five million. Every celebrity passing through town lobbied Jack for a slot; I myself was a frequent guest.

In late January 1949, Jack was leaving for a two-week Miami vacation with his wife and asked me to substitute for him as host. My visibility was hitting another peak: Paramount Pictures was just releasing *Make Mine Monica*, a film short about my life and career, and I had recently made the cover of *Parade*. I had plenty of engagements, too. But I wasn't feeling overly stressed, so I agreed to help Jack out. Who wouldn't want to gab with celebrities for a few hours in front of a microphone?

My mouth, it turned out, proved bigger than my stomach.

A sports non-nut, I got a bit nervous when I agreed to interview baseball's ruling slugger, Ralph Kiner of the Pittsburgh Pirates. He was a fine-looking 28-year-old, and a future Hall of Famer. Kiner won or tied the home run race every year between 1946 and 1952, and he led the National League in batting percentage three times during his decade-long career.

Beforehand I had arranged a hasty meeting with my brother-in-law, Bill Golub. "Tell me what I need to know about Ralph Kiner!" I pleaded. Bill filled me in on Kiner's Korner, the left-field area at Pittsburgh's Forbes Field where Kiner landed many of his homers. He told me that retired baseball great Hank Greenberg was Kiner's mentor and hero. Bill also gave me the batting average and number of home runs. I clutched a tiny crib sheet containing these details during the interview.

I never expected Kiner to be a dumb jock. But I also didn't expect him to recognize that I was ignorant of the sport. His attractiveness made me that much more vulnerable. About four questions into our live, on-air chat, Kiner narrowed his eyes.

"Miss Lewis, may I ask *you* a question?"

"Go ahead," I said, more intrigued than alarmed.

"What league am I with?"

I was on the business end of a lethal Kiner swing. The guy was with the Pirates. And that's all I knew! I had a vague thought that he was in the National League—my brother-in-law had assumed I could remember at least *that*. But it wasn't on my crib sheet, which I promptly wadded and tossed over my shoulder. Between my nagging guilt and the disarming charm of "Pittsburgh's Pride," I caved in grandly as millions of ears perked all over the Northeast.

"Ladies and gentlemen of the listening audience, I owe you all a tremendous apology," I announced. "I don't know what league Ralph Kiner is with. I don't know anything about baseball. But I couldn't resist having Ralph here. I owe him one, and I owe you—the fans—a lot of love for your patience."

Still on the air, my face burning from this confession, I turned to Ralph. "What can I do to make up for this?"

Flanked happily by Bob Hope and popular radio/television broadcaster Arthur Godfrey at a 1949 military fete in Minneapolis—with U.S. President Harry Truman's no-nonsense political partner, Vice President Alben W. Barkley, struggling to look comfortable amid the show business crowd. Bob and I were doing a special summer festival radio show in the city.

Kiner looked at me as if he'd hit a grand slam. He frowned momentarily, simulating deep thought.

"I have two great seats for *South Pacific* on Tuesday," he said. "I'd like you to accompany me."

I played right along, addressing the Copa crowd as well as the listeners. "What do you say out there? Should I go?"

The phone lines lit up. "Go!" everyone urged.

Ralph and I became sporadic date mates. He was very different from the creative types that normally caught my fancy; not only did he have forearms like fireplugs, he was very bright. He was also enamored of talent and celebrity, and he had an unusual affinity for show business and the theater. Ralph liked all the good things in life, not just baseball. There was no lack of conversation.

Ralph and I enjoyed hitting the town as much as the sack. Whether sharing rum or a rumba, we always had fun, and on the dance floor I was a sucker for his embrace. At the height of his summer season, I had engagements in Chicago, Atlantic City, and Minneapolis, where I also did a special summer festival radio show with Bob Hope. Ralph would fly in to meet me between games. My schedule was such that I could attend only two Pirates match-ups—and both times my very favorite player cracked homers.

Although columnists asserted that Ralph wanted to marry me, ours wasn't anything like a Marilyn Monroe-Joe DiMaggio romance. The subject probably came up in our travels; one night, after a few drinks, Ralph may have said, "What do you think about making it legal?" It was neither a serious consideration nor even a conversation. Both of us preferred playing the field, and the ninth month of that year also would be our ninth and final inning. For no real reason other than mutual ennui, I kissed my Boy of Summer goodbye and he strode confidently back to the dugout. Eventually Ralph married and became a sports commentator and author—and very rich.

Like the rest of the country, I thought TV was the greatest thing since, well, radio. And thanks to my shots on *Toast of the Town*, *The Milton Berle Show*, and others, everyone thought I was made for it.

I started plotting my escape from New York. I was spurred in part by a scary personal crisis—my father had just suffered a massive heart attack. It was the first time anyone in my family was seriously ill. I was very worried for his health, convinced that New York's killer pace and cold weather were to blame. I canceled every appearance requiring travel to assist my mother with his recovery. It was a much-needed period of extra closeness for all.

As my father improved, I resumed my full work schedule. But the dearth of studio talent scouts on the East Coast—and the fact that TV was still in the wind-up stage as a tool for mass exposure—meant that some of my best work was going unnoticed. Frustrated, I hired Henry Rogers, the premier publicity man to the stars, whom I sweet-talked down to $500 a month—one-quarter his normal client fee. I then had an urgent meeting with MCA's chief executive, Lew Wasserman, who was in Manhattan on business from Los Angeles.

Me partying it up in New York with Kirk Douglas and popular radio and nightclub comedian Danny Thomas—later the star of the TV hit *Make Room for Daddy* and founder of the world-renowned St. Jude Children's Research Hospital.

Lew swiveled in a high tufted-leather chair as I sat before him, his eyes large behind thick glasses. (It would be a couple decades before he adopted his trademark outsized power goggles.) I wondered aloud why MCA was not booking me in Hollywood.

"Singing is my calling card," I said. "I can't go out there and say, 'Here I am. Put me in movies.' I've got to show them." Lew rolled a gold pen on the blotter. "You're absolutely right," he said. "We should have done this a long time ago."

Indeed. For several years I had been stuck between being a starring performer and a star. With my current level of experience and exposure, a film contract looked like a snap. A studio deal—not just a motion picture guest shot—would enable me to relocate my family to the warm California sunshine, where my father could recuperate more comfortably and my career might flourish.

Further fueling my "Go West" impetus was the success of Kirk Douglas, with whom I had just ended an affair. He was hot off his turn as a selfish boxer in the screen drama *Champion*, for which he would soon be nominated for an Academy Award. And he was...*hot*.

Chiseled charms notwithstanding, Kirk had initially hooked me with a declaration over drinks at the 21 Club. "Talented people," he said, clasping my hand, "are the only true aristocracy."

KIRK DOUGLAS

My affair with Kirk in late 1949 was sparked in the most mundane of show business ways: by a press agent. When any of the big male movie stars traveled to the media hub of New York from Hollywood to promote their latest films in print and on radio, their publicists scrambled to arrange the highest-profile arm jewelry. I'd brace myself for the call: "Could I take you to dinner? I heard your show was wonderful...." Blah, blah, blah. I knew that these men were in positions of power. But I also had to wake up with myself in the morning.

Kirk had served in the U.S. Navy for several years before pursuing acting in radio, stage, and finally film, debuting opposite Barbara Stanwyck and Van Heflin in the 1946 drama *The Strange Love of Martha Ivers*. He was a married father but separated from his wife—a fact that was irrelevant to our mutual media wrangler, the star-making publicist Henry Rogers. Although I was cowed, Henry persisted, saying it would just be a friendly introduction. I gave in.

At that time, being in our prime, Kirk and I viewed our situation as a *Why not?* Neither of us had any illusions of developing a relationship; a divorce wasn't yet in the works for him. On the other hand, we did not just say hello and pounce on the mattress. We behaved socially—going to plays, having dinner, doing the town. But preliminaries be damned, it boiled down to doing each other.

I'm not the first to reveal that Kirk exhibited breathtaking sexual prowess. So let it suffice for me to say that I had an extra spring in my step during our time together.

More important, for such a young actor, Kirk had commanding talent, manners, good humor, and impeccable style. He also was rare in that he had an intellect and inquisitiveness that superseded self-love. Kirk was looking and searching and thinking, as was I. We were trying to figure out what was going on in the world, not just what our next gig would be.

Kirk went on to make some eighty films (including *Lust for Life*, *Spartacus*, and *Lonely are the Brave*) and earn three Academy Award nominations, and he ultimately landed on the American Film Institute's list of the top twenty-five male actors in Hollywood's first 100 years. Yet the Bigger Picture dominated our respective marquees later in life, when I started politicking actively and Kirk, in addition to becoming a Goodwill Ambassador for the U.S. State Department in 1963, wrote books and became a patron of the arts—donating generously to cultural institutions. His humanitarianism now bridging two centuries, I have the utmost respect for him.

I started dying my hair at eighteen. I went from dark to auburn, and then to red, carrot, and strawberry blonde, before flirting with tawny blonde, champagne, and gold. Here, at twenty-seven, I leveled it off with Hollywood-ready platinum.

This dovetailed with my own theory of talent, which I consider a miracle of the gene pool. You can teach music, but you can't teach someone to be Pavarotti or Placido Domingo or Frank Sinatra. You can teach algebra and medicine, but you can't teach someone to be Einstein or Jonas Salk. Everyone is born with a predisposition toward some kind of talent; when schooling or happenstance uncovers it, those individuals who protect and strive to improve it are the ones who deserve to reach the top.

I was determined to make the most of my talent. And I knew the only way to the top was through Hollywood.

A phalanx of photographers captured my April 1950 landing in Los Angeles. True to my latest press-appointed title, "Miss Sweater Girl of New York," I realigned my posture up and out as I descended the plane's stairs in a champagne turtleneck.

3 NICE WORK IF YOU CAN GET IT

"Start packing your bags for Hollywood, darlin'."

Lew Wasserman's phone message arrived on the tail of a terse Western Union telegram from Ed Sullivan: "Delighted to inform you that you are nominated for a Radio & Television Academy Award. Dinner at Waldorf-Astoria March 21. All proceeds to N.Y. Heart Fund."

March 1950 had come in like a lion indeed, and I was awash in a spring thaw of exceptionally good fortune. The Academy of Radio and Television Best Arts and Sciences had placed me, Dinah Shore, and Jo Stafford among the year's top vocalists during its first annual awards presentation. It was the closest thing we had to the Grammy Awards in those days, and earning my peers' official recognition was the confidence stoking I needed for my long-awaited trip west. It was a bonus that the event benefited the New York Heart Association, for which I had become an active fundraiser in the wake of my father's health crisis.

My Los Angeles debut was set for April at the Mocambo, the famous club on the Sunset Strip. It was one of the two biggest venues in the city, the other being Ciro's, and it had the hottest band anywhere. Owner Charlie Morrison was known for his adventurous bookings; he had seen me perform on *Toast of the Town* and signed me to a two-week run. My publicity for the engagement started before I left New York, with the news hitting the entertainment press like a tidal wave and earning me guest shots on radio and TV, including a singing appearance on the CBS variety program *The Alan Young Show*.

I broke the bank and went first-class all the way, lodging at the ultra-swank Beverly Hills Hotel—also known as the "Pink Palace." True to its sobriquet, the inn's spa treatments, doting twenty-four-hour room service, chic clothiers, and star-sprinkled Polo Lounge would tickle me that healthy color the entire time.

It was rewarding when people recognized me wherever I went. My newness in town, combined with the media coverage, had autograph seekers waving record jackets, napkins, torn print ads bearing my image, and at least one pair of boxer shorts. Frank Sinatra, Milton Berle, and Dean Martin were among the many who sent gifts and good luck notes to my hotel suite.

Wally Cox, the comedy half of my Mocambo marquee, led the welcoming committee. Wally was funny and brilliant; two years later he would hit it huge in the live TV sitcom

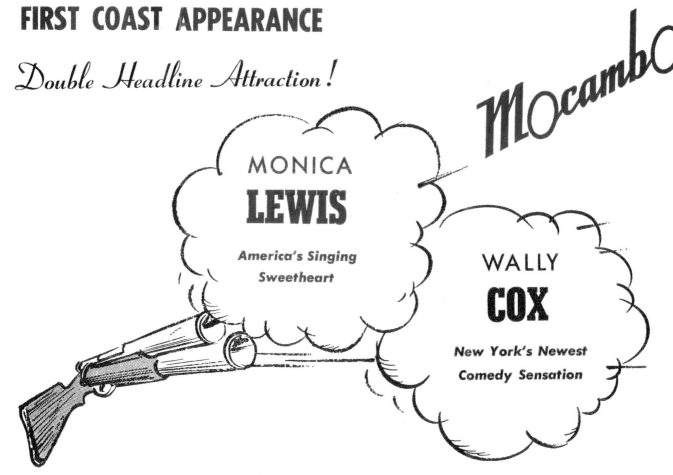

FIRST COAST APPEARANCE

Double Headline Attraction !

Mocambo

MONICA
LEWIS
*America's Singing
Sweetheart*

WALLY
COX
*New York's Newest
Comedy Sensation*

Opening . . **Wednesday Evening, April 12** . . CRestview 1-6171

Mr. Peepers as the eponymous nerd-cum-science teacher. He was also a peculiar little fellow, totally off the wall.

Wally and I got along fine. I couldn't put my finger on his sexuality—nor did I want to. I knew he was friendly with Marlon Brando and that they shared custody of a monkey. Or something.

Wally himself evidenced a certain simian weirdness one night while visiting my suite, where he detailed a plan to scale and "christen" the famous Hollywood sign on Mt. Olympus in the Hollywood Hills. "This town thinks I have no balls," he said, gesticulating spastically as he paced. "I'll give 'em balls! I'm going to climb that goddamn hill and micturate all over that fucking 'H.' They'll see my big balls for miles around!"

Whew. Regrettably, Wally also nearly caused me to piss away my own career on opening night.

I was a jumble of nerves before the performance. Charlie Morrison strutted about like a drill sergeant, barking at the lighting crew and generally raising hell backstage. I was seated at my makeup table, combing back a few wayward blonde strands but otherwise ready to go in my off-the-shoulder, emerald satin décolleté gown, when Charlie stuck his head in the dressing room door.

"You're gonna floor 'em, kid."

I forced a smile at Charlie's reflection in the mirror. But my stomach was roiling. Wally noticed my discomfort as I tottered to the restroom. A few moments later, he came to my dressing room door with a tiny pill and a glass of Coke.

I looked at the pill. "What is it?"

"It's a stomach-calmer," he said.

"What kind?"

"The kind that calms your stomach."

I was on in five minutes, so I washed the capsule down. The pill I had taken in desperate, unknowing haste was Phenobarbital—a muscle relaxant. It was a terrible mistake for me to use such a powerful drug before stepping in front of the curtain.

You're gonna floor 'em, kid.

My buddy and all-around entertainer Danny Kaye helped make L.A. welcoming—introducing me to friends like Vivien Leigh (*Gone With the Wind, A Streetcar Named Desire*) at Ciro's, a popular star nightspot. Operatic baritone Robert Merrill, a pal of mine, joined us this particular evening.

Onstage, my judgment was clouded, my movements leaden. Contrary to my normal persona, I avoided eye contact with the audience and focused vaguely on the rear of the room. By the time I took my final bow I could barely stand upright. The dizziness was completely overwhelming.

Sheila Graham, the big entertainment columnist who was also the lover of author F. Scott Fitzgerald (creator of the term "Jazz Age"), delivered her telltale review the next day. "We were very disappointed about last night's performance at the opening of Monica Lewis, who was touted as being so wonderful," she wrote. "I have loved her records, but something was amiss…."

It was crushing. I was so miserable over blowing my big opening that I called my mother in New York and cried.

"Oh, don't fret dear," she said. "You'll be great tonight!"

Mama was right. My second night at the Mocambo, with the medication out of my system, was nothing short of magical. Joe Pasternak, the big Metro-Goldwyn-Mayer studios-based film producer who'd discovered Judy Garland, was in the audience. I didn't learn of his presence until he came backstage to introduce himself and congratulate me.

The next morning brought a dream-come-true call from Lew Wasserman: "MGM wants to keep you here for a screen test."

Preparations for my MGM screen test required me to remain in L.A. four weeks beyond my Mocambo club run, and MCA was already discussing the recording aspect of a possible contract with the studio. Feeling like a movie star already, I retained my $80-a-night suite at the Beverly Hills Hotel. The room, plus my new habits of sipping sidecars in the Polo Lounge and loitering in the boutiques, all but exhausted my budget. But I didn't care. It was the vacation I never had—borrowed against the riches I was certain were just around the corner.

The interest expressed in me by Hollywood's most important production entity was immensely gratifying. And with my immediate attraction to the newness and creative energy of L.A., I eagerly immersed myself in the local social scene—hopping between the Mocambo, Ciro's, and other hot clubs. "Fun" was the operative word.

My backstage experience with Wally Cox notwithstanding, comics had long fascinated me; I was drawn naturally to their humor, and I learned from them how to ad lib and quell hecklers. I also learned that, while actors hog the mirror, comics whine—and that my living with any of them would be impossible. It just didn't jibe with my personal philosophy, which still holds: To get through this crazy life, you have to learn to laugh at yourself.

Still, I dated many comics on both coasts. Milton Berle, also known as "Mr. Television" for his early role in establishing and promoting the medium, was not one of the whining comics. I had known Milton since my late teens in Manhattan; we met through our respective mothers, who were friends. I had appeared on several of his radio programs, including

Although I gave Milton Berle the slip, I dated many comics in New York and Los Angeles—including Phil Silvers. Phil was older and a compulsive gambler, but he was also truly funny...and unmarried. Best of all, unlike most dysfunctional comics, he was really okay with being Phil Silvers.

64

MGM's recording division wasted no time issuing this promotional image once I signed my all-encompassing contract with the studio.

Let Yourself Go and *Texaco Star Theater*, as well as his hit TV version of the latter. I learned from those around him that Milton really loved sexy, built women; he married Joyce Matthews, a beautiful showgirl, twice! Earlier, Milton's mom decided that Milton and I should be married. She would call my mother every two weeks, pleading, "Jessica, why can't we get the kids together? Your daughter is such a doll and you have such a nice family." Mama always responded, "Darling, it's really up to them, you know." Milton's eyes were elsewhere and so were mine—he was in love with Joyce and I was about to marry Bob Thiele.

Always friendly, Milton's ego was more intact than that of most comics—even if he did have a God complex and could not imagine being wrong. Although I knew he had gotten his start as a boy model and was discovered by Charlie Chaplin before striking it rich in vaudeville, I never figured out what drove him. But being "off" for Milton was not a happy place.

After I arrived in Hollywood, Milton called and invited me to dinner. I didn't yet know many people in L.A. and was nervous about the MGM screen test, so I accepted. By that time, with the massive success of his TV program, my old friend *was* entertainment's equivalent of God.

My parents and I had barely been resettled in L.A. a month when I showed them the pleasures of the Mocambo Club in July 1950..

VIC DAMONE

MGM signed Vic Damone and me at about the same time in 1950. The gossips tried like hell to make an item out of us, but we were just good friends from similar singing backgrounds; Vic enjoyed his first big hit with "I Have but One Heart" in 1947. The sad irony is that the studio really had no plan for either of us once we were onboard. It even tossed us both into the jazzy 1951 drama *The Strip* just to keep us busy. There we were, two young but largely seasoned performers used to choosing our own songs, arranging music, and orchestrating our entire acts...and we were treated like teenagers!

Aside from Judy Garland, MGM's singers were mainly high sopranos; the studio's idea of a great vocalist was tenor Mario Lanza, and after that, basso cantante (and great guy) Howard Keel. The company brass was not particularly enamored of recording artists from the pop world.

Vic, who enjoyed career support from the likes of Frank Sinatra, Perry Como, and Tommy Dorsey, did not seem fazed by any of this. After leaving to serve in the U.S. Army from 1951 to 1953, he returned to marry the Italian actress Pier Angeli and claim starring roles in two MGM musicals: *Hit the Deck* and *Kismet*. And he continued to sing.

I always liked Vic's style. I still love his music.

We had a nice dinner, he told me lots of jokes, and I was pleasantly distracted for the moment. And then, as we glided back to the Beverly Hills Hotel in his giant limousine, Milton slipped his arm around me…and stuck his tongue in my ear! It felt like it went straight through my head and out the other side.

Kindly, I said, "Not tonight, Miltie. I have an early morning call. I must get a good night's sleep and hope to look beautiful tomorrow morning."

He settled back in the seat, disappointed. "How could you look any other way? Okay, kid, knock 'em dead. I'll call you." The next day he sent me magnificent roses. And he never called. I was relieved.

From what I had been told by girlfriends who went all the way with him, Milton's ego wasn't the only thing that was huge. I can only testify that Uncle Miltie had the biggest tongue I'd ever seen—or felt.

My finances were almost depleted by the date of the screen test. But there would be additional sacrifice en route to MGM's Culver City lot. Shortly beforehand, the studio's legendary drama coach, Lillian Burns—a homely, domineering stub of a woman who stood about chin-high to my five-foot-three-inch height—advised me that the camera adds weight and I should have a dehydration shot to shed five pounds. Leery of dealing with the studio's in-house M.D., I called a physician recommended by my brother. The doctor advised me there was nothing to worry about, other than that the treatment would cause me to spend forty-eight hours in the bathroom and become very thirsty.

I had the shot, losing two pounds of water in as many days. Next, there were repeated cab trips to the lot (only established stars were granted studio limousine service) for makeup tests and a new coiffure by hairdresser extraordinaire Sidney Guilaroff. Sidney was absolutely darling. We became friends on the spot.

Despite the buildup, my black-and-white screen test was a relatively simple affair directed by Joe Pasternak. I wore a black off-the-shoulder crepe dress. The set we used was barren save for a rotating stool and a piano replete with studio accompanist. I spoke my name and sang a song as instructed. For the close-ups, I perched on the stool—turning left, spinning right, and smiling all the way. As a favor to my brother, Kathryn Grayson, a coloratura soprano and MGM contractee (*Ziegfeld Follies*, *Show Boat*) who was married to my old co-host Johnnie Johnston, was on hand to offer suggestions and moral support.

The test turned out beautifully. No other studio knew how to package people like MGM; they made you look smashing.

The studio was impressed enough by my screen test to offer a two-year contract. At last, I felt that doors large enough to accommodate my biggest dreams were opening. But there was one major hitch: MCA forbade me to sign the agreement.

MGM's deal called for $500 a week—minus commissions, taxes, and Screen Actors Guild dues. That was a fraction of the $1,500 I was accustomed to earning weekly. Moreover, the contract would be all-inclusive. In addition to incorporating a twelve-week paid

In creating my MGM publicity portfolio, drama coach Lillian Burns ordered hairdresser-to-the-stars Sidney Guilaroff to shorten my hair and darken it from platinum to tawny—similar to one of the studio's top female draws, Lana Turner.

hiatus during which I could not make public appearances (including TV and radio) unless sanctioned by the studio, I would be forced to abandon Decca for MGM Records.

My reps deemed the terms terrible and the compensation beneath me. MCA wanted to stall for a richer, less restrictive one- or two-picture deal. But I was stubborn and vain: I wanted to return to New York with a big contract. That my pal and fellow singer Vic Damone was weighing a similar deal made me that much more impulsive.

After much arguing, I ditched MCA and signed with MGM for both acting and recording through an L.A.-based agent named Paul Small, who, it turned out, was married to the sister of Dore Schary—the studio's chief of production. I didn't know I was putting myself in an inferior position. Rather than a seasoned entertainment professional, I was behaving like a naïf fresh off the bus!

Everyone I knew had sided with MCA's caution over MGM except Leon and Jessie Lewis. They knew I worked hard to reach this point and supported my wishes. Yet neither of my parents, whom I was partly supporting while my brother and sister raised their own families, was keen to the idea of relocating to California. I appealed to their sense of adventure and convinced them that it would be fun—and especially good for Dad's health.

By June 1950, the three of us were settled into our new home in the Sunset Plaza Apartments above the Strip. It was a small but lovely one-bedroom flat (I took the fold-out couch in the living room). For $180 a month, it included a tennis court and pool access as well as a terrace with a panoramic view of the Hollywood Hills.

The traffic in L.A. was a trickle compared to today. Yet for me, having grown up using New York subways and cabs, learning to drive was daunting. Once I obtained my license, it took me a couple months to muster the nerve to maneuver my hotter-than-hot mint-green Pontiac convertible beyond the two or three roads I took to Culver City and back. Gradually,

I enjoyed an unprecedented sense of control over my life as I grew more comfortable in the driver's seat. Career-wise, however, I still wasn't completely behind the wheel.

At the behest of Lillian Burns, Sidney Guilaroff had shortened my hair and darkened it from platinum to tawny to make me look like Lana Turner, MGM's most bankable blonde. Sidney did it reluctantly, confiding to me that MGM would be smart to accentuate my natural attributes.

"They don't yet know what they have with you, dear," he whispered, wielding his scissors deftly as I reclined in the plush styling chair in his studio salon. "Hopefully they won't obscure a good thing. If they left you in my charge, they sure wouldn't."

I extracted as much knowledge as possible from the performance training, dance classes, and publicity MGM offered its players; I loved working with tap and dance teacher Willie Covan, who instructed Donald O'Connor and others. Finally, the day came when the studio drama coach, Lillian Burns, called me in to read a scene for her.

Joe Pasternak had been talking me up to Lillian. He raved, "Pay close attention to Monica Lewis. She can sing, and she can dance. I think we have a regular Betty Grable."

I appreciated Joe's boosterism. But Lillian had not earned her reputation and weighty position at MGM by being easy. She was the dean of all the studio's performers, and she made it a point to remind me that she had made Lana Turner a star.

Working with tap and dance teacher Willie Covan on the MGM lot was a joy. He taught Donald O'Connor and others their smooth, stylish footwork.

"Take a pencil and roll it between your fingers. That's how I taught Lana to use her hands," she told me. As I listened to this crap, I was dying inside because I had been taking bows half of my life!

I chose a scene from the early 20th century character drama *Our Town* for the reading. When I was growing up, my sister played piano off-stage for performances of this Thornton Wilder play, and I used to watch the rehearsals every day after school. I convinced Lillian to let me read a very touching mother-daughter scene that would always make me cry. So I did. And I cried and cried.

Lillian, aware that singing was my primary experience, was floored by my emoting. She got on the phone to Joe and said, "We don't just have a regular Betty Grable, we have a regular Lana Turner!"

Afterward, MGM-based producer Pandro Berman (*National Velvet, Father of the Bride*), whom I had befriended during my first visits to the lot, said Joe described me as "the female Lena Horne" in the studio commissary. Pandro said it was hysterical, because Joe had meant to say "white" instead of "female" in his awkward comparison to Lena, who was also an MGM player at the time and one of a handful of African-American actors with a major studio contract. Flustered and frustrated, I said to Pandro: "Do you think I'll ever find out if I'm Monica Lewis? And that it's okay to *be* Monica Lewis?"

Fortunately, there were some show business movers and shakers who really loved me for being me. One of them was an actor named Ronald Reagan.

I first met Ronnie in Manhattan in the fall of 1948 through some very good friends, Sonny Werblin and his wife, Leah Rae. Sonny was a key force at MCA before it moved into the picture business—he oversaw the company's East Coast talent operations while Jules Stein and Lew Wasserman ran the West Coast. (Eventually, Sonny would head up Madison Square Garden and purchase the New York Jets football team). He thought Ronnie, who had just been divorced from Jane Wyman, would make a fine match for me and arranged for the four of us to have dinner at the 21 Club.

At first I mistook Ronnie's politeness for stiffness, even if he did look stunning in a white polo coat. But the more he spoke, the more I began to simmer, and by the end of the evening I was completely taken with his manners, grooming, and confidence.

"The pleasure has been all mine, Miss Lewis," Ronnie said, kissing my hand when it came time to depart. I couldn't help but giggle when I caught the Werblins exchanging satisfied glances.

Ronnie and I spoke on the phone the following evening, and over the next several weeks, the two of us returned to the 21 Club and visited all the other hot nightspots. The hottest spot proved to be Ronnie's apartment at The Sherry-Netherland hotel, where we made love on our third date. The next day, enough flowers arrived for me at my parents' apartment to throw a funeral! Despite Ronnie's nickname, "Dutch Treat" was not in the Reagan lexicon.

Ronald Reagan and I enjoying ourselves at the Stork Club in New York before I moved to Los Angeles. I am wearing his special gift: a medal of St. Genesius, the patron saint of actors, which Ronnie had custom-made for me.

He preferred the most traditional of male-female gestures.

Unfortunately, Ronnie left for London in December 1948 to shoot the screen version of playwright John Patrick's war drama *The Hasty Heart*, which became one of his very best films. But for the better part of a year he maintained a romantic pilot light between us via thoughtful, moving letters and phone calls; not a week would pass without one or the other. These communications strengthened our bond in ways that purely physical contact could not. It was a true meeting of hearts and minds, and I valued that.

We tried to pick up where we left off after Ronnie returned to the States, but the usual scheduling conflicts—my touring tethered me to the eastern half of the country, while his film work and duties as president of the Screen Actors Guild kept him mostly in Hollywood—made fidelity impossible, and both of us dated others. We made up for it after I moved to Los Angeles. Our relationship also became a working one when MGM's vice president and general manager, Louis B. Mayer, wanted me to sing and be seen at different functions, especially Democratic fundraisers. Ronnie, conservative as he may have been socially, was ideologically liberal at the time and wrote the speeches I made at these events.

They were never less than rousing.

RONALD REAGAN

Although our careers kept us mostly on different coasts, Ronald Reagan was a constant in my life as the late 1940s turned into the new decade. Beyond my family, he was my sturdiest emotional bridge between New York and Los Angeles, and there was nothing at all the matter with this towering Illinois native and former radio announcer—almost. He was handsome, endearing, gentlemanly, polished...and stubbornly low-voltage.

As our romance was growing, Ronnie was at an ebb in Hollywood, being several years removed from his star peak in early-1940s movies like *Knute Rockne, All American,* and *Kings Row.* But his screen credits were the furthest things from my mind. Our chemistry developed gradually, and I became riveted by the stellar Reagan performance that unspooled during the times we shared in public and in private.

No one can argue that Ronnie's ultimate role in politics was absolutely Academy Award-caliber. He was vital and vigorous within his own parameters, and I admired his determination (I continued to do so even after he abandoned the Democratic Party for the GOP). He evidenced no lack of ambition or intelligence when we were closest; as president of the Screen Actors Guild, he engaged in legitimate debate over performers' rights.

While I appreciated everything Ronnie offered, the fact that spontaneity and creativity were real chores for him weighed heavily in my emotional decision to decline his hand in marriage. The last time I heard from Ronnie was the week before he wedded Nancy Davis in 1952. He called me at home from our favorite booth at Ciro's.

"Would you have a drink with me for old times' sake?"

"I don't think it would be helpful," I replied.

"I'd just like to see you again before—"

I knew in my heart he was not angling for a final fling. Ronnie truly just wanted to have one last toast for moral support before he took what he knew would be his resolute plunge.

"You know, honey, I really think it's not a good idea," I said, failing to choke back years' worth of feelings. "I will always cherish what we had. I wish you all the happiness in the world."

I do not regret my decision to part with Ronald Reagan. Fate works in mysterious ways, and I tend not to live life attempting to second-guess its inscrutable design. If it weren't for the Presidential Seal, this long-ago suitor would be just another page in my memory, albeit one of legal-pad length. Yet I cannot escape remembering that I nearly married a monolith, which shifted its intellectual axis, though never its moral foundation—and planted itself for eight years in the White House.

74

Ronnie's generosity extended to my parents, whom he lavished with an expensive sterling silver bar set and various trinkets from Tiffany. Gossip columnists reported that Ronnie had given me his medal of St. Genesius, the patron saint of actors. Actually, he had a special piece made expressly for me by William Ruser, a well-known Beverly Hills jewelry designer. The medal was about two inches across, made of solid, beautifully hand-engraved 14-carat gold. It was magnificent. And it must have cost a fortune.

While my parents adored Ronnie, many of my friends were not convinced our relationship would work. One skeptic was Cy Howard, a pal of mine and a successful comedy writer (*My Friend Irma*, *That's My Boy*), who never missed an opportunity to propose marriage to me. He was a very funny guy—a real maniac and a congenial cynic. But as with Jerry Lewis, one of Cy's major employers, a little of his personality went a long way.

Cy tossed in his two cents after spotting me with Ronnie at Chasen's, one of L.A.'s biggest celebrity eateries. "Was he whispering to you or nibbling on your ear?"

"What are you talking about?" I asked.

"Do you really like this guy?"

"Yes. So?"

"Well, don't ask him what time it is. He'll explain how watches are made."

Cy's smart-assery did circumscribe a nagging dilemma: As wonderful a human being as he was, Ronnie wasn't what I considered hip or cutting-edge. He was neither a rapier wit nor a Method actor. If I was steeped in avant-garde jazz, Ronnie was strictly ballroom.

Comedy writer Cy Howard was my cynical confidante while I was dating Ronald Reagan—and he tried to steer me away from the actor.

Earlier, this was a problem for Jane Wyman. After their initial passion wore off, Ronnie couldn't keep pace with his wife personally or professionally. Jane was an *actress*—the prototype of who gets to the mirror first. She wasn't terribly concerned with the politics of the nation as much as with those of the studio. Jane, not unlike myself, had had a checkered past with men. She saw in Ronald Reagan a safe haven—a handsome, young, healthy, moral man. But at some point she became bored with his straightness and longed for a more kicky life.

Ronnie told me his rift with Jane had much to do with her lack of fulfillment. He held out hope that she would give him a second chance, but that was unlikely after he and I had been linked in the press.

There was, to be certain, no love lost between Jane Wyman and me. One day in late 1950, I was lunching with Cy Howard at Chasen's and ran into Jane in the ladies' room. She was touching up her makeup, eyeing me in the mirror as I struggled to re-zip my dress. "The way to do that is to lie down flat on your back," she said, snapping her compact. Then she glared at me and added, "You're good at that."

I was shocked beyond response as she stalked out. I had heard every profanity in the book but had never been attacked outright by such a lousy personal remark. I felt wounded, and evidently looked it, when I returned to the table.

"What's the matter with you?" Cy looked concerned.

"Jane Wyman. She just blasted me in the powder room."

"Oh, don't worry about Jane," he said, nursing his scotch. "She snores and doesn't suck."

I laughed so hard my dismay evaporated instantly. Sweet as Cy could be, he also was frightfully "sheet"-smart—thanks no doubt to his involvement in a Hollywood prostitution scandal that took him years to live down.

In hindsight, I can understand Jane Wyman's spitefulness. After all, I received the gratification Ronald Reagan could not or would not give her in their final years together. It must have been a thorn for her. For me, it was a horn of plenty.

If Ronnie was a model of charm and urbanity in public, he was considerably less reserved behind closed doors. Regarding his dissolved marriage a highly personal failure, he had evidently embarked upon, to use an acronym for which he later would become famous, an SDI—or Sensual Development Initiative—after Jane left him. Ronnie was not a carnal prude, nor was he a minute-man. He was patient and painstakingly adept in the bedroom. It was the only place where he would relax his rigid decorum. And it was a most satisfying off-stage duet.

Inevitably, there had to be a day of reckoning. Ronnie was never a big swinger; he was anti-clique and had a pronounced coolness. I never saw him hanging out with any buddies. He was very much one-on-one and wanted desperately to have a wife. But I was looking for a combination of danger, great humor, and God-knows-what in an eternal partner.

After we diverged, Ronnie's path took a surprising turn when he switched his affiliation from the Democratic Party to the Republican Party very openly. As were most of us who had spent our formative adult years in the cloistered realm of show business, Ronnie was searching—looking for a new direction in life and work. MCA had struggled to get him good acting roles, unable to do much better than the silly 1951 chimpanzee comedy *Bedtime for Bonzo*. In 1954, the agency finally engineered his long-running job as host of CBS's *General Electric Theater*. Then they sent him to do promotional speeches for MCA, which brought him great public acclaim, and he relished the adulation. No one knew those cheers were the birth cries of a future chapter in world history.

When he successfully ran for governor of California in 1966 and 1970, and again in 1980 when he

I attended the American Legion's "Red, White, and Blue Revue" with Ronnie in L.A. in 1950.

campaigned successfully for President, the Democratic National Committee—of which I was a mammoth supporter—asked me if I would dish any dirt. I gave an emphatic "No!" There are those who were always a little over-anxious to smear Ronnie; even though he wasn't my choice for President, I have nothing but good things to say about his character. I did, of course, disagree strongly with some of his policies; whether he himself ever fully believed in everything he did, we'll never know. The public surely loved him enough to give him two terms in the White House.

I never knew Nancy Davis well. She, like I, had been under contract to MGM in the 1950s. She wanted Ronnie, and she got him. God bless her. She was an asset to her husband always—shaping him, making him happy. Nancy was and continues to be a tough gal, loyal and courageous. The Reagans enjoyed some fabulously exciting and revolutionary times in Washington, D.C. My admiration for her is boundless for the way she tirelessly cared for Ronnie during his final courageous years battling Alzheimer's.

Despite the constraints of my MGM contract, I managed to issue some well-received tunes through their label. These included my debut record, "I Never Knew I Loved You," which climbed the charts in the spring of 1950. My overriding hope, though, was for a great film role.

My very first week on the lot, I did get cast in a small part—a cameo, really—as an 1870s saloon singer in a romantic drama called *Inside Straight*, starring David Brian, Arlene Dahl, Barry Sullivan, and Mercedes McCambridge. (I was billed somewhere between Lon Chaney, Jr., and Barbara Billingsley.) The film was black-and-white, but that didn't stop the studio from trying umpteen shades of blonde on me in pre-production.

There wasn't much for me to do in *Inside Straight* but look pretty in a padded costume. I performed the requisite song, a corny number called "Up in a Balloon" (definitely not my kind of tune), in one take before lunch. I thought I was through and started to leave, but I was intercepted by the director, Gerald Mayer.

"Darling, we have to do your close-up," he informed me. "But we won't get to that until six tonight."

Unaccustomed to the snail's pace of filmmaking, I asked, "What do I do all day?" Mayer walked away without answering. But

I played an 1870s saloon singer in MGM's romantic drama *Inside Straight*, released in early 1951. The small part was my first film role.

MGM publicity head Howard Strickling loved my willingness to participate in parades and pose for any kind of photo. But soon I started feeling adrift without a...well, paddle.

I knew I wasn't going to sit around primping or reading. So I observed the production process with the intensity of a cinematographer or continuity person—looking for the best camera angles and taking note of where an actress set her prop pocketbook down between takes. I was so eager to learn about the business that I was determined to make the most of my captivity on the set.

Meanwhile, while the studio tried to figure out where I might fit in on its upcoming film slate, I became the darling of the MGM publicity department. I rode on floats in parades, attended store openings, and generally gave the MGM lion a run for its money as the company mascot. Howard Strickling, the studio's head flack, thought I was the Second Coming because of my versatility and willingness.

"I can put you in a rain barrel," Howard stated. "It has nothing to do with the dress, the stockings, or the fishnet hose."

I asked, "What are you talking about?"

He answered, "Sex appeal," but I just felt like a college liberal arts major.

By the end of my second week as an L.A. resident, I was dubbed "Miss Hollywood Everything." Perhaps others wouldn't have complained: My photos were, after all, in every movie magazine. But the publicity was far greater than anything I was actually doing. There would be announcements that I was going to make the next big film with Mario Lanza or whomever, but these projects were just happy talk—lacking even the minimal substance of hype. I was a headline in search of a story.

The breezy press junkets did have some benefits—notably, they were opportunities to introduce myself to my contemporaries from other studios and talent agencies. I met Marilyn Monroe in early 1950 when we both appeared at the launch of a Navy ship in Long Beach. Although MGM had released her to Twentieth Century Fox shortly before I arrived in L.A., Marilyn seemed upbeat and optimistic. I thought she was sweet.

The studio had photographed Marilyn in a black dress that she made famous; the costume department gave me the very same outfit to wear for my first big photography session. I recall asking the photographer, "Who wore this before?"

He answered, "Some kid named Marilyn Monroe who was fired."

"Is that an omen?"

He smiled. "She was cute, really cute. But they didn't think she had anything."

As everyone from moviegoers to world leaders would soon notice, Marilyn did have *something*—that is, aside from the increasingly supercharged sexuality of her voice and look. But I doubt even she herself could accurately identify what *it* was. *It* may have been lost somewhere in her mirror.

Even as Lillian Burns and Co. mulled my positioning on MGM's star roster, my patience began to pay off by the end of that summer. I was assigned a one-scene role in *The Strip*, a music-heavy, Los Angeles-based pseudo-film noir starring Mickey Rooney, Sally For-

My performance of the tune "La Bota" for the film-noirish 1951 drama *The Strip*, my second screen appearance, was deemed commercial enough for radio airplay.

MICKEY ROONEY

There are few Hollywood stars as versatile or enduring as Mickey Rooney. Some of my best moments on the MGM lot were spent filming my brief part for *The Strip* and getting to know Mickey between takes. He was a total team player, and he had a generous way of keeping everything on the set lighthearted and comfortable.

Mickey was born with natural talent to vaudevillian parents. An experienced performer by the time MGM signed him in 1934 at age fourteen, he played just about every musical instrument and role amazingly well. His 1937 turn as Andy Hardy in *A Family Affair* begat a thirteen-picture film franchise for the studio, and his work opposite Judy Garland that same year in *Thoroughbreds Don't Cry* led to their teaming in several hit musicals. His dramatic breakthrough in *Boys Town* arrived the next year, and memorable roles in movies like *National Velvet* (1944), *The Bridges at Toko-Ri* (1954), and *The Black Stallion* (1979) followed in succeeding decades.

Mickey's been at it since 1927, when his title role in the *Mickey McGuire* series of short comedy films launched his career, and as of this writing he's still going strong. He's a dear guy and deserves all the credit in the world.

rest, and William Demarest. Essentially playing myself, I was a club singer and performed a Latin-beat tune called "La Bota," which enjoyed significant broadcast outside of the picture and brought me the kind of talent-based attention I desired.

I quickly parlayed that minor success into a featured role in *Excuse My Dust*, a period musical comedy with Red Skelton, Sally Forrest, and Macdonald Carey. My part as a bubblehead belle named Daisy Lou Shultzer required me to don an 1890 Lillian Russell costume and talk with a helium-high Southern accent, and it brought me wonderful reviews. *The Hollywood Reporter* enthused: "…a young lady who makes news is Monica Lewis,

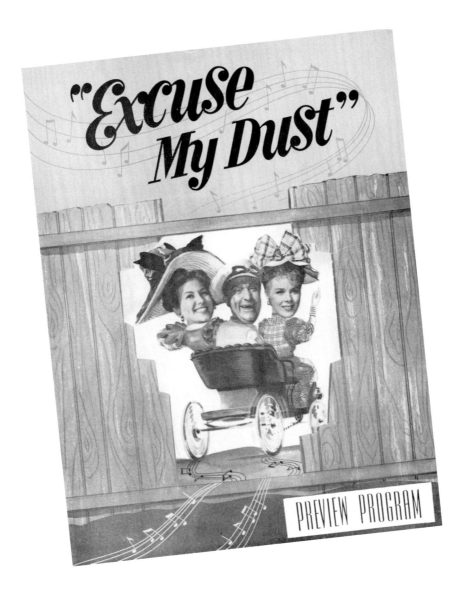

playing a turn-of-the-century 'flirt' with a penchant for French malapropisms culled from two weeks in Paris. Saucy, pert and with eyes that rove as freely as her hips, pretty Miss Lewis wraps up every scene for a big personal hit." And the *New York Sun Telegram* hailed: "[Monica Lewis] is a merry comedienne with a roguish relish for her role. The pleasant memories about *Excuse My Dust* are likely to recall…that this was the picture that first brought [her] to the screen." Finally, the work and the press I craved! I was thrilled.

In the still-considerable downtime between movie projects, I found time for fun on both coasts—dating, among others, *New York World-Telegram and Sun* columnist Frank Farrell and film producer Arthur Loew, Jr., whose grandfather founded MGM and father became a president of the studio. And I continued doing junkets. In 1951, one of the most ambitious was a multi-day visit to Mexico City for its annual Spring Festival, where I donned a "Miss Hollywood" sash and served as ambassador for the U.S. film industry. More importantly, I continued making music. "I Only Have Eyes for You" and "Nevertheless" were two of my best efforts that year, as was "Out of Breath"—one of several duets I did with singer Johnny Desmond.

EXCUSE MY DUST

The musical comedy *Excuse My Dust*, released in 1951, brought me my first featured role. The marvelous cast included Sally Forrest, Macdonald Carey, and top-billed clown extraordinaire Red Skelton, who played a late-1800s small-town eccentric struggling to work out the kinks in a gas-powered vehicle he invented. The film had a sprightly original score by Dorothy Fields and Arthur Schwartz (who was simultaneously enjoying success on Broadway with *A Tree Grows in Brooklyn*) and dance numbers staged by Fred Astaire's choreographer, Hermes Pan, who was my leg-crossing etiquette instructor at MGM. My two solo song-and-dance numbers, "That's for Children" and "Lorelei Brown," were pure, fluffy fun, as was the experience of the entire production.

October 17th
1 9 5 0

Monica dear:

May this be the beginning
of many good ones for you.

Good luck and a happy picture.

Love

Lillian

OFFICE OF
DORE SCHARY
VICE-PRESIDENT
IN CHARGE OF PRODUCTION

October 17, 1950

Dear Monica:

You're going to make a very cute Daisy Lou in
EXCUSE MY DUST, and I know we'll all be very
happy with your performance.

I'm sure it will be a good comedy and you'll
have fun making it.

Sincerely,

DS:mb

Miss Monica Lewis
c/o EXCUSE MY DUST

GROWLINGS IN THE LION'S DEN

MGM's Golden Age dominance of the movie business came to an end after World War II. Much has already been written about the studio's political infighting during this transitional period in entertainment, when television began vying with film for the public's attention and the Hollywood studios were competing for slices of a shrinking industry pie. Beyond my immediate, mostly civil dealings with MGM drama coach Lillian Burns and production executive Dore Schary (see their accompanying notes about the role I won in the studio's *Excuse My Dust*), I can offer only my limited perspective as a tiny cog in what was a sputtering machine.

To bolster its chances for survival, MGM diversified into other media when, in 1946, it founded its recording division, and the studio made a more determined shift toward screen spectacle to exploit TV's obvious limitations. But the company's most consistently popular output remained the film musical—thanks mainly to the sensational dance moves choreographed or directed by the likes of Hermes Pan, Stanley Donen, and Michael Kidd, and performed by incredible hoofers such as Fred Astaire, Gene Kelly, and Ann Miller. (MGM's musical production unit, led almost autonomously by Arthur Freed, worked hard to keep the genre fresh through the early 1950s with hits like *An American in Paris*, *Singin' in the Rain*, and *The Band Wagon*.)

When Dore Schary replaced MGM founder Louis B. Mayer as president in 1951, it was evident that he wanted go in a less theatrical direction. Marilyn Monroe just didn't do it for him. And in my case, while I think he liked me, he didn't seem interested in pulchritude and charm. He was not a big fan of larger-than-life personalities or even escapist fare.

Schary's leadership cast a pall over the lot.

The were other big factors stressing MGM, including the Supreme Court's 1948 antitrust ruling requiring the studios to divest of their movie theater holdings—ending controlled film distribution, and by extension, landing a debilitating blow on profits and talent contracts. But Dore's myopic stewardship hastened the decline of MGM and was another sign of the Hollywood studio system's coming demise.

Enjoying an evening at New York's elegant Barberry Room with columnist Frank Farrell, who was one of my most ardent supporters as well as an infrequent date. My stylish hat, sleek black crepe dress, and scooped neckline wowed club patrons.

I practiced ballet at the studio daily and had regular scene-reading exercises with Lillian. Sometimes Lillian's sessions would stray from business into personal advice: how to live, who to date, who not to sleep with, and so on. I just wanted to slap her.

MGM had a repertory group, and for some reason I was put in with the younger performers—the "training group," as the studio brass dubbed it. They tried to make me up like Jane Powell because I had dimples. They were putting Loretta Young dresses on me and pinning them in the back because she was so tall. Despite this novice treatment, I was always on time and ready—and I gave them what they wanted.

They wanted clones.

I laughed knowingly when the great dancer Moira Shearer, who three years earlier had become famous as the star of the classic ballet drama *The Red Shoes*, said to me in the commissary, "They have a regular passion for grooming here, don't they?"

Much as I loved that I was in L.A., professional satisfaction remained elusive. There was no dramatic breakthrough where I was getting anything challenging to do. I was just being compliant. My brother Marlo knew I was unhappy. I felt like wailing when he took me out to dinner for a heart-to-heart talk during one of one his visits from New York. "I'm doing everything I ever wanted," I said, "but when I drive through the lot, they greet me like I'm a little girl. I can't stand it."

"You have to stop being the learner," Marlo counseled. "I don't mean that you should stop learning, but you've got to establish firmly that you're not straight from the farm. Don't let them think or say, 'We discovered you.'"

Marlo was right. But I also knew that, after a year on the lot, it was too late to change perceptions, let alone renegotiate contract terms. Had I arrived at MGM two years earlier,

Budding actor and producer Arthur Loew, Jr., grandson of MGM founder and movie theater magnate Marcus Loew, was a sweet friend and occasional escort.

the situation would have been different. The musical as a cinema form was now on its way out—and that was clearly where I belonged as an actor and singer. I wasn't ready, nor did I particularly wish, to do Euripides's *Medea*.

I met Judy Garland in Hollywood in March 1951, well before she became a legend. This was more than a decade after she established herself as a major force at MGM with *The Wizard of Oz* and a few years before she starred in the big George Cukor remake of *A Star is Born*. We shared a dressing room while performing in a special radio broadcast revival of MGM's hit 1948 musical *Easter Parade*, founded on Irving Berlin's song of the same name, and we had a ball. Fred Astaire and Peter Lawford reprised their roles as Don Hewes and Jonathan Harrow III, respectively, while Judy, of course, was back as Hannah Brown. I played Nadine Hale—the role originated on-screen by Ann Miller—and my big song was Berlin's "How Deep is the Ocean," which replaced the movie's splashy dance number "Shakin' the Blues Away."

Judy impressed me in so many ways, but I was perhaps most amazed that she could scarf down pastrami sandwiches and pickles and then go on the air and belt without belching. Her daughter Liza, who was just five, was almost always with her. Perhaps because she was always surrounded by cabaret-type performers, Judy dug me and loved jazz musicians in general; I always got the feeling she was picking my brain on the subject. In the time I spent with her, she was never less than warm and down-to-earth.

It was rare of Judy to confide any of her problems to anyone, but while we were doing *Easter Parade*, she admitted

Working with Judy Garland—a true child of MGM—was such a pleasure for me. The inspirational power of Judy's voice triumphed over her personal troubles to make her a legend.

to me that her famous vibrato was becoming too much of a tremolo—her voice was starting to quiver excessively. "I've got to work on my breathing again," Judy said. "If I let go, I'm starting to sound like a Hawaiian houseboy."

"Do your 'lu-lu-lu's and your 'mi-mi-mi's," I said, recommending a common vocal exercise. "Just do them softly."

"I know, I know," she responded, waving at me with a little laugh. But she wouldn't do the exercise in front of me.

But, whatever personal demons she had, Judy was always good-humored—and sometimes downright funny—when I ran into her at parties and social functions. Often I would find myself in a corner gabbing with her; she always had offbeat takes on things. And if she drank too much, which was the norm for most of us at such affairs, she became very "British" to avoid slurring her words.

Growing up at MGM, Judy learned every secret of presentation. She and Mickey Rooney were virtually born of show business and experienced every pleasure and pang of adolescence against the surreal studio backdrop. Their almost symbiotic maturation crystallized with their work together in the Busby Berkeley musical *Babes on Broadway* in 1941. They could sing, dance, and play drums—and they both became awfully good actors. Whether on screen or on stage, Judy never needed special effects or backup singers. Her voice radiated power and love. It is tragic that the comfort she fostered with the camera and the audience never quite extended to her. Perhaps with today's advances in addiction-curing and psychiatry, she could have had a longer and happier life.

I had great times with Judy. I wish there could have been more of those great times for me—and for everyone who was touched by her talent.

While Judy Garland harbored concerns about her voice, I knew my own was getting lost in the daily studio bustle. Worse, I developed a not-so-healthy attitude: If I was going to dance away my career at MGM, I would have the grandest, damnedest time doing it.

There were deep-seated issues I needed to resolve. One was my irritation with how sexuality, more than talent, attracted people to me. Perhaps this was silly; looks *are*, after all, a huge part of show business, and I certainly flaunted mine in advertising and publicity. But it also fueled the lingering childhood sense of inferiority I felt in relation to the rest of my family's talent. There wasn't one thing I really did better than anybody; rather, the many things I did very well comprised a brightly packaged commodity.

And then there was my inability or unwillingness to give myself over completely to love—to look beyond the fun of a romp and say, "My God, this is something real." The random dalliances were little more than Band-Aids applied haphazardly to my battered post-divorce ego. True romantic fulfillment remained out of my grasp.

A performer without self-involvement is in trouble, and I could no longer deny that I needed help. On the recommendation of Bill Golub, my sister Bobbe's husband, I contacted

MGM had me play everything from soft to sultry in publicity shoots. The problem was that the studio didn't really know what it wanted me to be.

a highly regarded Beverly Hills psychiatrist named Leo Rangell. I scheduled daily appointments early in the morning or during my lunch break.

Dr. Rangell helped put my life in perspective. He showed me how to check the frustration arising from my desire for stronger movie roles and higher billing and demand the best songs and photographic angles—all the stuff that goes with the territory but can lead a female entertainer to a very unhappy old age. For two years, through both in-person sessions and correspondence, I leaned heavily on Dr. Rangell's therapeutic brilliance and gradually realized that he was the best investment I ever made in myself. (Six decades after I first met him, he was still publishing articles and serving as honorary president of the International Psychoanalytical Association.) Without his patient ear and advice, I can't fathom having enjoyed a wonderfully full-bodied romantic relationship with a very special man in the latter half of the 1950s.

But first, I still had some hard lessons to learn in love and life.

In July 1951, my folks and I were having dinner at Chasen's—the new center of my social universe—when across the room I noticed two men sharing a table. One was Ben Roberts, a noted screenwriter (*White Heat, Captain Horatio Hornblower, R.N.*) whom I knew from New York, where he sometimes collaborated with Sidney Sheldon. The other clearly

After my split from Ronald Reagan, I fell so hard for screenwriter Liam O'Brien that it set me on a new, and unexpectedly challenging, course toward marriage.

was Irish—with gorgeous black hair and blue eyes—and I batted my lashes at him shamelessly during the meal. Afterward, as we were waiting for our car, Ben emerged from the restaurant and greeted us, introducing his friend as Liam O'Brien, also a screenwriter.

Both men were chewing gum. I asked Liam if he had any to share. "I'm sorry, dear," he replied with a wink, making sure Ben was distracting my parents. "But if there is anything else you need at any other time, give me a call."

A couple of weeks later, MGM held a grand Hollywood premiere for *Show Boat*, a musical starring my friends Kathryn Grayson, Ava Gardner, and Howard Keel, and directed by George Sidney (*Anchors Aweigh*, *Annie Get Your Gun*). The studio publicity department wanted me to accompany Clark Gable to the event. Clark had long been my idol; I had seen *Gone With the Wind* about two hundred times. But by this time Clark was fifty, and I had the hots for a guy somewhat closer to my age who I hardly knew. So I told powerful MGM publicity head Howard Strickling that I wanted to choose my own date. He chided me for being foolish in forsaking such a big media opportunity but didn't force the issue.

I had already done some research on Liam O'Brien—discovering that, in addition to co-writing the Glenn Ford-starring Civil War drama *The Redhead and the Cowboy* and the Frank Capra comedy *Here Comes the Groom* with Bing Crosby and Jane Wyman, he was the older brother of actor Edmond O'Brien. Under contract at Twentieth Century Fox, he was also unmarried.

I phoned him.

"Hi, love, what can I do for you?" Liam asked.

"You can keep your gum," I tried to joke. "I've been ordered to the opening of *Show Boat* and I need an escort."

"They didn't supply someone wonderful?" he teased.

I was so nervous the handset was knocking my ear. "Yeah, they did," I answered, and then blurted: "But I'd prefer going with somebody I think might be better."

He chuckled. "You've got a deal. But I'll have to get my tux out of mothballs because I never go to those goddamn things!"

On the night of the premiere, Liam picked me up at my apartment. With gentlemanly manners, cultured wit, and the natural charm of a bard, he made a great impression on my folks. At the theater, we strode along the red carpet together and posed with Dore Schary and some costumed extras in the lobby. Everyone took our pictures.

My parents joined us following the screening for an after-party catered by MGM. We all enjoyed the evening, and my folks went home early. Liam and I remained parked at a

My first date with Liam O'Brien (left) was the September 1951 premiere of the MGM musical *Show Boat*. Chatting up one of the live entertainers here is none other than Dore Schary, who had risen to studio head from production chief that June following Louis B. Mayer's resignation.

LIFE AS A "LANA"-LIKE

Establishing my own identity at MGM was pretty futile. The comparisons between me and company box-office force Lana Turner—star of late-1940s hits like *The Postman Always Rings Twice, Green Dolphin Street,* and *The Three Musketeers*, as well as several pictures with Clark Gable—began as soon as my studio contract talks got underway in the spring of 1950, with columnist Hedda Hopper declaring me "a combination of Lana Turner and Betty Grable."

Catching me completely off guard one day on the Culver City lot, the iconic blonde herself stopped me as I left one of the sets. "Hi, I'm Lana Turner," she said with big smile. "I saw your show at the Mocambo and loved it. You're fantastic! I hope the studio finds something decent for you to do. You really should be in Arthur Freed's production unit because he makes the best musicals here." Lana kissed me and wished me good luck. I was awestruck! She then added as she walked off: "Don't let them try to make you like me. You just be you."

"God, I'm trying!" I yelled back with a wave.

The visual linkage between the two of us was strengthened further in February 1951, when *Parade* magazine ran a story titled "Lana-types" featuring up-and-comers including Mary Beth Hughes, Marilyn Monroe, and me. The article reported that after my first makeover at MGM, my publicity photos "came out looking so much like Lana that Monica was rushed back to the beauty parlor and given a new shade of hair."

It was silly and annoying.

Before too long, Lana became pregnant and stopped working. MGM was furious with her, so in early 1952 they started grooming me in earnest as a "threat." The studio planned to cast me opposite Vic Damone in an updating of *The Merry Widow*, a role intended for Lana. They even airbrushed Lana's head onto my body to create a publicity photo. But then she miscarried—and she returned to the studio to do the picture with Fernando Lamas. It premiered in September 1952.

With one "Lana Turner" too many, MGM pretty much let me languish. And within a few years, as the industry underwent a forced evolution, it had no use for Lana, either.

Rosemary Clooney and I did several radio shows together and were friends in jazz musicianship. Here, she was still flying high with her 1951 pop hit "Come On-a My House"—a song she despised—on the Columbia label, and we had started discussing china and linens to register for her impending wedding to actor José Ferrer.

cozy corner table with drinks and talked until four o'clock in the morning. There was no question this was going somewhere, although not on this particular date. "This has been the most amazing evening," Liam said, holding my hand as it came time to part. "I picked you up, not knowing what to expect, and you were darling. Then I meet these two adorable, beautiful people—your parents. How could I figure this was a one-nighter when I met all of you and saw the love?"

He drove me back to my apartment and we said our last goodnights. The following day, I was exhausted, but I went to work anyway. I was worried that he wasn't going to follow up with a call or other gesture. But with no fanfare, Liam phoned and suggested a quiet dinner. And so it began. Something different was happening to me—I was experiencing love for the first time as a fully realized and newly self-aware adult. Suddenly, everything shone under a warmly optimistic light. I was sharing the sunny clime of L.A. with my parents. I was making money. I was in the movies. All aspects of my life, at last, appeared to be coming together. For the moment.

Hanging out at Ciro's with fellow MGM players Fernando Lamas (*The Merry Widow*) and Anna Marie Pierangeli, who had shortened her native Italian name to Pier Angeli (*Teresa*, *The Devil Makes Three*). Keeping it all in the MGM family, two years later Anna Marie was married to Vic Damone and Fernando to studio contractee Arlene Dahl.

♫

Far, far from Hollywood, the tense period of economic competition, espionage, and nuclear arms proliferation following World War II—i.e., the Cold War—was erupting anew. After the previous decade's global conflict and the surrender of Japan, the Allies agreed to divide the Korean peninsula into a communist north and a democratic south. In June 1950, North Korean forces invaded South Korea. President Truman, likening the spread of communism to earlier threats posed by Germany's Hitler, Italy's Mussolini, and Japan's Tojo, threw U.S. military support behind the United Nations Security Council's effort to halt the aggression.

Our forces were in the thick of battle near Korea's 38th parallel by late 1951. During and after my transition from the East Coast to the West Coast, I had remained an unflagging supporter of the U.S. Armed Forces through military hospital visits and a prior deal I had made with World Transcription Service, for which I recorded songs each week for globally syndicated radio airplay. So when my very energetic and dear friend Danny Kaye—inspired by the troop morale-boosting tours completed overseas by Bob Hope and others with sponsorship by the United Service Organizations (USO)—opted to undertake a similar journey to Korea financed by the U.S. Department of Defense, I was thrilled when he asked me to accompany him. With nothing firm project-wise on my MGM schedule, I asked the studio for a one-month leave to spend the holidays with Danny and the troops in Korea. There was no expense involved on MGM's part, and seeing the potential publicity benefits it could reap, the studio quickly gave its blessing.

I knew this was the chance of a lifetime—and possibly my best exercise in greater-perspective development since I began my therapy with Dr. Rangell. It would also be an opportunity for me to return to being *me*: a seasoned professional who knew her craft and enjoyed every second of it. I was unfazed by the impending discomfort and danger of traveling and performing within a combat zone (which I will describe fully in the following chapter).

Upon returning from Korea in January 1952, I acknowledged to myself definitively that I was not getting career satisfaction at MGM and that my own identity was getting lost. Journalists described me as a "freshly-scrubbed Lauren Bacall" and compared my voice endlessly to Dinah Shore's. One even wrote: "She not only looks like Lana Turner, but does it better." Taking a kind of insurance policy out on one of its biggest female stars, the studio continued to style me in Lana's image. It was beyond aggravating.

If not for the income from my Chiquita Banana promotional work and my arrangement with World Transcription Service, I would have been broke. But I resisted complaining because I valued the knowledge I was gaining—particularly the different styles of acting required by drama, theater, and comedy. I learned how to make love with the camera.

To make matters worse, shortly after I returned from Korea, Louis B. Mayer—my highest-ranked cheerleader on the lot—resigned after a long period of political maneuvering between him, Dore Schary, and Nicholas Schenck, the chief of Loew's Inc. (MGM's corporate parent). Schary became the new head of MGM, and everything seemed to shift very conservatively.

One day I had an appointment to meet with Dore Schary and the rest of the newer players, who included Pier Angeli, Leslie Caron, Carleton Carpenter, and Debbie Reynolds. Appropriate to the weather, I arrived at the studio wearing a beautiful strapless summer sundress and looked just great.

Lillian Burns sized me up and down, shaking her head. "Not for Mr. Schary," she stated, acknowledging that L.B. Mayer may have approved…if he was still around. "I want you to wear white gloves and a high-neck dress."

I stood my ground. "But I am who I am, you know?"

"You'll be whatever we need you to be so you can be what you want to be," Lillian snapped. "If you want to get out of this group and get the good parts, you'll do as I say. I'm telling you that Dore doesn't date theatrics."

Lillian sent me home. Back on Sunset Plaza, I put on a navy skirt with a navy sweater and a string of phony pearls and white gloves, exchanging my sandals for pumps and hose. I nearly had a heat stroke by the time I returned to the lot. "That's the look," Lillian approved.

It didn't help. Dore Schary could see that the outfit wasn't really me. After examining me briefly, he leaned back, swiveled ever so gently, and said, "What's a nice girl like you doing in a place like this?"

I wanted to kill myself.

In addition to seeing Liam O'Brien, I found myself serving as his muse. He had been writing a play—a romantic comedy called *The Remarkable Mr. Penny Packer*—and had managed to finish only the first act. When he wasn't playing tennis, he would just sit at his desk and sharpen pencils for hours. I talked to him about how important it was to focus on the work, and we discussed it over meals and during long walks. After months of subtle whip-cracking, I helped him unblock. He completed the play and it opened in New York in 1952, with Burgess Meredith in the title role. It was a smash.

While my romance with Liam provided a new focus in my personal life, my regular sessions with Dr. Rangell helped level out the rollercoaster emotions tied to my status at MGM. I kept myself from stalking off the lot long enough for the studio to come up with another movie for me: *Everything I Have is Yours*, a 1952 Technicolor release featuring the popular married dance team of Marge and Gower Champion. I was given three songs to perform, including the title tune, as well as several key dialogue scenes.

Again, my hopes were raised.

The storyline was typical Hollywood pap. Marge and Gower were Pamela and Chuck Hubbard—a married dance team (what a stretch!) headlining a big Broadway show. On opening night, Pamela discovers she's pregnant. Her understudy, Sybil Meriden (me), must take her place, and over the run of the production Sybil becomes a big star. Flirtations intensify between Chuck and Sybil while Pamela remains stuck in a nice country house with the baby—painting and otherwise occupying herself as her jealously builds. Whether Marge and/or Gower demanded it or the screenwriters lost the courage of their convictions, nothing physical happens between Sybil and Chuck, save for one dynamite production number.

EVERYTHING I HAVE IS YOURS

Released in 1952, *Everything I Have is Yours* was another modest musical in which I played a featured role. Working with husband-and-wife dancers Marge and Gower Champion—in their first top billing—was a total delight. Other aspects of the production, namely the script and the lazy treatment of my character, were not so great. Still, I had a relatively substantial amount of dialogue and sang several songs, including the title number and a show-stopping set piece called "17,000 Telephone Poles." According to columnist Frank Farrell, when I "turned up for hoofing rehearsals in a set of snug pants that started camera crews whistling while they worked, MGM realized it had only half-exploited its talented find." But by then, I had decided to leave the studio.

In June 1952, the Society of Illustrators named me America's "Miss Leg-O-Genic." I posed on a stage for press photographers and something the group called its Committee on Anatomical Nomenclature. Members Walter Klett and Floyd Davis sketched me while Society representative Arthur William Brown (left) offered some amusing algebraic measurements.

Marge and Gower were talented and inventive, and it was a joy to work with them. We became lifelong friends. But the script and the handling of my character in *Everything I Have is Yours*, I felt, were a mess. As with my earlier small parts, I was reduced to token singing appearances that were silly from an acting standpoint and poorly integrated into the story.

There was no reason why I shouldn't have been given a shot at doing the sort of light-comedy roles, for instance, that my friend Doris Day—who also came out of radio and recording—enjoyed at Warner Bros. Doris could have wound up a second banana like me, but she got very lucky and had the right enthusiastic people behind her. She did some really wonderful work, like her portrayal of Jazz Age torch singer Ruth Etting in *Love Me or Leave Me* (1955).

Interestingly, MGM never failed to issue a print movie ad without my image in it—even though my roles usually were too small to warrant such play and the studio had no contractual obligation to do so. My countenance was always there along with the faces of Mickey Rooney, Sally Forrest, Red Skelton, and the Champions. I could sell tickets, but—no matter how well I tested for a part or was rated by preview screening audiences—I could not get a meaty role in a well-written script.

Positive notices never failed to come my way, albeit from some unexpected places. In June 1952, shortly after I began my summer hiatus from the studio, The Society of Illustrators—an organization of famous illustrators (including Norman Rockwell and James Montgomery Flagg) whose work appeared in newspapers, magazines, and books—named me "Miss Leg-O-Genic." They gave me a big plaque describing me as "the most leg-o-genic girl in America"—the designation intended to be more dignified than, say, slang terms like "gams," "pins," or "cheesecake." MGM publicity found it harmless and amusing. I accepted the award with gratitude and grace.

The next month, my fellow MGM singer-actor Carleton Carpenter and I were granted permission by the studio to appear in a theater production at the very prestigious La Jolla Playhouse—named for the lovely southern California resort town in which it was located. Titled *Remains to be Seen*, the play was a comedy-whodunit written by Howard Lindsay and Russell Crouse, who had enjoyed an extended run with it on Broadway.

Gregory Peck, Dorothy McGuire, and Mel Ferrer served as the La Jolla's board of producers; it was Mel who had offered to Carleton and me the lead roles originated onstage by Jackie Cooper and Janis Paige. I played Jody Revere, a Manhattan band singer whose wealthy uncle has been murdered and who is the prime suspect. Carleton, who had teamed successfully at MGM with Debbie Reynolds (their rendition of "Aba Daba Honeymoon" from *Two Weeks with Love* became a huge hit) and had just scored the lead in the comedy-western *Sky Full of Moon*, played Waldo Williams—the manager of a high-end apartment building where the crime has occurred.

My fellow MGM "newbie" Carleton Carpenter and I in the comedy-who-dunit *Remains to be Seen*, a summer 1952 production of the La Jolla Play-house. The experience gave me a level of professional satisfaction I wasn't getting at MGM.

I had a special affinity for the story because Jody was a young woman who auditioned for Benny Goodman. In addition to being an instant publicity hook, my parallels to the character gave me the confidence to add some flair in the form of dialogue and song bits, high-kicking, slapstick, and other tried-and-true performance tricks. (I personally cleared these embellishments with writers Lindsay and Crouse.)

After a week of intense rehearsals, we did a full week of shows. Carleton and I got a million laughs and the reviews were fantastic. We had a ball.

Summer 1952 brought another surprise: My Society of Illustrators honor had drawn the attention of hosiery manufacturer Burlington Mills, which then signed me to be the face (and legs) of a $1 million nationwide promotional tour. MGM immediate seized upon the publicity value of this nine-week, coast-to-coast promotion—the tour was set to begin in September, the same month the studio had slated the release of *Everything I Have is Yours*—and raised no objection to the deal as long as I promoted the film and its soundtrack album in all twenty-six of the scheduled cities along the way. Although this arrangement was not professionally rewarding, it was very lucrative and a necessary evil: It would help me pay off my bills and regain control of my destiny.

Every day of the tour was pretty much the same: rising early, downing lots of coffee, and jumping into another round of radio and TV interviews and press conferences. And then it was on to a great department store, where I sat on a high stage while hundreds of women chatted with me, sought autographs, and bought hosiery. I made many new friends, but the pace was taxing—and I wasn't singing.

I was more than ready to get back to my creative source by the time the tour wrapped in early November. Upon returning to the MGM lot, I asked to be released from my acting contract. The studio did not challenge me, and I had no regrets. As aggravating as it had been, I embraced my experience at the studio as a gigantic leap forward in knowledge.

All that spring and summer, Liam and I had discussed at length my career status, his ongoing projects, and our mutual feelings—and we reaffirmed our deep love for each other. We decided to make it official.

Because I had been married previously, we had to cede to Liam's religious affiliation and get a dispensation from the Catholic Church. We were hoping to obtain one called the Pauline Privilege locally and quickly, but according to the Church, I had a major impediment: My first husband, Bob Thiele, was a Methodist whose Catholic aunt had him baptized in the Catholic Church. The Church actually investigated all this—and decided that my divorce was invalid. We were told we needed a dispensation from Rome called the Petrine Privilege, which was based on St. Peter's code.

I was fit to be tied. I didn't want all of this—I just wanted to get married. I consulted my friend Jo Stafford, a top vocalist who was enjoying a big success with her cover version of country crooner Hank Williams's "Jambalaya." She had to abandon atheism and become

STOMPING FOR BURLINGTON MILLS HOSIERY

On the heels of my "Miss Leg-O-Genic" title, I was tapped by hosiery manufacturer Burlington Mills in August 1952 to headline a two-month fall national tour on behalf of its Bur-Mil Cameo brand. Promoting the hosiery with the "face-powder finish" (warned the ads: "When a girl's stockings shine—she doesn't!") was a well-compensated deal. And it placed me among the rarefied group of women to have had their legs insured for $1 million through Lloyds of London.

During the tour, as I had done almost daily for years, I wrote to all the columnists in New York, Hollywood, and elsewhere to tell them where I would be and what I was doing. I kept a record of all the disc jockeys, including the names of their wives and children and even their birthdays. I worked harder than most for my plugs; it set me apart from other celebrities and ensured that some kind of reception or coverage would always be waiting. Henry Rogers, my personal publicist, was so impressed with my promotional acumen that years later he invited me to be a partner in his firm. (I declined.)

a Catholic to marry the great music arranger and conductor Paul Weston. I asked Jo, "What if you really don't believe all this stuff?"

"You can believe whatever you choose," she said.

"Do you believe it?"

"All you have to worry about is your immortal soul," Jo replied. "Take your chances, Monica."

Liam helped me with the initial religious instruction, and he was completely supportive of my decision to leave MGM and return to live performing. He understood my need to work consistently, and as someone who had to travel frequently between Hollywood and New York, he knew that his bi-coastal existence would make it easier for us to maintain our relationship. My parents, of course, were fully behind whatever career decisions I made, and they looked forward to a return welcome from their wealth of friends in Manhattan. It would be a fonder farewell to L.A. than I could have hoped.

Just before I relinquished my apartment, I received a call from Scrappy Lambert, a former pop vocalist who was working as a talent scout for RKO Radio Pictures (the studio that delivered the classics *King Kong* and *Citizen Kane*) and its owner, Howard Hughes. Scrappy had been impressed by my performance in *Remains to be Seen* and told his boss about me. Howard wanted to discuss a possible starring role for me in a feature drama called *Affair With a Stranger*, which concerned the repercussions of an erroneously reported split between a successful playwright (played by Victor Mature) and his ex-model wife (Jean Simmons). I was in Howard's sights as "the other woman."

In preparation for my meeting with the reclusive tycoon, Scrappy instructed me to speak loudly at Howard, who was partly deaf. The appointment came just a couple days after I had one of my wisdom teeth pulled, so my face was completely swollen on one side—which I knew wouldn't help matters.

At RKO's big, beautiful office building in the heart of the Sunset Strip, I was ushered into a cavernous conference room with views so expansive they seemed to stretch a hundred miles south to San Diego. Howard was already seated and paging through a script. I was directed to a plush conference chair about fifteen feet away from him (it was no secret he was paranoid about germs). Once I was seated, he lifted his craggy, mustachioed countenance and proceeded to be very charming.

"I've heard so much about you, and it's a pleasure to finally meet," he said. "What did you think of the script?"

Holding an ice pack to my face self-consciously, I yelled, "Oh yes, Mr. Hughes—I like it very much. I think I can do a lot with the part."

Howard smiled and replied, "Welcome to RKO, dear. You're a beautiful and talented young lady. I know that you'll be wonderful."

That was it. There was no audition. I thanked Howard from afar across the conference table and left.

My role in *Affair With a Stranger* was substantial and heavy with dialogue, and all of my scenes were with Victor Mature. In one scene I sang a song that had been commissioned for me, "Kiss and Run," and played piano. Another scene had me unzipping my dress in a

provocative way—a big deal in those days. The scene turned out to be quite cute and funny. Nothing showed; it was all attitude and movement. And if it had a bit of extra zest, it was because I considered it my symbolic shedding of MGM and its bad contract.

Affair With a Stranger would be one of Howard Hughes' last pictures. But it was the first time on a film set that I was treated respectfully as an artist, and it brought me a good deal of money. I grabbed my loot, packed up Mom and Dad, and blew a kiss to the apartment before leaving it for the last time. En route to the airport, we reminisced about the mostly marvelous two-and-a-half years we had enjoyed as a unit in the City of Angels. Although it was goodbye, I knew it wasn't for good.

We flew to New York first-class for the first time in our lives.

Resettling in Manhattan was like slipping into an old shoe. Before the end of December 1952, I signed up with the William Morris Agency for live performance representation and honed a new act. I was hungry for the New Year, a revitalized career, and my impending married life.

Although I visited New York a number of times after moving to Los Angeles, I had done no performing in the city since inking my pact with MGM in early 1950. So my return engagement at the Plaza Hotel—one of the Big Apple's oldest and most beautiful buildings—was a big deal both for me and the press, who welcomed me back with open arms. I was set to open at the hotel's Persian Room on January 8th, 1953, for a full month. Grand and elegant, with a gorgeous stage and a dance floor in the center surrounded by booths, the Persian Room was one of the top venues for hearing

Securing the part of Janet Boothe, the "other woman" in RKO's 1953 Jean Simmons-Victor Mature drama *Affair With a Stranger*, was the sweetest parting gift from L.A. that I could have hoped for immediately after I left MGM. The role wasn't just another musical interlude; I had several key dialogue scenes with Victor (opposite). For my sexy turn at the piano, I sang a tune called "Kiss and Run"—which was also the film's presumably less titillating original title.

music—the most expensive such ticket in the city. It served the best food, the best wine, and had the best acts in New York.

My opening night sold out. In addition to the media, Liam, my family, and many of my oldest friends were in the audience. Danny Kaye was there, too, and I introduced him in his booth from the stage.

The next night, the hotel had to double the number of waiters to handle the crowd. The ninety-minute show I assembled was colorful and eclectic. I brought in a bongo player along with my pianist and pulled out all the stops—mixing some of my own hits with offbeat tunes. I performed a popular song of Greek origin called "Miserlou" (fully Americanized and immortalized by The Beach Boys on their *Surfin' USA* album ten years later) and even included a Korean folk song, "Arirang," that I had picked up during my overseas military tour. And I had special material for the show titled "What Kind of Woman Do You Want Me to Be?"—the story, really, of my adult life—written by songwriter Irvin Graham ("I Believe," "You Better Go Now"). Between sets, I shared with the audience some of my experiences in Hollywood and Korea.

From sound to lighting to the air temperature maintained in the room, I was a stickler for presentation. And with my new-found Hollywood film-set experience, I wasn't letting anything slip—especially with my wardrobe. One of the great joys of playing the Persian Room was my re-teaming with Burton Miller, who designed gorgeous costume dresses and boas for me. I wore a four-inch heel with only two rhinestone straps to hold it on. My makeup and hair were just as impeccable.

The show, like the Persian Room itself, was classy, gorgeous and intimate. I had a fantastic opening and run—and it was made all the better because Liam was in town with me

The Persian Room at the Plaza Hotel was among Manhattan's grandest music venues—the best place for my return to New York and live performing. I happily renewed my creative collaboration with my close friend Burton Miller (inset), who designed this and other fantastic stage outfits for me.

for most of it. I received great notices, including one in the ever-discriminating *New Yorker*. The operative critical word was "spectacular."

It was a wonderful homecoming.

WHAT KIND OF WOMAN DO YOU WANT ME TO BE?
By Irvin Graham

What kind of woman do you want me to be?
What kind of woman do you want me to be?
Tell me, and darling, I'll try diligently
To be the kind of woman that you want me to be...

Shall I be a goody-goody who won't smoke or drink
Who comes to you with downcast eyes and wears nothing but pink?
A little lady, winsome and coy
Who calls you "great big adorable boy"
Always so starched and purty
You won't dare talk dirty
Which I happen to know that you just love to do...
But darling if you want a goody-goody...
I'll be a goody-goody just for you...

What kind of woman do you want me to be?
What kind of woman do you want me to be?

Shall I be the intellectual who's read all the books
Who believes that culture's more important than looks
And every time we're alone just we two...
I'll explain flying saucers to you...
I'll be brilliant and clever and haunt you forever
With evidence of my far higher I.Q!.
But darling if you want a brilliant woman
I'll gladly go to night school just for you.

Or what kind of woman do you want me to be?
What kind of woman do you want me to be?

Would you like a wicked woman in a black negligee
Who makes love all night and sleeps right through the day
A fancy woman who walks with a slink
And whose favorite color is mink
I'll wear diamonds, and diamonds, and diamonds, and diamonds
Spend money 'til honey you haven't a sou
Yes, darling, I'll be a bad, bad, woman
If you think a bad, bad woman's good for you.

I'll be a
good woman, bad woman, happy woman, sad woman
redhead, blonde, brunette, bashful, coquette
shrewd woman, dumb woman, gay woman, glum woman
Any kind of woman in the world you ever knew
Oh darling if you'll only let me
I'll be all kinds of women to you
Yes, darling if you'll only let me
I'll be all *woman* for you!

The Persian Room gave me the boost I needed to advance on all fronts. With new material, new gowns, and a buoyant new raft of publicity, I confidently severed my last tenuous tie with MGM as a recording artist. The label's executives were not hip enough, frankly, to compete with power-house companies like Columbia; with the exception of my album, *Easy Come, Easy Go*, I felt that most of my efforts for MGM were relatively minor. Recording artists, I realized, were not of serious interest to the studios.

Subsequently, I contracted with a little New York label called Jubilee, for which I did several successful records—most notably *Fools Rush In*, an album of standards. Another small but very hip label, King, approached me to do a sophisticated rendition of a song of French origin that it owned, "I Wish You Love." It, too, charted highly before Keely Smith turned it into a standard. I then signed a long-term contract with Capitol Records, a wonderful major label with great musicians and arrangers like Nelson Riddle and Billy May. In October 1953, my Capitol debut, "Autumn Leaves," became a Top Ten hit.

Being a compulsive workaholic, I didn't want to waste a minute. In addition to pushing me for appearances at events and guest shots on radio and TV, William Morris got me booked for nightclub appearances all over the country. But the agency wasn't doing

Dean Martin and Jerry Lewis were among the friends who attended my January 1953 Persian Room opening. My young niece Joan Golub tried to keep from giggling when the guys posed with her backstage. I had spent enough time with the duo to know how she felt—and also to observe that while Dean was naturally straight-man funny, Jerry really wanted to be everything...most of all, Dean Martin.

anything that any other could have done, so I went back to MCA, where I had felt most comfortable. Thanks to my film work, I was able to command higher perform-ance fees: $5,000 a week, versus $50 when I first started out.

My relationship with Liam O'Brien remained strong through this period, and our efforts to clear the way for matrimony continued. Before leaving L.A., I had taken instruction in Catholicism at Loyola University and was baptized, with Jo Stafford and Paul Weston serving as my godparents. When I moved back to New York, the pre-dispensation application process and counseling continued at the St. Patrick's Cathedral chancery and in private with a Jesuit priest. I had great arguments with the priest about how the Holy Mother Mary ascended into heaven. (I could only visualize singer-actress Mary Martin doing that onstage in *Peter Pan*.) The priest, in his Irish brogue, admonished, "Ye have to take it on faith."

My family had to partake in several meetings with the Catholic Archdiocese; during these sessions, Liam sat in a waiting room with my sister's miniature poodle. My mother was an inadvertent hoot during one of the interviews. "You know," she confided, "my husband and I like Liam O'Brien a lot. In fact, we love him, and we think he's quite good enough to marry our daughter."

The priest raised an eyebrow. "That's very nice."

"Before you say anything else," Mom added earnestly, "my daughter is the most wonderful person in the world!"

It was quite a scene, and when I told Liam about it, he was very embarrassed. Although he was not a fully practicing Catholic, he was a devout and—based on my observation—sometimes tortured one.

After two years of submitting to the proper motions and rituals, I appealed to Rome for the dispensation in late 1953. I was informed it would take another year for the Vatican to respond.

To this day, I am astonished by the set of hurdles that delayed the ultimate consummation of my love for Liam. My final thought on religion: If something gives you comfort and solace and it doesn't hurt anyone else, I am all for it. It's your right to believe in anything you like politically, religiously, or otherwise—as long as you do not insist that I believe in it, or start a religious or political war over it.

My Persian Room run marked the end of my association with MGM Records; the album *Easy Come, Easy Go* was my best effort for the label (it was re-released later on the jazz-focused label Verve, which MGM bought in 1961). *Fools Rush In* was a successful album of standards I did for boutique label Jubilee before I signed with Capitol Records.

112

AUTUMN LEAVES

English Lyrics by **JOHNNY MERCER**

French Lyrics by **JACQUES PREVERT**
Music by **JOSEPH KOSMA**

MONICA LEWIS

PRICE 60c (In U.S.A.)

ARDMORE MUSIC CORP.
1730 BROADWAY, NEW YORK, N.Y.

My Capitol Records debut rendition of "Autumn Leaves," a jazz and pop standard with lyrics by Johnny Mercer, became a Top Ten smash in the fall of 1953. Like "I Wish You Love," it was a song of French origin.

$\square$

Between the protracted marriage preparations and my nonstop work schedule, I decided I needed some time off after 1954 rolled in. I gradually cut back on my travel. Instead of committing to engagements lasting a week or more, I flew into a city, played two nights at three or four clubs, made my money, and returned to New York.

I couldn't have been much happier, or more in demand, as a live entertainer. Yet I felt something was missing in my training all those years, and it had to do with my not really ever receiving intensive, professional acting lessons—not even at MGM. So in the summer of 1954, I attended the acting program headed by the influential acting teacher Sanford Meisner at the Neighborhood Playhouse, off Broadway. I was encouraged to do so by my friend Bob Fosse, a dancer and choreographer, who was doing the same thing. We shared a good laugh because most of the students were aspiring young actors, and there *we* were: two old show business pros!

I had known Bob since my early days in Manhattan, when he was part of a dance act called Fosse and Niles (he married dancer Mary Ann Niles at age seventeen). He aspired to be another Fred Astaire and was a real imp, with a wonderful sense of the ridiculous—and I guess he had to develop one, since he was raised in a brothel. He wasn't tall enough to be a movie lead or love interest; MGM, not surprisingly, didn't know what to do with him, so they had him dancing background for Ann Miller. But Bob was naturally smart and clever with a real vision. Somebody finally gave him a chance to show that vision, because he became one of the most famous choreographers of the 20th century and won an Oscar for directing the film musical *Cabaret* (1972).

Founded in part on the realistic approach to drama systemized by the Russian actor and theatre director Constantin Stanislavski, Sandy Meisner's technique involved improvisation and spontaneity, wherein the actor transfers a given character's existing emotions to a new time and setting and allows the character to "react" to the changes. Called the Meisner Technique, it was largely about increasing the performer's adaptability and extemporal resourcefulness, and it was one hell of an exercise. Sandy's course was fascinating and immensely helpful. It gave me a grasp on the method used by Robert Duvall, Grace Kelly, Gregory Peck, Tony Randall, and many other marvelous actors.

There were a number of people in my class who were quite good, but the one who emerged a superstar was Steve McQueen. At the time, Bob Fosse and I didn't know whether Steve understood what motivation was—he was very quiet and never let on that he was "getting" Sandy's approach. But his desire was evident. And despite the fact that he was an average-looking guy, he had an unusual set to his jaw and knack for taking and interpreting directions in surprising ways. It was all about restraint, and it really worked.

Nelson Riddle was one of the terrific arrangers with whom I collaborated at Capitol. Nelson worked with Nat King Cole, Ella Fitzgerald, Dean Martin, Judy Garland, Frank Sinatra, and other top vocalists through the mid-1960s and enjoyed a major comeback with Linda Ronstadt in the 1980s.

Steve would come to Sandy's class on his motorcycle, and soon he asked me out to lunch. We went Dutch because he only had a couple dollars. That I was virtually engaged didn't matter to either of us; for me, the meeting was strictly social. He had charm, but it wasn't a cultivated charm. I was struck by his ambition more than anything—that he had managed to scrape together enough money or rustle up a scholarship for that season with Sandy. Later, watching him in the western *The Magnificent Seven* (1960) and the World War II prisoner-of-war drama *The Great Escape* (1963)—both classics—I never felt Steve was less than a natural. He had a firm grasp on the camera's relationship to the screen and knew not to do anything larger than life. His performances always landed right where they needed to be, which gave him an iconic "cool." I was very happy for his success.

Pop icon Eddie Fisher and I appeared together more than a few times on national TV. Although Eddie could sing a ballad, he couldn't read music and he had no sense of rhythm; for duets, I had to put my arm around him and tap out the rhythms on his shoulder. No matter: Eddie had dozens of hit songs, including "Any Time" and "Oh! My Pa-Pa." And he sold millions of records.

I didn't have much opportunity to apply what I had learned from Sandy Meisner—not right away, at least. But I had plenty of work. My ongoing endorsements included ads for Chiquita Banana, Fannie May Candies, Golden Blossom Honey, and others. In March 1954, WABC-TV launched an evening TV version of my old short-lived radio show *Monica Makes Music* in the New York metro area, airing at seven o'clock five nights a week. On the program, I sang and interviewed personalities as well as expressed my views on current events, fashion, and entertainment.

And then there was dear Liam. After my bad first marriage and my series of fun but ultimately unfulfilling relationships, I felt I was ready to be married again. I thought Liam was The One.

But then something amazing happened.

One day in late 1954, while Liam was in California, I got a call from my brother-in-law, Bill Golub. Bill was my lawyer and had been helping me with all the dispensation documents. "I have great news for you," he began. "You've just received a papal dispensation. You are free and clear to marry O'Brien! Shall I send the papers up to your apartment?"

I was quiet just long enough for Bill to ask if I was still there. "Yeah…thanks, I'm here," I mumbled quietly.

He cleared his throat, obviously puzzled by my non-reaction. "So…?"

I continued flatly, "Bill, I would prefer that you file the dispensation under 'Miscellaneous.'"

Not only was I suddenly not excited, I could not go forward with it. And I couldn't quite explain why to *myself*, let alone Bill. Two years of being interrogated by the Church may have taken a toll. Or maybe it was just fate. I just realized that I had given everything. Liam had given me love, yes—but I had been offered love before. Perhaps it was because I was so knocked out over him for so long. I had been working, recording, and doing everything for my Mom, Dad, and Liam, and I was exhausted emotionally. I had given up so much that this just wouldn't work. I called Liam and told him I had received the papal dispensation.

"Great!" he shouted happily into the phone. "I'm flying right in." I told him not to. We both cried. He then got angry and demanded, "What in the world is going on with you?" I told him I didn't know.

My angst over my plans to marry Liam O'Brien, and the endless pre-dispensation application, drove me into social refuge. The Harwyn Club in New York, at 112 E. 52nd Street, was one of my comfort zones—and here it's kick-back time with Broadway light Elaine Stritch, actor Gig Young, and my best buddy Burt Miller.

Liam suggested that he fly east anyway and we should talk, but I said that it would only make things worse. He was so distraught that he had his MCA agent and frequent tennis partner Jennings Lang—a tall, very confident, and incredibly brilliant fellow who had just sold the film rights to Liam's *The Remarkable Mr. Pennypacker* to Twentieth Century Fox—call me and try to persuade me to change my mind. Jennings failed.

Liam accepted that it was over. Already needing a vacation after a very busy year—two of his bigger recent writing credits were the Rosemary Clooney musical *The Stars are Singing* and the Doris Day-Frank Sinatra musical drama *Young at Heart*—he retreated to Ireland for a month. From there he sent me a harsh letter. "By now we could be picking out curtains," he wrote in conclusion, "but I'm sure at this moment you are thinking about changing agents."

In my very fragile emotional state, it was a really hurtful touché. It also turned out to be prescient.

All the columnists in New York picked up on this story, and once again, my family was in shock. Liam was the first fellow they had truly liked. My parents sat down with me and said, "You may never find anyone else as nice, fun, or wonderful. But if this is your decision, you must have a good reason."

I began to think I had broken everyone else's hearts along with Liam's. I felt so empty and displeased with myself, and I went through months of heavy soul-searching. As the famous old song goes, I had to pick myself up, dust myself off, and start all over again.

Good tune. Good advice.

Actor (and later *Today Show* reporter and consumer advocate) Betty Furness snapped this candid shot of me on the town with all-around entertainer and *Tonight Show* host Steve Allen, a longtime friend, and New York radio and TV personality Eloise McElhone.

With a vague awareness of changes occurring within me, I set out anew. I had never thought about having children, but I began to feel as though I would like to have them; I just didn't know if I should do anything about it. Maybe it was coincidental, but after breaking off with Liam, I did several childhood disease-related fund-raisers including the hugely successful United Appeal Telethon in Charlotte, North Carolina, in December 1954. Beyond making me feel useful and boosting my self-esteem, my participation in such events gave me deep personal satisfaction.

Early in 1955, I resumed my comfortably random worker-bee ways on the nightclub circuit—dragging my pianist to posh venues in New Orleans, Chicago, Minneapolis, Las Vegas, and other major cities. I even agreed to appear at auto shows, which were prestige-free but big money. I was working, showing off, recording; altogether, I was more in charge of myself than ever before. Yet I became less enchanted with what I was doing. I was a celebrity but not a star.

That spring, I endeavored to cash in on a social investment in the form of Richard Rodgers, of the musical hit-making duo Rodgers and Hammerstein. I had befriended Richard (I called him Dick) when we were all guests on the first installment of Ed Sullivan's *Toast of the Town*. He was after me for many years for many things—wanting me in shows, offering feedback on my records. He was always complimentary.

Dick's erudition was mirrored in his stockbroker-smart sartorial style. He was careful with his innuendoes, always inquiring gently as to my personal status. I kept our friendship platonic by concocting stories about whomever it was I was romancing. Dick was substantially older and financially flush, but I wasn't interested in a sugar daddy or even a big brother. (I already had a perfectly great dad and big brother, thank you.)

I just wanted a chance to stretch my abilities.

Call it guts or plain stupidity, but I so loved the ballet music in Rodgers and Hammerstein's *Slaughter on Tenth Avenue* that I wrote lyrics and a little scene for it. It was a melodramatic girl-meets-boy-and-boy-dies piece in which I acted, sang, danced…and then ended up on the floor crying over my dead lover! I thought it would be a prodigious "audition." I asked my dad to play it on his piano beforehand to make sure I had all the notes. I was positive it was perfect.

Participating in the United Appeal Telethon in Charlotte, North Carolina, in December 1954, was personally fulfilling. And meeting all those wonderful kids stirred my maternal instinct.

I told Dick I had a surprise for him and performed the scene in his Manhattan office. Cueing my accompanist, I warbled, whirled, and wailed—finally collapsing into a weepy, trembling heap in front of Dick's massive oak desk. He sat there wide-eyed, and after a pause, he quickly applauded and thanked my accompanist. Then he helped me to my feet. "Sweetie," Dick said, walking me to a wing chair, "that was really great, just stunning. Only I promised that if I ever granted rights to that music to be done with lyrics, I'd give the first crack to Hammerstein."

It was a sobering moment—at least until Dick took me out for a consolatory double scotch. He recommended that I do summer stock in order to master performing without a

Resuming the nightclub circuit was part of my marriage-cancellation recovery. Here I'm helping Billy Reed, owner of the Little Club—in the East Fifties near Central Park—celebrate his establishment's eighth anniversary with singer-actor Janis Paige, my actor pal Robert Wagner, and stage star Julie Wilson (then appearing on Broadway in *Kismet*). It was much-needed fun.

Rehearsing with my father the lyrics I wrote for the ballet music from Rodgers and Hammerstein's *Slaughter on Tenth Avenue*, shortly before I "slayed" Dick Rodgers himself with my stealth performance of them.

microphone, because he wanted me to star in his and Oscar's next Broadway musical: *Pipe Dream*, based on *Sweet Thursday*, John Steinbeck's sequel to his best-selling novel *Cannery Row*. It was set to open in November.

When we parted, Dick gave me a hug and a peck on the cheek. Between the alcohol and his generous offer, I was floating on air.

120

Richard Rodgers

488 MADISON AVENUE · NEW YORK 22, N. Y.

Telephone MUrray Hill 8-3640

July
5th
1955

Dear Monica,

I finally got
myself a phonograph in the country
and listened to your album. It's
really quite wonderful. It has
warmth and intimacy and, best of
all, awfully good musicianship.
I am proud to be represented in
it and I am very grateful to you
for letting me have it.

Love,

Dick.

I immediately instructed my MCA agents to book me in a summer stock production somewhere in the Northeast. While they were looking, I was cast as the female lead in dramatic installments of two TV anthology series, *General Electric Theater* (hosted in wraparound fashion by my old flame Ronald Reagan) and *Appointment with Adventure*, airing just one week apart in June 1955. The first had me performing with Richard Kiley, an actor-baritone who a decade later won a Tony Award for his signature Broadway role as Cervantes/Quixote in *Man of La Mancha*; the second found me opposite Paul Newman, who the following year successfully portrayed boxer Rocky Graziano in the feature *Somebody Up There Likes Me*. Both stints were invigorating, and the latter had the side benefit of leading to a close friendship with Paul and his future wife, Joanne Woodward, for life.

MCA eventually located a good summer stock gig for me: *Best Foot Forward*, a Broadway musical-comedy revival at the Oakdale Musical Theatre in Wallingford, Connecticut, in August 1955. In the lead role, I essentially played myself—a movie star invited by a cadet to a military academy dance—just as Lucille Ball did in the 1943 movie version. It was an in-the-round production inside a giant tent with only one microphone hanging above the stage. Without the crutch of a mike on stand, I had to project my voice and find creative things to do with my hands. It was a wonderfully freeing and confidence-boosting experience. By this time, I had a new man in my life: Liam O'Brien's former agent, Jennings Lang, a widower and single dad who was now production head for MCA's television subsidiary, Revue Productions. A few casual, conversational dinners in the spring had led us to steady dating over the summer. When I moved temporarily to Wallingford for *Best Foot Forward*, the cast was lodged in a motel with no in-room phones; I had the telephone company install a line in my room so I wouldn't miss any calls from Jennings. After the show's run, he brought his two young boys, Mike and Bob, to New York to meet me. They adored me and felt instantly comfortable with me, and the feeling was very, very mutual.

Following a romantic weekend with Jennings in Las Vegas, I had to inform Dick Rodgers

For several years after I left MGM, and certainly thanks to all the publicity I did for the studio, my image continued to appear on magazine covers around the world—including these examples from Germany, Chile, and France.

121

A few months after ending my engagement to Liam O'Brien, I was taking up regularly with his dashing and dynamic MCA agent, Jennings Lang. Here we're on our first date at The Harwyn Club in New York. Jennings admitted to me that this holiday card produced by MGM publicity, featuring me as a lady St. Nick, had caught his eye years earlier.

that I was in love and wouldn't be able to commit to his Broadway show. I was that certain I had found The One.

Jennings encompassed so many of the things I wanted in a guy. He figured out what he had to do and did it. He had a live-life-to-the-fullest vitality and an intellect that I found highly desirable. In addition to being studied in law, he had an appreciation of literature and theatre that meshed with my own. Sure, Jennings couldn't sing or play the piano—I already knew plenty of people who could—but he was naturally funny without being brash. One night on the town, I said to him: "You never tell me I look good." And without a pause, he replied: "I take you out in public, don't I?" I had never encountered such a combination of humor and strength in one potential mate. What surprised me most is that I was able to give myself over to it completely.

The first five eventful and trying years of the 1950s prepared me not only for the second half of the decade, but the second half of my life. It was, all in all, a necessary break from routine that rendered me more adaptable and adventuring, and—beyond the yearning, heartache, and missed opportunity—more capable of placing the tribulations of each day in perspective.

My awakening began in 1951 with my tour of Korea with Danny Kaye and was crucial to bringing the Big Picture into focus. The best way for me to explain how is to show you.

I made many new buddies while touring South Korea—including this sweet Korean boy, who had ingratiated himself with the 1st Marine Division stationed in Inje. This photo appeared in the *New York Daily News* and newspapers across America a few days before Thanksgiving 1951.

4 SOMEONE TO WATCH OVER ME

For the briefest moment after I took the makeshift stage at the base of an otherwise barren, massive hillside in Wonton-ni, near the frontline in South Korea's battle with North Korea, I was overwhelmed by the sight before me: some 15,000 soldiers—a veritable sea of fatigues—waving and applauding wildly. I had deliberately averted my eyes from the anti-aircraft guns surrounding the site and the fighter planes buzzing watchfully overhead; I was focused on performance, not safety.

Just before my customary professionalism and gift for song and dance kicked in, I was struck that this not only was my biggest audience ever, but my youngest. The faces I glimpsed read late teens or early twenties, and despite the smiles, they revealed the stress of kids coping with a very adult situation. But as soon as I stood before the microphone, I let them know that it was okay to stay and play awhile.

The Korean War was a long way from sunny Southern California. But even here in the fall of 1951, in the middle of a bleak, chilly, foreign landscape rattled by not-so-distant artillery fire and streaked with thin plumes of smoke, the stage was my home away from home. There I knew exactly who I had to

A moment of repose during one of my many U.S. Army hospital visits in the spring of 1951. Despite the contractual constraints placed on me by MGM, I continued to contribute to the war effort.

WELCOME HOME, USS MANCHESTER

When the USS *Manchester*—a Cleveland-class light cruiser warship—returned to port at Long Beach, California, in June 1951 after deployment along the eastern coast of Korea, the crew of the self-anointed "fightin'est ship in Korean waters" chose me to be their homecoming queen. Two nights of celebration at the Lakewood Country Club in Long Beach culminated with the crew's surprise presentation to me of a three-and-a-half-foot high, sixteen-pound silver loving cup—the largest ornamental vessel of its type ever made in Japan. "What's an Oscar compared to this?" was my grateful and widely quoted response.

The USS *Manchester* sailed on into history, returning to Korea about five months later. First launched in 1946, it was the last of the 27 ships in its class remaining in service when it was decommissioned in 1956. The ship and its brave, spirited crew will always hold a special place in my heart.

To kick-start the USS *Manchester*'s homecoming, I arrived at the Lakewood Country Club in Long Beach, California, with a Marine honor guard. Later, four representative shipmates—(left to right) Marine Staff Sgt. Richard C. Martin, John P. Dawson, SH1, Kenneth L. Thomas, FN, John W. Starek, FCs, and Marine Staff Sgt. George A. Anderson—posed with me and my "Miss Manchester" honorary loving cup at MGM Studios.

be and what I had to do: *entertain*. It wasn't until I exited—when I returned to being myself, wearing the required military-issue clothing—that I was able to mingle with these brave men and begin to comprehend the scope of the job at hand.

Their sense of duty filled me with joy, sadness, and pride. I just wanted to pack all the guys up and take them back with me to where it was safe and warm.

When my pal Danny Kaye, a huge star and versatile showman, called me to ask if I would travel with him to Korea and perform for the troops, I gratefully accepted his invitation (with the blessing of my home studio, MGM, which had no pressing work for me at the time). I neither paused nor suffered any trepidation over the idea of traveling so far to such a foreign and dangerous place; the trip was made under the aegis of the U.S. Department of Defense, and it felt like a natural extension of my lifelong roles as a singer and a true-blue American.

In fact, after Danny's request, I recalled my earliest pangs of patriotism, which dated to grade school. The concepts of democracy and equality having been spoon-fed to me at a very young age by my parents, I wrote a composition about my sincere admiration of this wonderful country titled "Why Do I Love America?" The prize for my winning essay was a $25 certificate, which was presented to me by New York Mayor Fiorello LaGuardia in a public ceremony at City Hall. There I was at age 12, a proud, beaming, and diminutive American. I could not have imagined then that one day I would be anywhere near combat.

I was heard and seen overseas by our servicemen during World War II and the Korean War long before I arrived at a real frontline. From the mid-1940s through the 1950s, my voice traveled far and wide with V-discs, the military radio program *Voice of the Army* and the Armed Forces Radio Service (AFRS). And my frequent publicity-related coverage in the military newspaper *Stars and Stripes* cemented my status as a

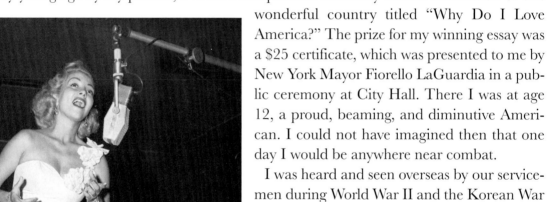

Servicemen around the globe continued to hear me all through the 1950s thanks to the Armed Forces Radio Service (AFRS), which distributed my music to more than sixty overseas radio stations twice a week via a program called *Personal Album*. AFRS described me as the "most-heard singer in the world"—with my voice reaching an estimated 90 million people. My recordings for AFRS were done quickly and informally, with basic instrumental accompaniment, at Capitol Records in Hollywood each week.

darling of the U.S. Armed Forces. I gave every moment I could spare to the war effort and turned nothing down. (My brother Marlo did his part for the U.S. Special Forces, also known as the Green Berets, until he was honorably discharged for an inoperable eye condition.)

During the waning years of World War II and the start of the Korean War, I toured hundreds of army camps and hospitals, visiting with and singing for the GIs. In June 1945, I did a three-day benefit tour of servicemen's hospitals in New England with Eddie Cantor—the manic comedian who would later go on to the make his mark in TV on shows like *The Colgate Comedy Hour* and *Eddie Cantor Comedy Theatre*, and continued to work even after a heart attack slowed his pace in 1952. We entertained some 7,000 wounded vets at Camp Myles Standish in Taunton, Massachusetts, which served as a welcoming area for hundreds of thousands of U.S. and Allied soldiers as well as a prisoner-of-war compound.

Jimmy Stewart and I, along with Lt. General Ira C. Eaker, promoting the fifth annual U.S. Air Force Association reunion at the Hollywood Bowl in August 1951. The event drew 2,000 veterans as well as guest appearances by Bob Hope, Betty Grable, Lana Turner, Ava Gardner, and Cary Grant.

Volunteering for the war-bond drive also deepened my sense of community. One clever promotion in November 1945 found me in Baltimore, Maryland, playing the mysterious, red-masked "Miss V"—visiting bond sales booth locations in shopping centers and hotel lobbies, where I tapped people at random to purchase a $25 Victory bond before my identity was revealed. I raised $11,000 in "E" Victory Bond sales in just one evening.

My efforts on behalf of the military continued through my transition to Los Angeles, where I helped organize hospital and army base visits with Hollywood friends like Elizabeth Taylor, Keenan Wynn, Debbie Reynolds, Jim Backus, and Howard Keel. Two or three times a week, several of us took two-and-a-half-hour military transport flights from L.A. north to Travis Air Force Base in Fairfield, California, where we personally visited with, entertained, and generally boosted the morale of GIs wounded in Korea. Some of our performances there were taped for broadcast distribution by AFRS.

I was repeatedly commended for my participation in the U.S. Army and U.S. Air Force Recruiting Program; from the servicemen themselves, I averaged about 3,000 letters a month. Yet even being a very active member of the Women's Army Corps (better known as WAC), often I asked myself: *Is it enough?*

I did several of Bob Hope's military camp shows around the U.S. in 1951. Other singing talents from the MGM stable appeared, too—like my pal Debbie Reynolds, here giving me a hair assist backstage.

Once Danny Kaye assembled his Korea touring troupe—in addition to me, there was Danny's accompanist Sammy Prager and accordionist June Bruner, who had just toured the Far East with comedian Jack Benny that summer—there was an incredible amount of preparation for the tour. For me, handling the dozen required vaccinations covering everything from smallpox to cholera was tough. They made me queasy, and one of them left me with a raging fever and sore arm for more than a day. Journalists joked that I'd had every shot except "anti-wolf serum."

Several higher-level Army personnel briefed Danny and me. There were certain rules we had to follow, including that we were always to eat our meals with the soldiers. We were given some guidelines regarding what kind and amount of clothing we could take (my luggage could be no more than one duffle bag, one clothing bag, and one makeup case); otherwise, everything we wore would be military issue. I was given big, baggy, olive-drab pants, a jacket, a helmet and boots. The boots, particularly, were too large for me, so I had to stuff them with socks.

We also were told what to expect in case of capture. My one passing moment of concern arose when each of us received our Noncombatant's Certificate of Identity, a photo identification card issued by the adjutant general's office of the War Department in Washington, D.C. It was stamped in big red letters: "VALID ONLY IF CAPTURED BY THE ENEMY." The card clearly indicated the bearer's civilian status, and my understanding was that the Geneva Conventions provided for special treatment for anyone carrying it.

I knew the trip to Korea was incredibly long, but I was excited. We were scheduled tentatively to do almost two dozen shows in as many days! The air journey began October 27th, taking us from Los Angeles to Honolulu—my first time ever in Hawaii, where we enjoyed a brief layover—to Tokyo and then on to the South Korean capital of Seoul. We flew in an Army transport that had long rows of bucket seats along each side of its stark cabin, and I passed the time by singing, talking, and napping. I was amazed to see goony birds for the first time when we refueled in Guam, where it was very hot and sticky. And we had a lot of fun with the soldiers, who seemed similarly impressed to find celebrities hitching along as travel companions.

The Danny Kaye Troupe's work officially began after it alighted from Seoul and landed at Taegu, South Korea, for a tour of the 8th Army Units. There we pitched our theater tent five miles behind the North Korean and Chinese enemy lines. Our entertainment unit included servicemen who were skilled at setting up the sound system and portable lights and erecting the stage, which was more than large enough to hold Danny, me, Sammy Prager, and June Bruner, plus a fold-up piano. The surrounding mountains created a natural amphitheater. A few chairs were provided, but the audience was just as happy to stand or sit on the ground. Afterward, our crew broke it all down and we traveled either by jeep, helicopter, or Cessna L-19 "Bird Dog" light plane to another base, depending on the distance to the Army's next division.

ELIZABETH TAYLOR

By the age of eighteen, Elizabeth Taylor was already a tent pole for MGM, having starred in the 1940s classics *Lassie Come Home, National Velvet,* and *Little Women* before enjoying her first major acting success as an adult in the 1950 romantic comedy *Father of the Bride.* It was while she was killing some time on the studio lot in the summer of 1951, awaiting the premiere of her landmark drama *A Place in the Sun,* that I invited her to join me in some morale-boosting for our Korean War servicemen. She wholeheartedly accepted.

Liz was on the verge of getting an ulcer at the time. She was seeing director Stanley Donen, the "King of Musicals" (*On the Town, Singin' in the Rain*), after her divorce from socialite and hotel heir Conrad "Nicky" Hilton, Jr. But her mother felt Stanley was too brash and liberal for her daughter. Being a guest of the loose military entertainment unit that I had formed with some other MGM players, including Debbie Reynolds, Keenan Wynn, Ricardo Montalban, and Arthur Loew, Jr., was just the diversion Liz needed.

At least two weekends each month, we traveled to different army bases around the West Coast, visiting recovery wards and generally cheering up the soldiers. We also put on shows. Liz was concerned that she could not contribute because she didn't sing or dance, but we came up with a most irreverent use for her. While Ricardo and I did a duet of "Baby, It's Cold Outside," we had Liz sashay around the stage, prattle off a few throwaway lines...and then Arthur came out and hurled a cream pie in her face! The crowd broke up seeing her gorgeous violet eyes peering through that mess. She was an awfully good sport.

Elizabeth Taylor has a great heart and a fabulous survival instinct. She has lived her life passionately through multiple marriages and umpteen personal ills, all the while using her worldwide stardom to promote the welfare of others—particularly in fundraising and the fight against AIDS. She is a tremendous force for good.

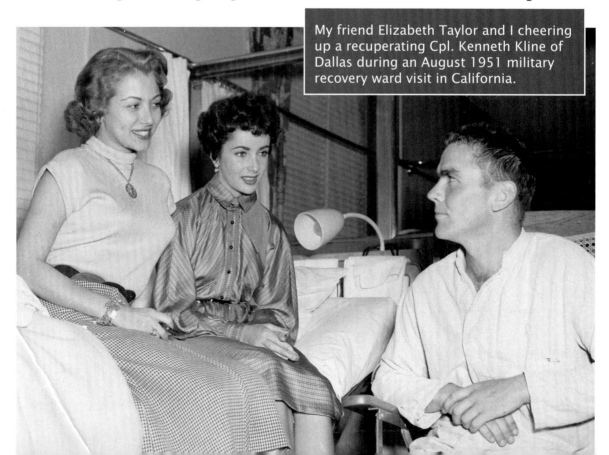

My friend Elizabeth Taylor and I cheering up a recuperating Cpl. Kenneth Kline of Dallas during an August 1951 military recovery ward visit in California.

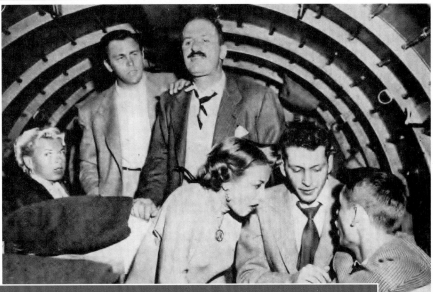

Some of the regulars in my MGM military entertainment unit, which was dubbed "Operation Starlift" by the media, posing before a flight to Travis Air Force Base in Fairfield, California. Pictured along with a uniformed officer (top, left to right): Jim Backus, Debbie Reynolds, Keenan Wynn, me, Howard Keel and Eileen Christy. Midflight on one of our jaunts, I am shown at center conducting a rehearsal in the noisily reverberating, frill-free cabin with (bottom, left to right) Beetsie (Mrs. Keenan) Wynn, Howard, Keenan, Arthur Loew, Jr., and Carleton Carpenter. Our base shows were taped for the Armed Forces Radio Service.

134

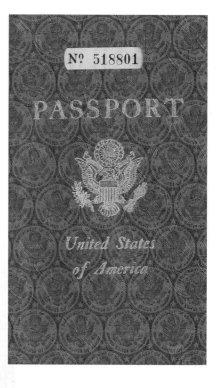

Photograph of bearer

Monica Lewis

PHOTOGRAPH ATTACHED
DEPARTMENT OF STATE
WASHINGTON

4

This passport, properly visaed, is valid for travel in all countries unless otherwise restricted.

This passport, unless limited to a shorter period, is valid for two years from its date of issue and may be renewed upon payment of a fee of $5 but the final date of expiration shall not be more than four years from the original date of issue.

American citizens traveling in disturbed areas of the world are requested to keep in touch with the nearest American diplomatic or consular officers.

American citizens making their homes or residing for a prolonged period abroad should register at the nearest American consulate.

SEE PAGES 6, 7, AND 8 FOR RENEWAL, EXTENSIONS, AMENDMENTS, LIMITATIONS, AND RESTRICTIONS.

5

My special military passport to Korea—and the adventure of a lifetime.

Renewal, extensions, amendments, limitations, and restrictions

This passport is not valid for travel to or in any foreign state for the purpose of entering or serving in the armed forces of such a state.

This passport is valid only for travel in the countries herein named and for the purpose herein stated.
JAPAN, KOREA AND NECESSARY COUNTRIES EN ROUTE - ON OFFICIAL BUSINESS FOR THE DEPARTMENT OF THE ARMY.
X X X
X X X
R. B. SHIPLEY
Chief, Passport Division

6

Renewal, extensions, amendments, limitations, and restrictions

LIMITATION
This passport is valid for 2 MONTHS
It will expire on
DEC. 23, 1951 and shall not be extended without the express authorization of the Department of State.

7

After deplaning in Honolulu en route to Korea in late October, Danny Kaye and I were greeted by a military commander with leis—and a phalanx of photographers—on the airstrip.

Our shows began roughly at five o'clock in the evening, when the setting sun provided warm, flattering light and a dramatic backdrop. Each performance was followed by dinner in the mess hall with the troops. The meals were simple Army food but not K-rations; in those days, I didn't have a problem with my cholesterol, so I enthusiastically ate whatever they served. After dinner, it was back to the tents for sleep. Our accommodations were minimal: sleeping bags atop cots. Danny shared a tent with Sammy, while June and I had our own.

Since there was no running water, bathroom routines had to be carried out via latrine and sponge bath; only twice did we visit camps that had a portable shower. I washed and rinsed my hair in an overturned helmet. The latrine was a basic bench-with-hole affair inside a tent. Two MPs escorted June and me to the latrine and stood outside. I always took a portable radio with me, as it helped me accomplish the business at hand. Between the cold and the fatigues we had to wear, things we normally took for granted were quite a task.

Each morning we awoke early, moved on to the next division, set up camp and did the whole thing over again. I seemed to lose track of the days; they all went by in a flash.

Everything I saw in Korea was an eye-opener. Sure, I was used to the hospital scene, as I had sung in so many of them—both in auditoriums and sitting bedside in the wards of the non-ambulatory. And I was familiar with the use of aromatic tobacco to mask the stench of bloody bandages. But nothing prepared me for what I saw in the real war. While I did not observe actual combat, I watched the Lorries pour in with broken men, attended operations performed in open tents on damaged bodies, and witnessed enormous bravery.

The military P.R. person would find GIs who had special stories, and I or other members of our troupe would be asked to meet with them. Sometimes such requests came from random personnel. On one occasion, I took up a battalion surgeon's suggestion that I visit the

Helping Danny make a precarious exit from our Air Force transport in Taegu, Korea, on October 30th—with our fellow trouper, accordionist June Bruner, following. We paused for an introductory chat with Lt. Colonel Martin W. Shrewsbury, special services officer of the 8th Army.

boys in the field hospital tent. So I did, and I discovered that a soldier was undergoing a minor operation. I felt so sorry for him that I asked the medic if I could give the patient a kiss.

"I wish you would," he said with a grin. "His blood pressure is very low."

It was like a scene out of the early-1970s film and hit TV series *M*A*S*H*, which the Korean War inspired. It certainly broke the tension and put a big smile on that wounded serviceman's face.

A few times, all hell broke loose in the field while we slept. One night the noise of artillery fire was so frightening that I ran to Danny and Sammy's nearby tent. Danny, having done USO tours in 1944 and 1945, was familiar with this kind of situation. He had us huddle together and sing loudly from fake books—bootleg collections of pop song lyrics from every recent decade—until dawn, when a somewhat irritated commander finally informed us that the enemy had fallen back.

Good thing we had nipped a little scotch. We needed it.

Our performances for the troops were incredibly gratifying. Seeing those young guys crowding our stage, sitting atop walls, and hanging from trees with binoculars to get a good look at us was something none of us would forget. Obviously, it wasn't like a club or concert setting where we might be judged critically, so vanity took a backseat to practicality. With June Bruner dressing rather plainly because she had to "wear" a big accordion onstage, I did what I could under the gritty circumstances to look my best. I had two different performance outfits that I wore with high heels: one was a large, flaring magenta skirt paired with a spangled off-white turtleneck sweater; the other was a straighter, less billowy chocolate-brown skirt that I could wear with a long-sleeve bone-colored top to ward off the persistent Korean dampness.

Our troupe's act was a combination of song, dance, and jokey repartee. Danny and I did a little comedy routine together, and being a natural clown, he also insisted on trying to crack me up while I sang beautiful ballads. He stalked around the stage making faces at me as if in awe—bowing and scraping. He was relentless! After one of our shows, I had really had it with Danny's excessive silliness and told him so.

"You're on plenty and you get plenty of laughs," I scolded. "I want these guys to enjoy one heartfelt love song. Let me do 'I'm in the Mood for Love' or whatever damn song I want, and for God's sake, let me do it by myself!"

"No one else I've worked with ever minded," he defended. His smirk became a pout. "Oh, you're a spoilsport."

It was the only time I had a disagreement with Danny, if you can really call it that. He was a smart and very complex man, and he was always enormously protective of me. We could be honest with each other because we were friends—surely the foremost reason he asked me to do the tour. He also knew that he had my utmost respect.

DANNY KAYE

There's never been another all-around entertainer quite like Danny Kaye. Accomplished as a singer, dancer, actor, and funnyman, he broke from the constraints of his Borscht Belt beginnings—lighting up Broadway in the early 1940s before heading to Hollywood, where he excelled in comedies and musicals like *The Secret Life of Walter Mitty, The Inspector General,* and *On the Riviera.*

I had first known Danny in New York, where he and my father shared the same doctor. He was one of the few big stars to welcome me immediately with open arms after I moved to Los Angeles in 1950, and he was terrific fun whenever I ran into him and his friends on the Hollywood club circuit. Danny's wife, Sylvia Fine, also was extremely talented and bright; she wrote all of his original material. She was his accompanist when they first started dating.

Humor was Danny's greatest gift, and he shared it generously with everyone, including me. I learned from him that comedy shouldn't come from dysfunction or an inability to cope with the world. Sure, you can make fun of bad things within the bounds of taste; that's a big part of it. But when it comes from a place of hate, it isn't that funny anymore. Personally, I've seen comics who are really hilarious for fifteen minutes and have people howling—and then they'll say one thing that is way out of bounds and the audience will straighten their backs. Danny knew where that

Danny and I arriving at the airstrip in Kapyong, Korea, on October 31st before hopping into a jeep en route to our show for the 2nd Infantry Division the next day.

line was and avoided it. "I can take anybody off the street, teach them a good dirty joke, put them in the Paramount Theater, hit the light, and teach them the timing," he said to me once. "They'll rock the place—and it has nothing to do with being funny."

After our tour of Korea, Danny continued successfully in film (*Hans Christian Andersen, White Christmas*) and launched a popular television variety show in the 1960s. His philanthropic drive, which included—among many charitable contributions—fundraising as an ambassador for UNICEF, remained strong until his death in 1987.

Danny Kaye wanted to be a combination of philosopher Alfred Schweitzer, medical pioneer Michael E. DeBakey, conductor-composer Leonard Bernstein, and President of the World. He certainly embodied the influence and innovation that characterized all of those men. But he succeeded perhaps beyond his own wildest ambitions at just being himself.

140

Danny Kaye greets the 3rd Infantry Division in Sinp'al-li, Korea, from a temporary stage erected in a rice paddy on November 2nd. Some 6,000 soldiers eventually gathered for our performance.

Brig. General Thomas J. Cross, CG, 3rd Infantry Division, personally thanks Danny and me at division headquarters after our show in Sinp'al-li.

Danny's philosophy was simple. "We're here to entertain," he said. "We're here to make these soldiers feel good. This is what we do best, and we're doing our best for them."

The troops showed their gratitude by streaming into our shows by the truckload. Only one of every three men on the battle line was tapped at random and given permission to attend. Although they were homesick, their faces managed to reflect adoration and pleasure toward our stage. And the joy was mutual. As I wrote to my mother in a personal letter from Korea that was reprinted a year later by *Parade* magazine: "If all of America could be here ten minutes, there'd be no problem about blood shortages; they'd give more blood than they'd keep!"

At the end of every performance, when it was getting dark, Danny would order the lights turned off and ask the audience to strike a match or click a lighter in a gesture of hope for victory. (Virtually all of the soldiers smoked.) We performed a final song before that constellation of proudly flickering souls, many of whom would never see home again before an armistice was declared in July 1953. It was a sight, and an emotion, like no other.

As I sang against a smoky, chilly backdrop in the Korean county of Chorwon on November 6th, I was warmed by the response of about 13,000 GIs from the 25th Infantry Division. Chorwon had lain entirely in North Korea just prior to the war; our show took place in a portion newly taken by South Korea.

I got a "kick" out of showing my oversize military-issue boots to wounded soldier Swen Larsson of Los Angeles during my visit to a 24th Infantry Division hospital tent. (Obviously, he did, too.)

By the official end of its South Korean field tour schedule in Pusan on November 16th, 1951, the Danny Kaye Troupe had entertained approximately 145,000 troops. In addition to my being the favorite pin-up of the GIs in Korea, an informal poll of frontline soldiers published stateside indicated that Doris Day and I were "the women they would most like to lead them in an attack."

Before departing, we celebrated an early Thanksgiving with the men of the 14th Infantry Regiment, also known as the Lightning Lynx. In addition to presenting us with personalized jackets and beautifully hand-drawn honorary certificates of acceptance into their ranks, the guys gave me a portrait of their insignia with the words "Monica's Guardian" emblazoned on it. Afterward, we did a climactic farewell-to-Korea performance for the men of the 3rd Bombardment Wing at Seoul's Chosen Hotel.

En route back to the U.S., we made a stop in Tokyo, where on November 19th we performed two shows for military hospital patients and personnel in the decidedly more controlled environment of the Ernie Pyle Theater. (The appearance earned me an oddly flattering mention two years later in *The Wise Bamboo*, a memoir by the former GI manager of Tokyo's Imperial Hotel, J. Malcolm Morris, who described me as "the most female-looking woman I have ever met at the Imperial…or anywhere else.") We followed this immediately with copious, self-congratulatory libations of sake. Thanks to the alcohol, I got as silly as I had once accused Danny of being. But heck, I felt I had earned it.

Two flights and three days later, Korea was a stark and historic memory.

Traveling within the 24th Infantry Division at Lanyang-ni, where the Danny Kaye Troupe entertained some 10,000 soldiers on November 8th.

Having fun trying on the helmet of Major Charles R. Cline of Los Angeles, 1st Cavalry Division air officer, at division headquarters in Wonton-ni.

Some 15,000 soldiers of the 1st Cavalry Division amassed for our November 9th performance on a Wonton-ni hillside. The appreciative audience was just as breathtaking from our stage-level vantage point.

146

Humbled by the huge 1st Cavalry Division crowd, Danny and I took our time thanking and warming up the troops before commencing the fun.

I happily played the curvy dervish for our selfless GIs, showing off my big felt skirt and spangled turtleneck sweater to their approving applause (which became a sustained roar with a little egging-on from Danny). It was one of just two performance outfits I had for the war zone.

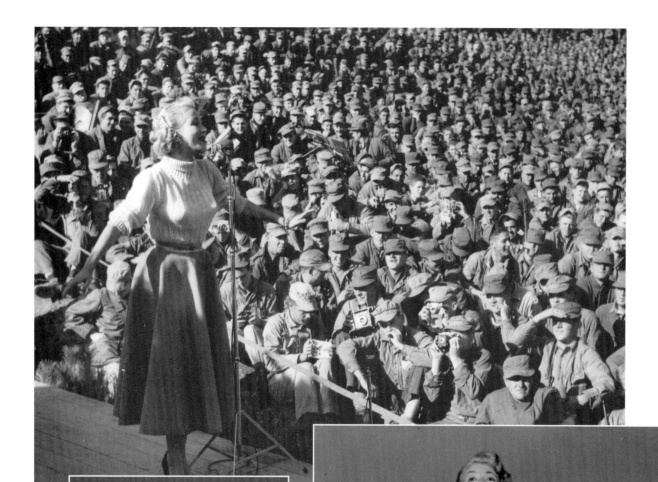

As dusk drew closer, I had the rapt attention of the 1st Cavalry Division.

I concluded the Danny Kaye Troupe's special evening in Wonton-ni with a sunset serenade to the real troopers.

After we entertained 10,000 soldiers of 1st Marine Division in Inje on November 10th, Major General Clovis E. Byers (far right) offered a personal thank you to (right to left) Danny, our pianist Sammy Prager, June Bruner, and me.

I lingered on the airstrip after arriving in Pusan before the entire troupe—June, me, Danny, and Sammy—gathered for a group photo prior to our November 16th performance for the troops of the United Nations Command.

Some enterprising soldiers renamed Pusan Stadium the "Monica Lewis Theater" prior to our show. I was both flattered and touched by the gesture.

I enjoyed a grandly protective military entrance as I descended toward the stage at Pusan Stadium.

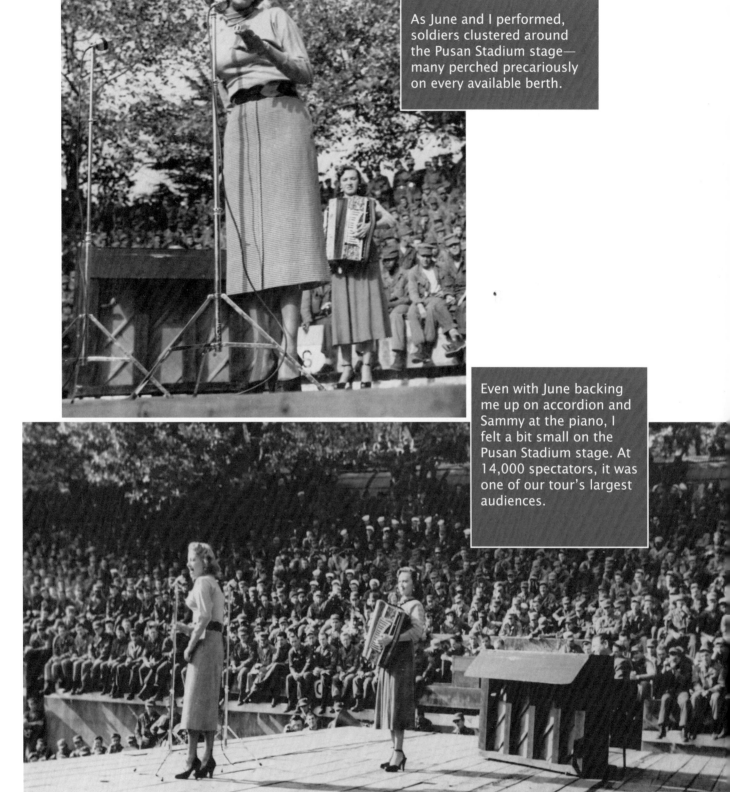

As June and I performed, soldiers clustered around the Pusan Stadium stage— many perched precariously on every available berth.

Even with June backing me up on accordion and Sammy at the piano, I felt a bit small on the Pusan Stadium stage. At 14,000 spectators, it was one of our tour's largest audiences.

DINNER WITH THE TROOPS

Before departing South Korea and beginning our multi-leg journey home to the U.S., I helped prepare, serve, and celebrate an early Thanksgiving feast with the 14th Infantry Regiment, also known as the Lightning Lynx, which "adopted" the Danny Kaye Troupe into its ranks.

As I left the regiment's frontline command post for the last time, I cried as I read the sign over the entrance: "The Home of Lightning Lynx and Monica Lewis." I have never forgotten these men, their sacrifices, or their wonderful spirits.

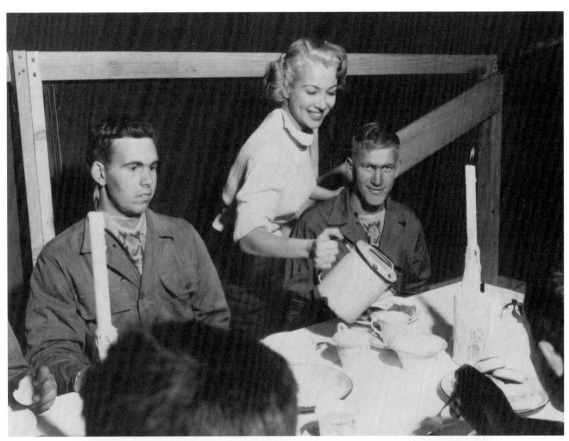

A farewell glance: June and I, proudly wearing our Lightning Lynx (14th Infantry Regiment) jackets, preparing to board our flight from Seoul to Tokyo.

Danny's hamming gets the better of me at the Ernie Pyle Theater in Tokyo, where we did two November 19th performances mainly for hospital patients and military personnel.

Retouching my makeup in my makeshift dressing room at the Ernie Pyle Theater between shows. The military police left nothing to chance, assigning backstage guard duty to Pfc. Alexander Waters of Camden, New Jersey (left), and Cpl. Charles Sutterfield of Pine Bluff, Arkansas.

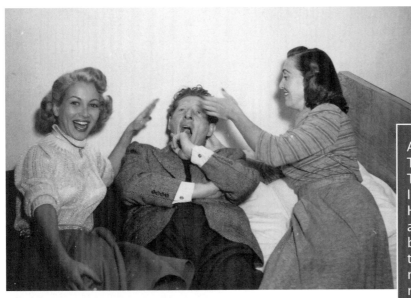

After our two Ernie Pyle Theater performances in Tokyo, Danny, June, and I returned to the Imperial Hotel, where we drank a lot of sake and kicked-back royally to celebrate the conclusion of our military entertainment mission.

At Tokyo's Imperial Hotel with my Torii Award, shaped and named for the gateway to a Japanese Shinto temple. It was presented to me by the Far East Air Forces for my outstanding personal contribution to troop morale while on tour with Danny Kaye.

Back in Hollywood, I had a new appreciation for the value of life. Our servicemen not only had purpose and courage under fire, but they were free of self-aggrandizement. They weren't fighting for a press release; there was no fussing with hair or fretting over singing the right note. The selflessness of combat made most of my concerns and perceived challenges appear positively tiny.

The word "epiphany" is overused. People have them, or think they have them, every day. All I know is that when I walked into the MGM commissary after those few incredible weeks in Korea, it didn't look so all-important. The studio trappings appeared as artificial as they really were compared with a mess hall and what that represented. Korea was not a movie set; it was thunderously, wondrously real.

I continue to thank Danny Kaye quietly to this day for choosing me to go overseas with him. While entertaining was both my drive and my reward, Korea made life crystal clear. It not only was the break of a new dawn, but my intellectual awakening to the world—and further impetus to find truer, deeper meaning in my personal life.

Jennings and me at our New Year's Day 1956 wedding reception at Chasen's, the famous celebrity hangout in West Hollywood. My new hubby was going great guns as vice president of MCA TV Ltd., selling primetime programming to all the networks.

5 THE FOLKS WHO LIVE ON THE HILL

Despite America's best wartime efforts, the close of the Korean conflict did not bring resolution, but rather, an escalation of Cold War tensions. In 1953, with Dwight D. Eisenhower succeeding Harry Truman as U.S. president and Joseph Stalin's death bringing the rise of Nikita Khrushchev as the Soviet Union's new leader, the opposing players on the global stage became more clearly defined. Paranoia and espionage were rampant, and eyes turned toward the skies as nuclear testing and the space race got underway in earnest.

Stateside fears of Communist takeover and atomic warfare were played out in science fiction movies and backyard bomb shelters. But it was our hunger for diversion—and increasing consumer appetite—that really exploded in the mid-1950s. Disneyland and McDonald's made their landmark debuts. Automobile sales soared into the millions. Television programs like *Gunsmoke*, *Lassie*, and *The $64,000 Question* kept families happily decompressed (or out-guessed). And especially for those of us immersed in music, rock rolled in with the force of a tidal wave, carrying with it the likes of Bill Haley and His Comets, The Platters, Chuck Berry, and of course, Elvis Presley.

Being a multimedia celebrity, I was naturally attuned to the rapid evolution of politics, technology, and culture. Yet with romance stealing my focus through the end of 1955, most national and international events seemed to occur in a parallel universe.

My relationship with Jennings Lang was a bicoastal one; he traveled often between Los Angeles and New York negotiating production deals for MCA's Revue TV division. He always called me the day before he flew in from the West Coast to make sure my schedule was free, and I often found myself holding my breath like a schoolgirl, waiting for the phone to ring. It was pure, pomp-free attraction, and I never felt taken for granted.

There was one problem. Whenever Jennings picked me up at my parents' duplex apartment at Madison Avenue and East 73rd Street, where I lived then, my mother refused to meet him.

"Monica, are you out of your mind?" she finally blurted to me privately, reminding me of my messy disengagement from Liam O'Brien. "You're going from the frying pan into the fire!"

Mama's heated reaction to Jennings was fueled by his involvement in a major 1951 Hollywood scandal. Jennings, who was married at that time, was the agent of movie star Joan

Bennett, the wife of the prolific film producer Walter Wanger (*Stagecoach, Invasion of the Body Snatchers*). That agent and client were having an affair wasn't lost on the gossips, and it evidently didn't escape Walter. One afternoon, the producer confronted Joan and Jennings in the parking lot of MCA's Beverly Hills headquarters, turned to Jennings, and—following an argument—aimed a .38-caliber pistol at groin level. He fired twice; one bullet struck.

Jennings survived the attack with a minimal wound. But the affair's emerging details were grist for the media mill and assumed mythic life—even partly inspiring Billy Wilder's classic 1960 comedy-drama *The Apartment*. Every tabloid asserted that Wanger's gun had claimed one testicle.

In truth, Jennings bore a scar on his left inner thigh where the bullet actually lodged. And I can testify that nothing was lost. (This chapter will affirm his ongoing procreative ability.) Now, I cannot fault Walter or anyone who has faced the pain of infidelity for reacting strongly to it, but I also can't condone the use of violence to resolve domestic situations. Fortunately, Walter's stint as the "Lone Wanger," for which he served just four months in a minimum-security prison after pleading temporary insanity, did no permanent damage. And had the gleefully lascivious press done just basic research into Jennings's injury, they might have learned a thing or—in this case—definitely two.

Nobody's past is perfect. And with my own resolve to remain face-forward, I loved Jennings for who he was presently. I saw nothing in him but good. That we each had endured our share of tribulations and bad decisions endeared him to me even more.

Winning my heart, alas, was just half the battle.

While Jennings had thoroughly impressed my dad with his smarts and charm, he continued to ply my mother with everything from flowers and perfume to chicken soup with matzo balls. Finally, she defrosted when my sister Bobbe convinced her to accept an invitation from Jennings to hear a marvelous jazz pianist named Dorothy Donegan at Manhattan's Embers Club. About an hour after we arrived and the music started, Jennings courted Mama royally and ordered a mild Mai Tai for her. A few sips did the trick. She turned to Dad, smiled, and said, "Leon, it must be a sin to feel this good!"

The next evening, Jennings returned to the apartment to pick me up. As we bid goodnight to my parents, my father asked, "Jennings, when are you going to make an honest woman of my daughter?"

Jennings chuckled. "I'm working on it."

As we waited in the hallway for the elevator, we could hear my mother, in full-throttle operatic soprano, scream: "How could you do that, Leon? How could you humiliate our baby that way?"

Jennings and I laughed, knowing in our hearts that we were already committed. I was thirty-three and he was forty; it was the right time for both of us. Here was a man with such a worldly embrace that a Monet painting excited him as much as a baseball player slugging a homerun. He was my dream guy.

With Christmas drawing near, Jennings asked my parents if they would approve of my staying with him and his boys in Los Angeles for a couple weeks "to see," as he put it, "if Monica can stand it." After all, I had never lived in a house, mothered children, or even tended a garden. Everyone agreed it was a good idea.

So, back to L.A. I went.

The Lang residence in super-upscale Brentwood was beautiful but comfortably lived-in, with plenty of household help. Mike Lang had just turned fourteen and, although he and his brother had met me earlier in New York, seemed suspicious of my sudden appearance under the family's roof. But he was polite, and I took it as a compliment when I overheard him say to Jennings in a decidedly adolescent way, "Monica doesn't look *anything* like my friends' moms." Bob, then nine years old, simply clung to my arm. I took the kids shopping for a Christmas tree and all the trimmings. We had such warm, loving fun making the house over for the holidays.

My Brentwood run with the Lang clan went so well, and so quickly, that I suddenly found myself staring at a prior two-week commitment to appear at a national gathering of chicken flickers in Kansas City, Missouri, starting January 4th, 1956. (Chicken-flicking was the hand de-feathering of poultry post-slaughter; machinery handles the task today.) Jennings suggested that we tie the knot before my departure, and I agreed that January 1st would be the ideal date. In just three days, we got our blood tests, obtained the marriage license, and flew my parents to L.A. in time to celebrate Christmas with us. Jennings covered the airfare of everyone who could attend on such abrupt notice. It was all a wonderful adrenaline rush.

We were married at the Beverly Hills home of Herbert Brenner, an MCA agent, and the reception was at Chasen's. Amid press descriptions of ours as "the first Hollywood wedding of the New Year," we managed a discreet two-day honeymoon in Palm Springs at the Racquet Club, a favorite desert escape of the stars. Meanwhile, my folks took the kids to Disneyland.

It was a new year—and another new life. I winged it to the Chicken Flickers Convention in a state of matrimonial euphoria.

At the outset, it was tough to give up any of the freedom I had enjoyed as a single woman and performer to become a mother and housewife. I missed New York, my family, and being able to sing whenever I wanted. For the first time, I wasn't the star of the show; I could relax and lean on someone other than myself. This was freeing in a different way, and one that required adjustment.

Becoming the lady of the Lang household allowed me to exploit my need to prove that I could do "normal" things. As a child, I had always liked using my hands. In Brentwood, I

My new role as Mrs. Jennings Lang and Mama Monica! Jennings gave me a new station wagon so that I could transport his two boys in style; the vehicle's raspberry-and-white color scheme made all the kids in Brentwood think I was the ice cream wagon. My husband had a blast with Mike and Bob on a jaunt to Mexico (opposite, top), and at home, Mike—pictured at the piano and in his school portrait—always enjoyed jamming with his buddies.

After we married, Jennings commissioned this extra-sexy publicity shot to keep me visible, and professionally viable, while I adjusted to being a Brentwood housewife and mom. It probably didn't endear me to the MCA executive wives' club.

became Mrs. Fix-All. I spent hours at the local nursery learning all about gardening. I wallpapered the bedrooms. I taught myself to repair a leaky faucet. I climbed ladders to change lightbulbs in the high ceilings. Jennings always peeked in at me mid-project, shook his head, and cracked up. "Please," he implored, "just shout if you need me!"

Most importantly, I learned how to interact with, and care for, two young boys. While Bob was occupied with school and requested my help with homework, Mike, who was already playing piano quite masterfully, took to challenging me on all manner of musical data and history. He was shocked to learn that one of his idols, the great jazz drummer Shelly Manne, was a friend of mine.

Mike's initial acceptance of me was complicated by his age and memories of his own mother. In his mind, I believe, his pop's new wife should have been some comfortable-looking, flour-and-apron-strings type. But he did demonstrate his loyalty to me when one of his pals offhandedly remarked, "Your dad married a great piece of ass." Mike socked the kid right in the jaw. He then came home and confessed to Jennings, suggesting, "Maybe Mom shouldn't wear a bikini while she's watering the garden." When Mike faced me about it, I thanked him for his chivalry but also explained that the situation should not have been settled by a fist.

I accompanied Jennings to New York several times that first year to keep up with my own family and friends there. On our first post-marriage visit to Manhattan, one of my husband's MCA associates and his wife held an elegant reception for us at their Park Avenue duplex.

Conducted by Frank DeVol and released by Verve Records in 1957, my album *Sing It to the Marines* featured twelve standards selected by the ranks of the Marine Corps—including "Nice Work If You Can Get It," "I Get a Kick Out of You," and "The Song is You." (The entire album has been reissued internationally under the latter tune's title.) Known as "Sweetheart of the Marines," I also appeared regularly on a Marine Corps-produced TV program, *Dress Blues*, which aired Sunday afternoons.

THE WHITE HOUSE

WASHINGTON

July 11, 1957

PERSONAL

Dear Mrs. Lang:

Thank you very much for having sent to me an album of your recording entitled "Sing It to the Marines." I know I shall enjoy the songs, as I did your performance on one of Danny Thomas' shows.

With appreciation of your thoughtful courtesy, and best wishes,

Sincerely,

Dwight D. Eisenhower

Mrs. Jennings Lang
456 North Bristol Avenue
Los Angeles 49
California

PERSONAL

I received this thank-you note at our Brentwood address from President Dwight D. Eisenhower after I sent him my album *Sing It to the Marines*. His surprise acknowledgement of my January 1957 appearance on *The Danny Thomas Show* gave it an extra-personal touch.

Co-hosted by Joan Crawford, the party was attended by MCA founder Jules Stein, Nanette Fabray, Alfred Hitchcock, Polly Bergen, producer Hal B. Wallis (*Casablanca*, *Gunfight at the O.K. Corral*), and many other luminaries.

Although I was no stranger to the celebrity social scene, being an MCA executive's wife, I discovered, carried certain expectations. These were channeled through Edie Wasserman, the spouse of Jennings's boss, Lew. Edie was dark-haired, immaculate, and, at the time, prone to offering instruction in comportment.

During an A-list party thrown for us by restaurateurs Dave and Maude Chasen a few weeks after our wedding, Edie and everyone else saw my husband and me share a lingering kiss perfectly befitting a newly hitched couple. The following day, Edie called to sternly reprimand me for what she deemed an immature display.

Next from Edie came lists of names and birthdays I was to remember, as well as forthright and completely unsolicited tips regarding appropriate attire for public functions. I never doubted that her advice was well intentioned; Edie was mapping what for me was new social terrain. Still, I needed to convey to Jennings my discomfort with the situation.

"You've always done things your way—and that's fine with me," he said, reaffirming my independent spirit. "Next case!"

It was wonderfully typical of the casual yet firm manner in which my husband dismissed matters he considered trivial. Including his associates' annoyingly persistent whispers that our union would last only two months. (They were wrong. We were together forty years.)

♫

Getting ready to wow a nightclub packed with Marine Corps recruits as a Southern Belle singer on the set of the Warner Bros. feature *The D.I.* (1957). Director and star Jack Webb offered me instruction on stage positioning in relation to the camera.

The job offers that continued coming my way during my first year of marriage also provided some needed ego stroking. By 1957, I felt settled enough at home to pursue a few more gigs.

The first was a guest appearance that January on *The Danny Thomas Show*, in an episode called "The School Teacher." I played the former college band-singer-turned-school-teacher of Danny's young son, Rusty. My big moment came when I surprised Danny with a spur-of-the-moment nightclub performance that dispelled his schoolmarm perception of me.

Shortly after that widely seen acting bit, I opened at the posh Venetian Room in San Francisco's Fairmont Hotel with Mort Sahl as the comic half of the marquee. (Within four years, Mort would be contributing jokes to President John F. Kennedy's speeches while influencing comedians like Woody Allen, Lenny Bruce, and George Carlin.) The success of my San Francisco run, combined with my work with the Armed Forces Radio Service, attracted Verve Records founder Norman Granz, who signed me to do *Sing It to the Marines*, an album of evergreens selected through voting by U.S. servicemen. It got tremendous airplay that summer and some record shops even used it for window displays promoting military recruitment.

Press coverage of *Sing It to the Marines* led actor-director Jack Webb to tap me for a singing part in *The D.I.*—a feature drama for Warner Bros. Jack, riding his success as L.A. police detective Sgt. Joe Friday in the long-running TV series

170

Dragnet, starred as a boot camp drill instructor breaking-in Marine Corps recruits at Parris Island in South Carolina. It wasn't much of a stretch, but I played a campy, crowd-pleasing Southern belle named Burt(!) and took the stage in a sparkling black dress.

Aside from another movie credit and the opportunity to work with Jack, who was the utmost professional in his multiple hats on the production, the role brought me an appearance on *The Jackie Gleason Show*, a print advertising tie-in with Luster-Crème Shampoo, and a call from Columbia Records. Mitch Miller, Columbia's artist and repertoire head, wanted me to press a single of the catchy novelty tune I performed in the film: "(If'n You Don't) Somebody Else Will," with music by Ray Conniff and lyrics by Fred Weismantel. Permission was granted by both Warner Bros. and my current label, Verve, and what *Variety* tagged a "sophisticated hillbilly song" charted better than anyone expected.

The biggest, most welcome surprise that spring—which may not have been lost on those who noticed that I looked bustier and curvier than usual in *The D.I.*—was when I learned I was pregnant. Jennings and I, and the boys, were overjoyed.

My husband called just about every place in the world to find the best prenatal care. He wanted to know everything that needed to be done, and he did everything so fast. It was

In performance and relaxing between takes on *The D.I.* The catchy tune I sang for the scene, "(If'n You Don't) Somebody Else Will," was issued as a single by Columbia Records.

like having a pair of giant arms encircling me protectively—but not so tightly that I could not move comfortably in and out of them.

On January 11, 1958, I gave birth to our baby: a boy. We named him Andrew Rockwell Lang, but no one ever called him anything but Rocky. It was a seamless experience, with no morning sickness and an uneventful labor. I was happy, healthy, and felt sensational. I fell totally in love with this little fellow the moment he was first placed in my arms.

Jennings behaved both as a loving dad and an excitable kid. If the sweat and ambition of being a young agent stymied his enjoyment of fatherhood in his early twenties, his level of success as the forty-something vice president of MCA TV Ltd. allowed him to savor it fully. Jennings's efforts had made the company's Revue Productions the go-to source for broadcast television programming, including hit series like *Bachelor Father*, *Leave It to Beaver*, *Tales of Wells*

I was the proudest and happiest first-time mom ever when Jennings and I welcomed our son Andrew Rockwell "Rocky" Lang into the world in January 1958.

Jennings's son Bob was the less outgoing but no less playful of my husband's two boys. He often held my hand, and there were times when he just clung to me. Bob found a convenient and very pliable play-mate in his new baby brother Rocky, and bath time was always a big production—with lots and lots of bubbles.

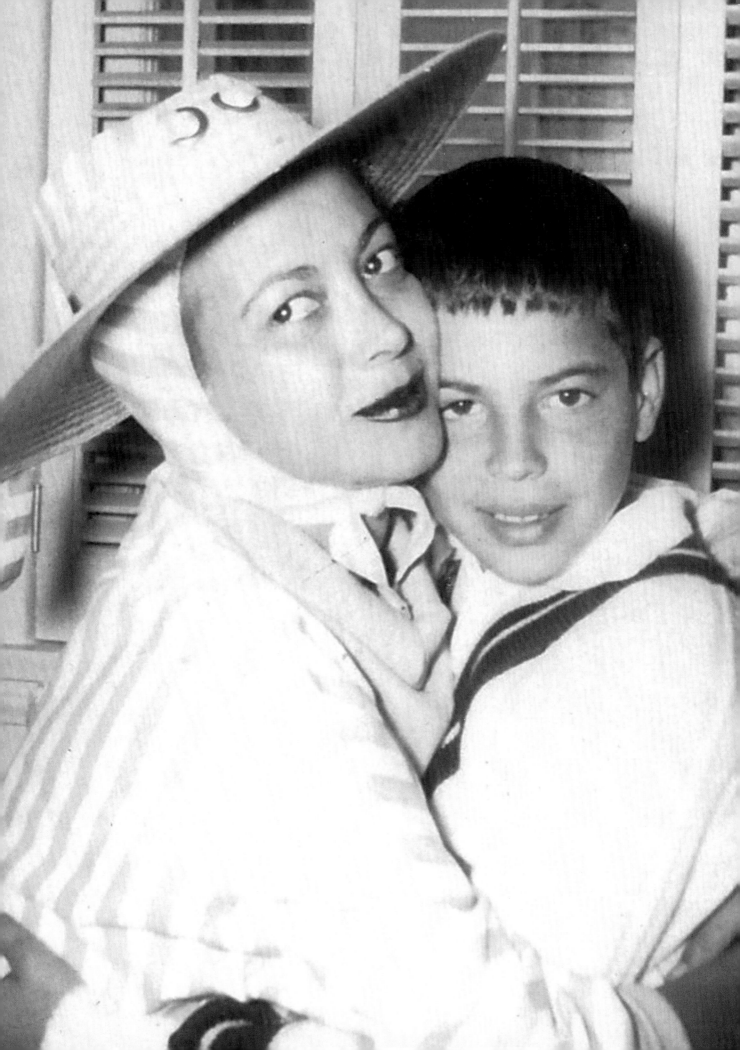

Fargo, and *Wagon Train*; that year, MCA purchased the sprawling Universal Studios backlot, with its extensive production facilities, to centralize and expand its television operation, renaming the site Revue Studios.

As his executive responsibilities increased, Jennings was still able to take time off, and we both gloried in our new baby. I wanted the two older boys to feel completely included in the newly enlarged clan. So, still in the physical recovery stage, I asked Mike to carry Rocky and Bob to haul the diaper bag—and we all marched into court, where I legally adopted my husband's sons. We were now officially a family. Mike and Bob cherished the baby; I never heard them utter the term "half-brother" in reference to Rocky. They were *brothers*. And I was their mom.

Three months later, with Rocky gaining weight and becoming more vocal, we permitted ourselves a break. I accepted an invitation to London from Great Britain's Granada Television to appear on *Chelsea at Eight* (also known as *Chelsea at Nine*), a popular international cabaret recorded weekly at the Chelsea Palace Theatre. Jennings saw it as a chance to enjoy the European honeymoon we had never managed to plan. Mike, then sixteen, was attending the prestigious Lawrenceville School near Princeton, New Jersey, so we lodged eleven-year-old Bob with my sister Bobbe and assigned Rocky (along with an expensive and fully vetted baby nurse) to my parents in Manhattan. Then we headed overseas.

The London press received my singing on the TV show brilliantly—so much so that Granada had me back for another appearance just before we returned to the U.S a couple weeks later. It was gratifying, but I couldn't wait to go home to my baby and the boys.

Once we were all back in L.A., my husband encouraged me to be more take-charge in the household. I hired a pool builder and sold my mink coat to pay for a walkway from the kitchen to the backyard. On the social front, having Rocky gave me the perfect excuse to bow out of the MCA wives' club; instead, I concentrated on raising our family and developing a social life that allowed us to relax. From the immediate neighborhood, our friends included Eddie and Margo Albert and my old flame Sidney Sheldon. People on our street met easily while out walking their dogs, and some of us became so close that we took turns dropping in for drinks.

It was great having my buddy Burton Miller around, too. Burt had more or less followed me to L.A. and wound up living with us in Brentwood for nine months while he sought an apartment. He was a huge help to me in redecorating the house, and Jennings and our sons took to him quickly—delighted by his humor, creativity, and loyalty. If Jennings and I had to travel, we knew the kids were happy to have Burt look after them.

Burt, of course, also was my fashion guru, and he helped me dress to impress for parties and special events, as well as those all-important MCA hierarchy functions I was not able to avoid. Jennings couldn't wait for him to outfit me in something avant-garde. I combined miniskirts with high boots and cute, stylish caps. I even sketched ideas for pieces that Burt could create.

Even in Hollywood, the climate for gays was not particularly hospitable then, and Jennings defended Burt whenever necessary to ensure that no prejudices would impede his ability to work. My husband ultimately landed Burt in Revue's costume department, where his talent flourished and he rose to the top.

Burt told me he had always wanted to be a dad. Jennings and I granted him the next best thing by formally anointing him Rocky's godfather.

My husband's relationship with his parents, who lived in New York, was not as close or visibly affectionate as the one I enjoyed with mine. His dad, Harry, was born in Hamburg, Germany; at age two he relocated with his family to America, where he eventually married Lilly, a woman of Russian descent. Harry never kissed Jennings in his life—instead shaking his hand as soon as he could walk. It undoubtedly primed Jennings for a lifetime of deal making.

Once Rocky was born, Jennings's father was like a dam bursting with emotion. He became so much freer to express his love, and it spilled over to his grandchildren and even his own wife. Jennings and I made sure they had everything they wanted or needed, including

Rocky was a preternaturally smart toddler. At age three, he told us he wanted his birth name changed from Andrew to his dad's name, Jennings. So Jennings and I took him before a judge, who asked him if he had any debts. "No, Judge," Rocky piped up. With the name change decreed, Jennings lifted our son over the bench so that he could kiss the judge.

air-conditioning for their apartment, which the frugal Mr. Lang had long resisted having installed.

Befriending my husband's parents made me want to be around my own more often. We frequently invited Mama and Dad, who were still in fairly good health, to Los Angeles and always had a joyous time together. That changed suddenly during one of their visits with us in 1960.

Jennings was on his weekly trip to New York at the time. Mama came into my room one night, tearful and frightened. "Monica," she said, "I think Daddy is leaving us."

I called our doctor, who came out to our Brentwood house followed by an ambulance. He determined that my father was in cardiac arrest. Mama left with my father in the ambulance while I remained behind and tried to find someone to stay with Rocky. Burt was away, and it took me a couple hours to reach one of our housekeepers. When I finally arrived at the hospital, I encountered my mother leaving Dad's room. "It's over," she said. "He's gone." The impact of her words almost caused me to stumble.

Jennings jumped on an overnight flight to be with us. Meanwhile, Mama handled the situation a lot better than I or my siblings did. I had trouble accepting my father's passing. And I had nightmares about it for a long time.

Eventually, I had to take Mama back to Manhattan. I brought Rocky with me and stayed there with her for several weeks until Jennings asked me to return home. He suggested that I see a grief counselor and even bought me a baby Yorkshire terrier. I told him that if I looked at the puppy, I was afraid I would fall in love with it—and have my heart broken again. He returned the dog.

Jennings tried to cheer me up with some overseas travel. My dad had written a symphonic piece called "The Israeli Suite," which was recorded in Israel; he never heard the work fully performed. While we were visiting Israel, Jennings used his American show business clout to arrange a meeting with Teddy Kollek, director general of the office of Israel's first prime minister, David Ben-Gurion, and the future mayor of Jerusalem. Teddy located a recording of Dad's music and gave it to us. He became our best friend in Europe.

Upon returning to L.A., I continued making weekly pilgrimages to my father's grave at Hillside Cemetery on Centinela Avenue. I played his music on a tape recorder there, changed the flowers, and talked to him incessantly. This went on for months before I finally realized that I had to spend more time with the living. Mama and the rest of the family needed me.

I only saw Jennings cry twice. The first was when my dad died. The other was when President John F. Kennedy was assassinated.

Jennings and I were passionate Democrats and donated substantial time and money to many causes supporting our political affiliation. We campaigned heavily for Jack Kennedy in 1960 and admired his intelligence, confidence, and fearless push behind the civil rights

In the late 1950s and early 1960s, I had small roles in several TV programs, including the anthology series *Studio 57*, the Westerns *Tales of Wells Fargo* and *Wagon Train*, and Blake Edwards's very cool detective series *Peter Gunn*, which had a modern jazz score by Henry Mancini. For this scene from *Overland Trail* (1960), I played a turn-of-the-century blind woman (actors Ethel Shutta and William Bendix also are pictured). My old acting coach, Sanford Meisner, told me to put on a blindfold and practice "acting by ear" to pull it off.

movement. Watching him debate a clearly uncomfortable Richard Nixon on television in the weeks before the presidential election that November was fascinating, and it was the first time TV influenced the course of politics in a big way—leading the youthful Massachusetts senator to the White House in January 1961.

In early 1963, the Democratic Party invited us to a major fundraiser at the Beverly Hills Hotel, where President Kennedy was set to appear. Couples making donations were seated at dinner tables for ten, which included a solitary extra chair. After addressing the crowd, Kennedy worked his way around the elegantly chandeliered ballroom and took the solitary chair at every table to chat with the guests. The visits were limited to ten minutes, at which point the accompanying Secret Service agent said, "Mr. President, we need to move on."

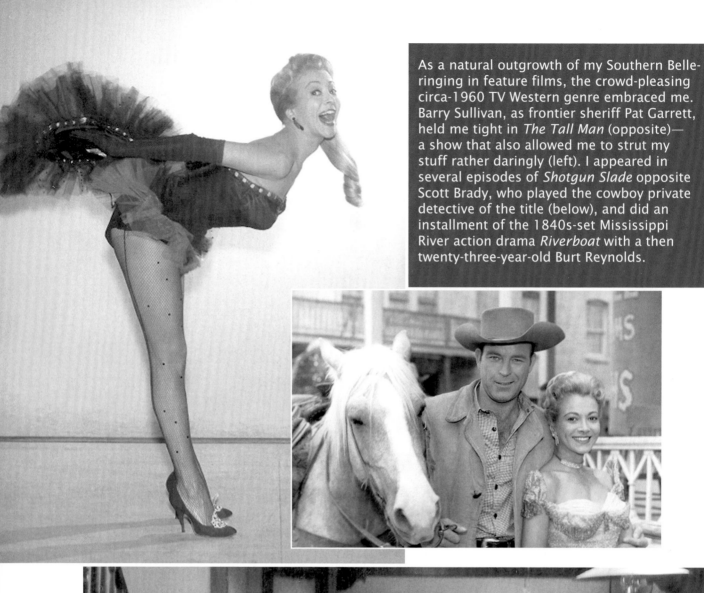

As a natural outgrowth of my Southern Belle-ringing in feature films, the crowd-pleasing circa-1960 TV Western genre embraced me. Barry Sullivan, as frontier sheriff Pat Garrett, held me tight in *The Tall Man* (opposite)—a show that also allowed me to strut my stuff rather daringly (left). I appeared in several episodes of *Shotgun Slade* opposite Scott Brady, who played the cowboy private detective of the title (below), and did an installment of the 1840s-set Mississippi River action drama *Riverboat* with a then twenty-three-year-old Burt Reynolds.

Jack gave no soliloquies during his table-hopping; it was all warm, fun, interactive chatter. When he looked at you, it was with rapt attention—you got the full force of his great humanity, and you felt as if there was no one else in the world. The overworked word "charisma" really should have been invented for him, because like no one else, he had it.

Each guest got about a minute of direct face time with Jack, if they wanted it, but a few people were either too shy or two awed to speak up. The exception at our table was actor Marlon Brando—he grabbed Jack's ear and just didn't want to let go.

When the President turned to me, I shared with him a brief story about Rocky, who had just turned five. Our little son was a total sponge at this point, and he seemed fascinated by the barrage of political ads that filled our living room (and everyone else's) thanks to TV. He would toddle into the kitchen and announce to Jennings and me, "Come see 'Votefur' Kennedy on TV!" Yes, between the tube and all the political conversations Rocky overheard in our house, he thought Jack Kennedy's first name was "Votefur."

The President laughed. I could see in his eyes—the same thoughtful, unwavering eyes that, just months earlier, caused Soviet Premier Nikita Khrushchev to blink and end the Cuban Missile Crisis—that he loved this genuine familial moment. A bit later, when he finished saying his final goodbyes, Jack passed by Jennings and me on his way out of the ballroom—bending over quickly between us and whispering in my ear: "Give my love to your son Rocky. When he grows up, I'd like him to run my campaign."

This memorable evening hung heavy in our hearts a few months later when, on November 22, 1963, John F. Kennedy was shot to death in Dallas, Texas. I was in my bedroom in Brentwood when my mother called from New York. "Turn your television set on," she said, sobbing. "They've killed the president."

The nation reeled. And the image of the Kennedy family walking behind the horse-drawn caisson bearing the President's flag-draped casket in Washington, D.C., climaxed three days of horror and sorrow.

While adults everywhere found this turn of events almost paralyzing, small children also found it difficult to absorb the tragedy's shockwaves. Less than a week later, through the kitchen window, Jennings and I saw Rocky and a couple of local kids carrying one of their friends on a makeshift stretcher made of sheets. They were marching solemnly through the backyard garden.

I went outside. "Where are you going?" I asked.

"We're going to have a barium," Rocky replied.

"A what?" Thinking of the so-named element, I could see that this had nothing to do with a periodic table. Or an enema.

"You know—a *barium*."

I finally figured out that the kids were referring to either "burial" or "buried him," which they had heard endlessly on the TV news. I suddenly had a vision of them digging a hole and putting the boy in the ground. I said, "Well, can I go with you?"

"Okay," Rocky said. "Have you ever been to a barium?"

"Yes," I answered solemnly.

I was simultaneously touched, entranced, and disturbed by this strange procession. I followed the children to the end of the garden and stood with them beneath a large tree while Jennings watched from the house.

Rocky looked at me. "What do we do now?"

I thought it best to end the scene. "Let's say your friend can get up and we had a nice barium."

"Okay," he answered, as he and his friends pulled the sheets back. "This was a nice barium. You can get up now."

I asked the kids if they wanted cookies, milk, popsicles, soda...*anything*. I just wanted them to get rid of that stretcher.

The speed of life in the Lang family paralleled the fast-track growth of MCA. Founder Jules Stein had taken the company public after buying the Universal Studios backlot, handing just over half of his sole ownership to his underlings (with the lion's share going to company president Lew Wasserman). The original backlot purchase agreement called for Stein to rent the property back to Universal Pictures and provide a direct line to MCA's star clientele, who included Doris Day, Cary Grant, Rock Hudson, and Jimmy Stewart.

MCA bought Universal Pictures itself in 1962. But before it could, the company was compelled on antitrust grounds by the U.S. Department of Justice (then headed by Attorney General Robert F. Kennedy, Jack's brother) to exit the talent business. At the time, my old record label, Decca, owned nearly ninety percent of the controlling stake in Universal Pictures; once MCA merged with and assimilated Decca, MCA wound up a major player in the recording business as well as a filmmaking entity. A year later, the company consolidated its executive offices on the Universal Studios property—and made an iconic visual statement about its newfound entertainment industry prominence—by constructing a gleaming fifteen-story high-rise of glass and black aluminum known simply as the Black Tower.

When MCA moved Jennings into this new building, he detested it. My husband skillfully wielded all the legal and negotiating tools for business. Yet he gravitated toward the creative side of production and had grown accustomed to hanging out on the lot at the writers' bungalows, on the sound stages, and in the editing bays. Always loyal to Lew Wasserman and serving the company's best interests, Jennings's efforts on behalf of Revue Productions—then newly combined with the motion picture division and renamed Universal City Studios, Inc.—set the foundation for the company's expanding fortunes. But he was not a corporate soldier and preferred synergy over hierarchy. It went against his grain to be boxed inside a starkly vertical structure with former agents and others who had never produced a movie or TV show or done anything creative. In quiet rebellion, he filled his office with an array of colorful contemporary art that contrasted sharply with the rest of the Black Tower's spartan décor.

Jennings had a flair for showmanship that matched his big personality. Often he was as involved conceptually with programs like *State Trooper*, *McHale's Navy*, and *The Munsters* as he

THE (R)EVOLUTION OF MCA

A few years after MCA acquired Universal Studios' 360-acre studio lot in Universal City, an unincorporated community in Los Angeles County surrounded by the city of Los Angeles, in the late 1950s, it bought Universal Pictures itself. The move sparked a period of rapid growth for the company that saw it evolve into the largest modern film production company and complex in Hollywood.

Through the 1960s, MCA/Universal founded its fortunes on the popularity of television and—largely through the salesmanship and show conceptualization of my husband, MCA vice president Jennings Lang—became the main source of TV network programming. By the mid-1960s, the company had expanded into the recording and themed entertainment industries, introducing a studio tram tour and opening its sound stages and filmmaking secrets to the public. The interactive tour experience became an attraction unto itself while promoting Universal's biggest film and TV hits.

Working under MCA/Universal chief Lew Wasserman, Jennings innovated, and subsequently developed and sold to the networks, the concept of the made-for-TV movie—creating a new profit stream for the company. And his late-1960s position shift to vice president of Universal Pictures helped make it a dominant player in global theatrical distribution. Domestically, my husband produced, supervised, or helped package the studio's biggest movies over the next decade, including *Airport*, *The Sting*, *Jaws*, and his very own blockbusting "event" movie, *Earthquake*.

The advent and explosive growth of home video in the late 1970s and 1980s increased profits further, and major corporations began to purchase the studios. This conglomeratization of Hollywood has continued. Since 1990, when Lew Wasserman sold the company to Matsushita Electric Corporation (now Panasonic), Universal Studios has been controlled by Seagram, General Electric (owner of NBC, the network that first rolled the dice on the made-for-TV movie), and the cable television giant Comcast.

---

was with selling them. Most significantly, Jennings, who introduced thirty-minute movies for TV at Revue in the early 1950s with *The Revlon Mirror Theater* and *General Electric Theater*, was the momentum behind long-form television—developing and supervising the first ninety-minute weekly film series, *The Virginian*, a Western, in 1962. The next year, Jennings accompanied Lew to New York to sell NBC on the idea of motion pictures made directly for TV. The networks top executives, including West Coast programming head Grant Tinker, bought the concept and the first of the finished telefilms to air—a crime drama called *See How They Run*—proved its Nielsen ratings viability.

NBC inked a multiyear deal with MCA to produce "World Premiere" telefilms with Jennings developing and supervising. And despite later efforts by others to claim the title, my husband became the acknowledged father of the made-for-TV movie.

Jennings's vast success in television and rising profile at MCA led Lew to begin preparing him for a shift to feature film production, which was lagging. So in 1965, with my mother now staying with us full time and our need for a home projection booth and screening equipment growing apparent, we sought a larger house in Beverly Hills. We found one—the Mountain Drive mansion of my old producer friend Pandro Berman, who had recently left MGM. Although the place was in disrepair, it was palatial—a steal at $240,000. And it had everything we needed and wanted.

It behooved MCA to ensure that its top executives had great homes because the properties inevitably doubled as places for Universal Studios business and social functions. Jennings worked out a fantastic deal with MCA that had the company reimburse us the property's purchase price and cover all the renovations and upgrades in exchange for a very reasonable rent. With the help of a company-supplied architect, we immediately set about terracing the backyard's steep grade and building a tennis court, a pool, and a pool house—all connected by elaborate brick patios and walkways. It meant several months of upheaval, but the results were gorgeous.

Our 10,000-square-foot Georgian Colonial in Beverly Hills was built in 1937 on a property almost two acres in size. We played host to everyone from Old Hollywood greats (e.g., Groucho Marx, Ginger Rogers) to then-contemporary 1960s music industry giants (e.g., Quincy Jones, Diana Ross) to media celebrities (including Tom Brokaw, who covered several of our fundraisers) during our twenty-seven years there.

That we had European affiliates of MCA overnighting at our house before long was testament to Jennings's knack for reaching out and making friendships and deals with international distributors (it helped that he spoke French, German, and Spanish reasonably well). Still, he never took profit percentages on his productions and stubbornly remained a salaried man—albeit one with a sizable expense account and a large block of stock. He didn't want to sit on the MCA board, preferring instead to run his own candy store. Yet in his new role as vice president of the film division, he continued to enhance the images of those for whom he worked as well as those he mentored, including up-and-coming company executives Sidney Sheinberg and Ned Tanen.

I felt Jennings was the unsung hero of that watershed period in MCA's history. He deserved everything the company gave him.

We were avid, eclectic art collectors. In addition to the large painting by Pierre Alechinsky that concealed the portholes for our living room's projection booth and could be raised and lowered by pressing a switch, we had original pieces by Calder, Picasso, Rodin, Vuillard, and even Grandma Moses—plus works from the European avant-garde movement, also known as COBRA (Copenhagen, Brussels, Amsterdam). It was fun to discover a young artist and watch her or him grow in reputation and value.

The Lang family's newly buffed and polished Georgian Colonial became "da place to be." While a pool and a tennis court were *de rigueur* for Beverly Hills residences of similar size, a self-contained pool house with full bedroom and bath, living room, kitchen, bar, and ladies' and men's dressing and restroom areas was not. We transformed the surrounding rear yard into a magnificent sculpture garden, and adjacent to the tennis court, we installed a covered viewing stand equipped with a refrigerator, television, and phones.

It was paradise.

The main house held an attraction unto itself: our magnificent home movie screen, which commanded our living room whenever it unfurled gracefully from the ceiling at the push of a button. At the opposite end of the luxuriously furnished room, on the wall behind an extra-long sofa, hung a large painting by the renowned Belgian artist Pierre Alechinsky that lowered electrically to reveal two portholes for the state-of-the art projection booth. MCA provided the exhibition equipment, 35mm film prints, and two on-call union projectionists who became our friends. Every Saturday night, we had sit-down dinner parties followed by screenings of new movies weeks ahead of their theatrical debuts.

Our manse became the scene of celebrity parties and politically driven fetes, forcing me to become an expert at making guest lists and planning menus; the always-reliable Chasen's was our caterer of choice. For the larger events, which typically found gleaming Bentleys, BMWs, Jaguars, and Rolls Royces strung through our circular driveway and along the front curb like tinsel garland, we had valet parking. Depending on the star wattage or political stature of the invitees, I asked MCA to supply security guards, who remained on duty until the last reveler departed.

Parties for political causes and for charity were regular events at the Lang residence. But for New Year's Eve 1966, my husband, son, and I pulled out all the stops for our guests—and feted fun for fun's sake.

The celebrity hobnobbing wasn't just at home in Beverly Hills, but behind home plate at Dodgers Stadium. My husband, a rabid fan of the Los Angeles Dodgers, arranged for Rocky to meet superstar National League pitcher Sandy Koufax during his last season with the team. Koufax was inducted into the Baseball Hall of Fame six years later, in 1972.

Fundraisers became our specialty. The American Civil Liberties Union (ACLU) and, much later, the investigative magazine *Mother Jones* and the advocacy group People For the American Way (founded by influential *All in the Family* TV producer Norman Lear), were among the progressive entities we supported. We were committed to all the causes of the underdog.

Our parties for the ACLU were particularly successful, attracting the likes of Lena Horne, Dinah Shore, Barbra Streisand, Frank Sinatra, and Dean Martin—all of whom also sang informally to our guests at one time or another. (Frank and Dean, along with Joey Bishop, Peter Lawford, and my friend Sammy Davis, Jr. were then known as the "Rat Pack" for their ensemble work in the 1960 Las Vegas heist movie *Ocean's 11* and many subsequent stage appearances together.) And our Democratic Party fundraisers were huge draws—with attendance numbering in the hundreds. For one event, we covered the pool with a temporary floor and rolled AstroTurf over both it and the tennis court to serve a backyard sit-down dinner for 500.

To describe these gatherings as colorfully inclusive would be an understatement. Picture Carol Burnett, Walter Matthau, and Jack Lemmon as a singing trio. Or great jazz musicians like Benny Carter and Hazel Scott performing while Clint Eastwood nodded rhythmically nearby. Established Hollywood royalty such as Lucille Ball, George Burns, and Groucho Marx mingled and listened as two young, extraordinarily talented composers named Lalo Schifrin and John Williams—both championed by and given some of their earliest screen credits by Jennings—played piano. (Lalo created the classic title theme for the TV series *Mission: Impossible*; John later did the indelible scores for *Jaws*, *Star Wars*, and umpteen other box-office smashes). Topping it all off was Massachusetts Senator Edward M. "Ted" Kennedy, who we had met and befriended at various Democratic functions after his brother Jack's untimely death, as one of our returning guests of honor.

Although prudent and proper when circumstances dictated, ours was a heady existence swathed in luxury and security: We were not merely in the fast lane, we *owned* it. But we were also largely of a generation that did not inherit wealth or make a killing in the stock market or through corporate mergers. Most of us had earned our money the hard way, and, now settled, we wanted the world to see what we had accomplished while remaining respectable and civic-minded.

That said, we neither courted nor went out of our way to avoid the bra-burning, acid-dropping, sexually swinging late-1960s counterculture immortalized by the music of The Beatles, The Doors, The Rolling Stones, and others. Our attitude was "Live and let live." We were primarily about making the world better and celebrating the good life through philanthropy—with plenty of food, drink, music, art, and fun, creative talk.

The conversations at our parties was not all party patter. There were very serious things going on locally and globally that frequently fueled debate. In late summer of 1965, racially-ignited riots in the Watts neighborhood of South Los Angeles erupted, resulting in thirty-four deaths and ominous, arson-caused smoke plumes billowing across town. Meanwhile, on the other side of the Pacific, the expansion of U.S. involvement in the Vietnam War under President Lyndon B. Johnson exacted a huge toll in American lives and had become a quagmire, sparking antiwar protests at home.

Beverly Hills was at a safe distance from these conflicts, but the pain they inflicted on people we knew and the country we loved penetrated our family's social conscience deeply—renewing our ideological call to action. We threw our full support behind yet another Kennedy family brother: Robert F. "Bobby" Kennedy, a civil rights activist and vocal opponent of the war.

Bobby had resigned his post as U.S. Attorney General less than a year after Johnson replaced JFK in office. He won the U.S. Senate seat from New York in 1964 and four years later commenced his own bid for the White House, becoming the leading Democratic contender in the spring of 1968.

In addition to donating generously to Bobby's campaign, we worked hard for him. I planned and organized small dinner gatherings at the homes of rich, influential people all

My family at our home with Senator Edward "Ted" Kennedy, who participated in one of our 1966 fundraisers to help re-elect Democrat Edmund G. "Pat" Brown governor of California. (Brown lost to my ex-boyfriend, Ronald Reagan.)

Jennings and I greeting Ted Kennedy, family matriarch Rose Kennedy, Patricia Kennedy Lawford, and Joan Kennedy at the home of MCA chief Lew Wasserman during a May 1967 Democratic fundraiser. (Jeanne and Dean Martin are in the doorway in the background.) Ted's brother and Rose's son, Robert F. Kennedy, formally declared his candidacy for U.S. president the following March.

over Beverly Hills and adjacent Bel Air, where Bobby himself often appeared and spoke. This intimate fundraising approach allowed donors to interact with him—and it loosened their purse strings impressively.

If Jack Kennedy was polished and dapper, Bobby was more raw and funnier in his discourse. He had probably spent the years since his brother's assassination reflecting not only on that loss, but on the arc of his family's very public life and the vicissitudes of being both wealthy and a parent of kids who faced an uncertain world. I understood the latter, as I was still raising a young boy.

Rocky was ten at this time and assumed our enthusiasm for RFK. He got on the phone to our friends and his friends and their parents, chirping: "Hi! This is Rocky Lang. How are you? I'm raising money for Bobby Kennedy. Can I come over and get a dollar from you? Okay, I'll be there soon. Bye!" Then he put on a political convention-style straw hat I gave him, hung a canvas bag over his shoulder, and biked around the neighborhood collecting. When someone gave him ten dollars, he flipped with joy.

Our family shared the optimism expressed by Bobby Kennedy in the quotation that he made his own—a line paraphrased from George Bernard Shaw's early-20th century series of plays *Back to Methuselah*: "Some people see things as they are and say, 'Why?' I dream things that never were and say, 'Why not?'"

These words echoed as sadly as the gunshots that rang out on June 5, 1968, at L.A.'s Ambassador Hotel. There, following his victory speech in the California presidential primary, Bobby was left wounded on the floor of the hotel kitchen by an assassin after exiting the ballroom en route to a press conference.

I was supposed to have been at the hotel with Bobby to help him celebrate. But my housekeeper was ill, and Jennings was on location with Paul Newman and Joanne Woodward at the Indy 500 in Indianapolis, Indiana, overseeing production of the racing drama *Winning*, his first major feature for Universal Pictures. So I remained at home with Rocky.

I had invited a fellow campaign worker, a single mom, over with her young son to spend the night. Her boy and Rocky watched the speech with us on TV but they were both asleep before Bobby said, "…on to Chicago!" My friend and I slipped into an adjoining bedroom to finish watching the telecast. It wasn't long before we were staring at the screen in horror. About an hour later, Rocky awoke and called for me.

"What did I miss?"

I didn't answer. But he could read me very well at his tender age. He sat straight up in bed. "Mama, did they hurt him?"

I told him Bobby had been shot and was in the hospital, and that everyone was praying for him.

"I don't care if he gets to be President," Rocky said. "I just want him to live to see his children." His teeth began to chatter, and he cried.

Jennings was as distraught as the rest of us when he called. He calmed Rocky down, told him to take care of me, and assured his son that he would be home in the morning.

My friend was wreck, so I put her to work. We made hot chocolate and lit candles. Everyone was soothed for the moment.

Bobby Kennedy died barely a day after he was shot.

The assassination of Martin Luther King, Jr., in Memphis, Tennessee, that April and the two Kennedy family tragedies topped a decade of shattering events that caused a loss of faith and trust in America. These personages were our last great hopes to unite the nation.

A year after Bobby was killed, the U.S. landed the first men on the moon—fulfilling JFK's ambitious goal to beat the Soviets in the most symbolic contest of the space race. Advancing relations within the human race should have been a cakewalk by comparison.

Having contributed substantially to television's entertainment dominance, my husband seized upon the dual challenge of growing MCA/Universal's feature division creatively and profitably during the late 1960s. He had his work cut out for him.

Although movies had made great technical strides in color processing, widescreen presentation, and stereophonic sound—and rolled out gimmicky innovations like Cinerama and 3-D—to combat TV, their profits dwindled. Baby Boomers, hardened by serial national tragedies and filled with anti-establishment fervor, turned away from musicals, historical epics, and other traditional Hollywood fare, demanding realistic, socially aware, often brutally

We took Rocky to Rome, Italy, with us for the late-1969 premiere of the Universal Pictures release *Story of a Woman*—one of Jennings's responses to the European-influenced "New Hollywood" after MCA/Universal promoted him to vice president of the film division. Our son appeared in the movie as an Italian urchin playing soccer in the street.

violent stories that spoke to their disaffected condition. Antiheros, unhappy or ambiguous endings, and psychedelic imagery in genre-bending pictures such as *Bonnie and Clyde*, *The Graduate*, *2001: A Space Odyssey*, and *Easy Rider* danced on the grave of the old studio system. In the so-called "New Hollywood," the major studios ceded almost completely to the artistic vision of a new filmmaking generation.

Jennings, a cultural weather vane well versed in overseas business-dealing, observed the influence movies from Europe and Asia were having on American cinema. That the rest of the MCA/Universal brass didn't know the French New Wave film movement from French toast failed to discourage him from trying to capitalize on industry trends. For example, the stateside success of Italian filmmaker Sergio Leone's "Spaghetti Westerns"—his latest, *The Good, the Bad and the Ugly*, appeared domestically in1967—convinced Jennings to offer $1 million to the gun-toting star of those films, Clint Eastwood, to play a rebellious Arizona cop on a New York City extradition stint in the 1968 action/drama *Coogan's Bluff*. And Universal's backing the next year of *Story of a Woman*, a romantic drama with international stars (Bibi Andersson, Robert Stack) and far-flung European locales, strengthened the company's foreign distribution connections.

When we weren't traveling to far-flung locations, I sought refuge amid the lush foliage and aesthetic harmony of our backyard sculpture garden. I loved this sculpture of a woman on a hammock, frozen in repose.

All of this meant considerable jet-setting for the Langs. And I welcomed it. With a succession of awful headlines emanating from L.A.—including the gruesome, panic-inducing August 1969 murders orchestrated by Charles Manson in the hills above the city just a few miles from us—I needed an occasional escape beyond our own backyard playground. Whether the travel was primarily for business or for pleasure didn't matter; invariably, it was a mixture of both.

In 1969, after our sons Mike and Bob were living on their own—Mike was in the National Guard and Bob had recently married—we decided it was time for something expeditionary. Jennings and I, along with Rocky, Bob, and Bob's new bride Marsha, went on a photographic tour in Africa—specifically, Kenya and Tanzania. The Serengeti plains were vast and the wildlife gorgeous, and we slept in thatched huts. On safari, Rocky saw a live giraffe for the first time and jumped out of the open truck to get closer to it; our guide yanked him back quickly. Seeing the archaeological and anthropological wonders of the Olduvai Gorge, also known in and out of Darwinian circles as the Cradle of Humankind, was as educational as it was exciting. And it was a kick for the kids to watch their own highly evolved dad command respect wherever we went.

In latter 1971, Jennings and I embarked on another exotic adventure in Prague, Czechoslovakia, where my husband's prowess as a hands-on film producer reached artistic fruition. There he managed a project that combined his personal passion for Europe, history, and unconventional storytelling: *Slaughterhouse-Five*, based on the antiwar science fiction novel by Kurt Vonnegut, Jr., about an American prisoner-of-war living at once in the past, present, and future. It was directed by George Roy Hill, who had been around a lot longer than the fearless young film school graduates making their names in the New Hollywood, but who also did his best work (*Butch Cassidy and the Sundance Kid*, *The Sting*) during this intensely creative period.

The 1945 bombing of Dresden, Germany, by Allied Forces during World War II played large in the book, and that event was recreated for the film in the Czech city of Most, about an hour and a half outside Prague and eighty kilometers south of Dresden. Most itself was still surrounded by abandoned, weathered Russian tanks and military equipment, and the Czech government wanted the old war-damaged areas razed so that they could build anew. Universal Pictures obtained permission to set fires and explosions and generally make any kind of mess as long as it handled the cleanup.

Prague was a beautiful city in that middle-European way, and I nearly got lost exploring it on foot. Kurt Vonnegut, who had actually lived through the Dresden firestorm as a POW, got along famously with Jennings and spent some time with us. It was a privilege to meet this lovely, funny, brilliant man.

After the movie's release in early 1972, we were all together again in France at the Cannes Film Festival, where *Slaughterhouse-Five* took the Jury Prize. While it didn't cause a stampede at the box office, I've always felt the picture—like the story's own protagonist, Billy Pilgrim, and other films from the New Hollywood period—was ahead of its time.

Look closely—those aren't leonine hair extensions, but my other "babies": Yorkshire terriers Tina and Misty.

There was no crystal ball to reveal the magic and prosperity that lay ahead for us in the 1970s—just the pervasive hum and flicker of projection equipment. Jennings and I devoted additional evening time at home, and he at the studio as well, fulfilling one of his work-related tasks: screening the dailies—the raw film footage created on the sets of various productions. This was very much a part of a studio executive's oversight, and unless the dailies revealed something obviously wrong with a project's direction or performances, the process for both of us was fun. The many miles of celluloid we reviewed indicated a healthy film slate at Universal; glimpsing the progress of imminent hits like *Airport* as well as Clint Eastwood's directorial debut—the thriller *Play Misty for Me*—gave us plenty of juice. Meanwhile, the increasing volume of celebrity traffic appearing on our premises (especially the tennis court) each week was proof my husband's tireless networking was paying off.

There was sadness, too, at the start of the decade when my wonderful mother Jessie passed away in April 1971. Mama's health had been in gradual decline since she suffered a stroke in New York a few months earlier. My sister cared for her until she was mobile enough to fly to L.A. with a nurse, and I'll never forget her arrival. She emerged from the plane slowly in a mink coat and with her hair done perfectly, waving and smiling. Her lower lip drooped slightly; her left arm and left leg were virtually paralyzed. But she could feed and dress herself. We took her everywhere with us.

It was easier for Mama to stay in our cozily appointed pool house because there were no stairs to negotiate. One peaceful, pink-hued spring evening, with Jennings out of town on extended business, I was down there watching TV with her when she started to feel ill. I called the doctor, who instructed me to give her a Valium.

"I really don't think this is what she needs," I pleaded, looking at my mother's unusually pained expression. "I'm calling an ambulance if you don't want to do anything about it."

The doctor assured me he would call for one instead and meet me at the hospital.

Mama rallied in the emergency room after the medical team stabilized her. And over the next ten days, she appeared to improve. But then she suffered a setback: kidney failure caused toxins to build in her system. She was on the brink of toxic shock.

The doctor needed my signature to perform additional procedures. With my nerves fraying, I asked Bob to pick me up and drive me to the hospital. Mama was in a deep sleep when I entered her room. She had a faint smile on her lips and looked so placid and sweet.

"Jessie…Jessie…," the doctor whispered, leaning over her. "Monica is here."

Mama opened her eyes—the most beautiful eyes I have ever seen. She smiled broadly as her heart monitor signal jumped wildly. Some nurses rushed in and gave her a shot, and she closed her eyes again. I put my hand on her and held her. And then I left.

The next morning, the hospital called to inform me she had died. Jennings felt terribly guilty for being away. I just told him I loved and missed him.

My grief lingered for months. But I did not go haywire like I did when my dad passed on eleven years earlier; I now recognized the inevitability of death.

I was blessed to have enjoyed such a fully involved and uniquely creative relationship with my parents, who had more *joie de vivre* than most people I have met. Jessie Lewis lived

My mother, Jessie Lewis, was still gorgeous before a stroke and declining health led to her death in 1971. Her many wonderful experiences included a performance with fellow operatic soprano Mary Garden at the White House during William Howard Taft's 1909-1913 presidency. The three Lewis children—me, Marlo, and Bobbe—supported each other after Mama's passing.

to the age of eighty-one and saw her three talented children become successful, articulate people. And she left this world in her familiar high style—an aristocrat, a flirt, and a lady who taught us all to love.

I like to think that I have taught people how to love, too, and in a few cases, I have introduced friends who became life partners. I once even endeavored to play Cupid between two Hollywood titans—Barbra Streisand and Clint Eastwood.

Drawn by our highly visible work for the Democratic Party, Barbra befriended us in the late 1960s. Branching out from theatre, TV specials, and record-breaking recording into screen acting with Broadway musical adaptations like *Funny Girl* (in an Academy Award-winning reprise of her smash stage role), the screwball comedy *What's Up Doc?* (1972), and

Jennings with Barbra Streisand at our home. While building a friendship with us based on shared political interests, Barbra sang at some of our fundraisers and sought advice from my husband in evaluating and purchasing artwork.

her hugely popular romantic pairing with Robert Redford, *The Way We Were* (1973), she was fully in control of her career. Recently divorced from actor Elliot Gould, Barbra had a production company of her own and was expanding her horizons.

Clint Eastwood, then estranged from his wife, former model Maggie Johnson, also had his own production company. Clint clicked with Jennings immediately when my husband hired him to appear in *Coogan's Bluff,* and we spent many hours socializing with him at our respective homes. Jennings was so impressed with Clint's acuity on both sides of the camera that, in 1971, he allowed him to helm *Play Misty for Me,* starring Clint as a late-night disc jockey stalked by a murderous female fan. It was one of seven pictures Jennings and Clint made together at Universal—others included the Westerns *Joe Kidd* (1972) and *High Plains Drifter* (1973)—and critics praised it as the work of a formidable director.

Somehow Jennings and I thought these two strong personalities would mesh. So we arranged a dinner party for twelve at our home and invited them both. Barbra was seated next to my brother Marlo, with Clint on the other side of him. As I normally did for a fancy multi-course meal, I spared no detail with the floral arrangements, glassware, and silverware. The table was aglitter.

Barbra sat there and stared at her elaborate place setting for awhile. Finally, she turned to Marlo. "Which fork do you use first?" she whispered.

"You know," Marlo answered sweetly, feigning uncertainty, "I think you always start with the one that's outside the farthest."

"Oh, I see."

As the meal got underway, Clint seemed lost in his food between idle pleasantries. And Barbra turned her focus to Jennings, who was giving her advice on buying artwork and had already shown her around New York's best galleries. She was a complex person but wasn't afraid to ask for help. I've always found that admirable in an otherwise supremely confident individual.

Marlo left his seat briefly at least twice—causing Jennings and me to glance at each other and engage in diversionary patter, hoping to encourage a spark in the nominal airspace between Barbra and Clint. Nothing. They continued to eat, lift their wine glasses, and look in every other direction.

Barbra called me the next day. I was expecting her to ask about Clint. Finally, after some preliminary chatter, she got down to brass tacks. "Okay, Monica," Barbra chuckled, "where did you find that little mother-of-pearl tissue box in your powder room?"

Yes, a bathroom accent, in the end, had upstaged my attempt at playing accessory to romance for two lovely and remarkable people. I swallowed my pride and promised Barbra I'd get her one.

From a mild-mannered celebrity matchmaker, I wound up a brassy lesbian brothel madam. It was a film part, actually, for the 1973 crime drama *Charley Varrick.*

Jennings gave Clint Eastwood his first shot at directing with *Play Misty for Me* (1971)—a smashing debut. Although Jennings lost Clint's *Dirty Harry* franchise to Warner Bros., Clint made seven films with my husband at Universal.

Jennings and I chat up the man of the moment, Pentagon Papers whistleblower Daniel Ellsberg, at our April 1973 fundraiser for his legal defense.

DEFENDING DANIEL ELLSBERG

America in the early 1970s was rife with political ugliness. To stem the many thousands of casualties we were suffering in Vietnam, President Richard M. Nixon—essentially admitting defeat—began a four-year extrication of our soldiers from the war. U.S. support of Israel during the 1973 Arab-Israeli War precipitated a major oil crisis stateside. And the breaking news of the Watergate scandal in Washington, D.C., in 1972 ultimately led to the president's resignation in disgrace two years later.

In the midst of this tumult, we threw the ultimate party for someone we deemed a hero and friend: Daniel Ellsberg.

While employed in 1969 as a military analyst at the RAND Corporation, a global policy think tank headquartered in Santa Monica, California, Daniel copied a set of classified Department of Defense documents—later dubbed the "Pentagon Papers"—that revealed years of disastrous government deceit in the handling of the Vietnam War. He slipped them to *The New York Times*, which published excerpts in 1971. The Nixon administration indicted Daniel on, among other charges, espionage, and his trial began in Los Angeles in January 1973.

Within a few months, Daniel was broke and could no longer afford his legal team. The ACLU stepped forward, asking Jennings and me—along with our good friends and Democratic Party allies, the award-winning lyricists Alan and Marilyn Bergman (hotter than hot that year with the song "The Way We Were")—to stage a star-studded fundraiser at our Beverly Hills home.

Invitations for the event, held on Daniel's April birthdate, went out by mail and phone. The guests included many big names from Hollywood and politics, including Diahann Carroll, Burt Lancaster, Billy Dee Williams, civil rights activist Julian Bond, L.A. mayor Tom Bradley, Pulitzer Prize-winning journalist David Halberstam (author of the 1972 JFK/Vietnam War account *The Best and the Brightest*), and the ACLU's Southern California Foundation head Stanley Sheinbaum.

The musical participation of Barbra Streisand and the super-talented composer Marvin Hamlisch, with whom she and the Bergmans had just worked on "The Way We Were," was the icing on the fundraising cake. For each contribution of $1,000, Barbra graciously sang the donor's favorite song. She and I also took turns warbling "Happy Birthday" to Daniel—much to his embarrassed delight.

The Beatles were also invited and arrived late, yet their musical set with Barbra on the temporary stage we had erected in our backyard was worth the wait.

And so was this surreal scene: At four in the morning, the music world's Fab *Five*—Ringo Starr, George Harrison, John Lennon, Paul McCartney, and Barbra Streisand—were crammed into my kitchen, snacking on leftovers. Barbra soon departed, and I encouraged the boys to make themselves comfortable in the living room. Then I dragged upstairs to my bedroom, where Jennings was already out like a light.

No sooner than I was under the sheets, our houseman, Charlie, knocked on the door.

"Mrs. Lang, sorry to disturb you," he whispered urgently. "Mr. Ringo wants some Jim Beam and I can't find any."

I shuffled downstairs, dug behind the bar, found the whiskey, and presented it to Ringo. He cradled it gratefully, as if it were warm milk, and resumed the British Invasion of my living room.

The next day, I swept through the house to survey the aftermath. The usual party refuse, spills, and scuffmarks were fully expected. But my nose crinkled as I passed the coffee table, upon which was perched our precious, $100,000 Joan Miró sculpture—a beautiful, strangely amusing piece with a sensuous round hole carved in the back. I looked more closely.

It was filled with marijuana cigarette stubs.

I laughed for a good half hour. If only the master sculptor could have seen how much The Beatles appreciated his art.

The minor damage was worth it: Our much-talked-about fete raised over $50,000 for Daniel Ellsberg's legal defense. The perfect denouement arrived a month later, when prosecutorial misconduct landed the case in mistrial—and Daniel was vindicated.

Me with Daniel Ellsberg and actor Billy Dee Williams, who was hot off his role as Chicago Bears football star Gale Sayers in the acclaimed telemovie *Brian's Song* (1971) and his turn as Louis McKay, the husband of singer Billie Holliday (played by Diana Ross), in the feature *Lady Sings the Blues* (1972).

Hanging out in our dining room during the Ellsberg affair (left to right): costume designer Bill Whitten, Billy Dee Williams, Jennings, and Barbra Streisand. Jennings and I discovered Whitten; he designed my dress for that evening and pretty much had the town sewn up with costume work for Neil Diamond, Elton John, Lionel Ritchie, and Michael Jackson (yes, Bill created Michael's famous solitary rhinestone glove).

With Rocky old enough to take care of himself, I had returned to acting—taking one-shot roles in *Ironside*, *Marcus Welby, M.D.*, *Emergency!* and other episodic prime-time TV series produced by MCA/Universal. Being the wife of Jennings Lang definitely got my foot in the door on these shows, but I still had to audition for them. And I worked for the basic pay scale set by the Screen Actors Guild like everyone else.

Jennings was the executive producer of *Charley Varrick*, and our always gracious, supremely funny pal Walter Matthau had the title role as a stunt pilot turned thief. It was veteran director, Don Siegel—my husband's frequent collaborator with Clint Eastwood (most recently, they had teamed on *Two Mules for Sister Sara* and *High Plains Drifter*)—who approached me personally to play Beverly, the den mother in a rural house of ill repute. My scene was to be shot at the famous Mustang Ranch outside Reno, Nevada, which had just become the state's first licensed brothel.

I told Don I'd do it only if Jennings appeared in the scene as a paying customer. My husband wasn't thrilled with this stipulation but wanted to see me in the movie.

"Okay," Jennings gave in, "as long as I have *no* dialogue. I'll just stand in line and it will be funny for our friends."

Jennings said he would fly with me to Reno and stay one night, after which he had to get to New York. Our room wasn't ready when we arrived, so I took a nap in Walter's room while he and Jennings visited the location and met with the ranch's flamboyant and storied Sicilian owner, Joe Conforte.

There was a hitch in scheduling and Jennings had to leave before his silent cameo as an impatient john could be filmed. I knew he was relieved. And I later jokingly accused him of pimping me out for the part.

The next day, I had a 6:30 a.m. makeup call at the ranch. A convoy of trucks, only a couple of which were related to the production, was lined up outside the place at daybreak. The property was ringed by huge fences, with vicious-looking guard dogs roaming the perimeter. Inside, I couldn't believe what I saw. Most of the girls were about nineteen and many were from the Deep South. Several, I learned, could not read; I helped them fill out the tax forms for the small appearance fees Universal was to pay them. They had no trouble handling their own time cards, which were pinned handily to their shorts.

In addition to being limited to fifteen minutes per customer, the Mustang's girls were told when to eat, sleep, and work. A huge "menu" with prices hung from the wall in the garishly appointed lobby; its offerings included "Regular," "French," "Greek," and "Around the World." They were not salad dressings.

We had to work around the parade of ranch regulars. I was moved by the arrival of one early-morning customer—a wheelchair-bound paraplegic rolled in by his mother for his weekly "fix." Everyone was so sweet to him. His favorite girl entered the lobby and wheeled him off, telling him how handsome he looked.

There was one prostitute, about twenty-eight, who was hipper and more self-assured than the rest. She told me she had been a casino card dealer and was a single mom of three children, whom she left in the care of her own mother for a few hours each day while working to provide for them. Turning tricks paid her three times as much as turning cards. She planned to continue at the ranch for two years, then get out and open a hair salon.

I suspect several members of our film crew took full advantage of the location. I had some good, clean fun playing Madam Beverly and interacting with Walter and the rest of the cast, but I was happy when it was over. Three days of shooting in that carnal "fast food" environment left me depressed.

Flying back to L.A., I pondered all that I had with renewed gratitude.

Raising kids in the high-living environs of Brentwood and Beverly Hills was fraught with its own pitfalls. Neither Jennings nor I were tyrannical parents, but we did have expectations. Our boys always had rules to follow and, even while living amid affluence, they were never spoiled. All of them were on an allowance and either attended summer school or had a job by their late teens. They abided by our rules of social conduct and decorum.

Following in his dad's footsteps, Rocky expressed an early interest in media and sports that led him to directing shows for cable television, making short films, and—during high school—doing an apprentice TV film crew stint with ABC Sports during the 1976 Summer

Jennings could never get enough tennis on our private regulation court. Among the high-powered Hollywood challengers in our backyard racquet club were Lloyd Bridges, Paul Newman, Grant Tinker, and Richard D. Zanuck.

Olympics in Montreal, Canada. While a history major at UCLA, he was admitted to the American Film Institute's Conservatory for Advanced Film Studies. In my son, I saw this wonderfully creative person emerging. Rocky had been exposed to so many artistic, influential, celebrated people growing up, yet he always remained his own person—realistic, compassionate, sincere, and ambitious, if lacking the killer instinct. He blossomed into a terrific tennis player, too, but for him it was always about savoring the game, not winning the cup.

Certainly, there were many powerful personalities who made a happy racket on our home tennis court, where Rocky and Jennings were willing challengers when available. Lloyd Bridges, Paul Newman, producer Richard D. Zanuck (son of legendary Twentieth Century-Fox film studio head Darryl F. Zanuck), and tennis champion Martina Navratilova all graced our competitive backyard space over the years. The foot traffic got to be such that we discouraged drop-ins and recommended enthusiasts schedule appointments through Maggy Martino, my husband's extremely bright and rigorously organized assistant at MCA/Universal.

We tried not to make the court regulations so ironclad that there wouldn't be some flexibility. People still would visit casually and take their chances, and if the court was already booked, they could always sit in the viewing stand with a drink and share laughs or industry gossip with whoever was on either side of the net. Depending on the guests and how busy I was, I sometimes played hostess and emerged with a tray of food or snacks.

We had our "A" and "B" lists of celebrity court regulars—but I'll never reveal who was on which. I will say that Paul Newman was the only visitor generous enough to bring a box of fresh tennis balls along with a case of beer every time. And producer Grant Tinker, then

As much as I tried to improve my tennis game, I preferred the courtside view—whether relaxing on the terrace in jeans (this pair was designed by my friend and celebrity costumer Bill Whitten) or just hanging out with my favorite guys, Jennings and Rocky.

married to Mary Tyler Moore and co-founder of the TV sitcom powerhouse MTM Enterprises (and later, head of NBC), made a tremendous contribution to the courtside ambience by giving us a professional umpire's chair.

Admittedly, I didn't rate highly enough as a tennis player to make either list. The end of the line for my would-be tennis game came during one of our many family winter getaways to Palm Springs, where I was taking my millionth professional lesson. When I finished, Rocky and I went to get some orange juice.

My son put his arm around me. "Mom, give it up."

I looked at him. "Why?"

"Because you don't like it," he explained. "You do everything else so great. But you keep trying and trying on the court, and every time the ball comes toward you, I think you're going to have a heart attack. You've done really well for hating it."

I stomped and stammered and insisted that I didn't hate tennis. And Rocky insisted that I did.

He was right. My best serve was lunch.

The American film renaissance of the early 1970s was something for those of us in the Hollywood community to behold. Young directors like Francis Ford Coppola (*The Godfather*), William Friedkin (*The Exorcist*), and Martin Scorsese (*Alice Doesn't Live Here Anymore*) were hitting their stride with artistically and commercially successful movies, some even achieving mega-hit status. Cinema was fresh, daring, and often brutally unflinching—but also literate and thought provoking.

At the same time, old-fashioned big-screen entertainment had not disappeared completely. The best evidence of this was Universal's own *Airport*, a multi-character melodrama with lots of familiar performers (including my old pals Burt Lancaster and Dean Martin) tossed into a plot concerning a jetliner with a mad bomber onboard. Based on Arthur Hailey's best-selling novel, it was the biggest film of 1970, with a gross of over $100 million.

Jennings, being the executive supervising the production for Universal, not only reveled in the film's success but was awakened to its implications. The capsized luxury liner scenario of *The Poseidon Adventure*, which Twentieth Century-Fox launched in December 1972 and sailed happily to huge returns over the following year, confirmed his line of thinking: that audiences, weary of Vietnam, Watergate, and inflation also wanted less ambiguous, less cerebral entertainment. As *Poseidon* proved, there was room for submersion as well as subversion; people wanted to see characters confront problems much larger than their own.

The disaster movie—which had been around in one form or another since film's earliest beginnings—was "escapism" in all senses of the word. And Jennings, having worked with every genre and variation thereof after nearly ten years in Universal's film division, felt it was a sure bet.

*I*NVITATIONS TO DISASTER

In addition to producing offbeat dramas and comedies like *Pete 'n' Tillie*, *The Front Page*, and *House Calls* for Universal Pictures in the 1970s, my husband, Jennings Lang—competing good-naturedly with producer Irwin Allen at Twentieth Century-Fox— became one of Hollywood's two showman-like "Masters of Disaster." Taking a cue from Universal's own box-office smash *Airport* (1970), Jennings produced a series of all-star air crisis movies incorporating that film's name. His genre pièce de résistance, *Earthquake* (1974), followed a similar multi-character narrative, as did *The Hindenburg* (1975). Also born of the trend, *Rollercoaster* (1977), about a ride-bombing theme park extortionist, was more of a cat-and-mouse thriller; still, it deployed the same vibrating sound effect called Sensurround my husband introduced with *Earthquake*. Disaster movies were the province of formula filmmaking, not auteur theory. As Jennings once quipped: "If Fellini did it, it wouldn't be *Airport*. It would be Fellini with four jet engines attached."

COURTESY OF RIC TURNER COLLECTION

"Honey," he said, "to get people out of the house, you have to give them an event. Or they'll stay home and watch TV reruns."

My husband had been gestating an idea ever since we attended a preview screening of the sci-fi film *The Andromeda Strain* in L.A. in February 1971. It was the night after a big earthquake centered in the northern San Fernando Valley rocked the area, and while we watched the movie, a strong aftershock shook the theater. Jennings excitedly talked about the experience all the way home, and then carried his enthusiasm for a temblor-themed event film right into Lew Wasserman's office the next morning. Lew told him to develop it.

My husband originally sought to hire a novelist to produce a bestseller a la Hailey's *Airport*. He approached Hailey about the possibility, but the author only wanted to work from his own scenarios. That same day, Jennings had lunch with a producer who had prior ties to Universal and also had a deal with Mario Puzo, author of the novel *The Godfather*. Jennings met with Puzo and commissioned a script for $100,000.

Puzo's screenplay, Jennings felt, was "rather amateurish" and would have required a budget of about $17 million—a prohibitive figure back then. After paying Puzo another $25,000 to rewrite the script, Jennings was still not satisfied, so he took Puzo up on his recommendation of another writer, George Fox. Jennings, in the meantime, had hired director Mark Robson, who was adept at staging both character drama (*Peyton Place*, 1957) and action (*Von Ryan's Express*, 1965). Robson and Fox rewrote Puzo's effort and delivered a filmable script, titled *Earthquake*.

The success of *The Poseidon Adventure* and the announcement by that film's highly visible (and competitive) producer, Irwin Allen, of an unusual, all-star joint studio venture between

In *Earthquake*, I was cast as Barbara, secretary to architectural firm chief Sam Royce, played by Lorne Greene (best known for the long-running TV Western *Bonanza*). These were my calmer moments in the picture.

Twentieth Century-Fox and Warner Bros. to make a skyscraper conflagration epic called *The Towering Inferno* really lit a fire under Jennings and Universal. Armed with a budget of approximately $7 million and a November 1973 production start date, Jennings went to town—marshaling the studio's best model builders and special effects technicians, including master matte artist Albert Whitlock (*The Birds*, *Hellfighters*), and assembling the actors. Charlton Heston, my old MGM friend Ava Gardner, George Kennedy, Lorne Greene, Geneviève Bujold, Richard Roundtree, former child evangelist Marjoe Gortner, newcomer Victoria Principal, and Yours Truly, were among the eclectic cast.

The roster of mostly familiar faces followed the tack established by *Airport*. "You don't want to have to spend too much time explaining personality in a disaster movie," defended Jennings, when asked by *Time* magazine why typecasting was common in the genre.

Besides, action and special effects were the true stars of the show. And Jennings's concept for Sensurround—an extended, extra-low-frequency bass sound effect that caused a rumbling sensation in theaters, realized brilliantly by Universal's sound department—generated a groundswell of media interest.

The critical reception of *Earthquake* upon its release in November 1974 was mixed, but it beat *The Towering Inferno* out of the gate by a month. It won the Academy Award for Best Sound and, for its panoramic depiction of L.A.'s destruction, a Special Achievement Award for Visual Effects. Most importantly, with more than 41 million admissions sold by the end of its run in 1976, the film was a box-office bonanza for MCA/Universal.

Jennings was a bona fide superstar on the studio lot.

At home, the welcoming Lang family atmosphere meant that we had friends hanging out almost every day. There was one slim, bespectacled guy in his mid-twenties who came around often—usually quiet, very polite, obviously intelligent. He would sit on the back patio and glow as Jennings regaled him with stories about the business. He'd talk to me about music, flowers, and his mom. He'd hit the pool and the tennis court with Rocky. And he'd discuss filmmaking with anyone who would lend an ear.

His name was Steven Spielberg. And until 1975, when he stunned Hollywood—and audiences everywhere—with his summer blockbuster *Jaws*, no one knew the extent of his capabilities.

Jennings had much more than an inkling. Steven, who got his big directing break at Universal Television with a segment for the 1969 pilot of Rod Serling's supernatural anthology series *Night Gallery*, had demonstrated a rare knack for pacing, suspense, and visual verve with the 1971 telemovie *Duel*—in which a traveling salesman is menaced on a desert highway by a hell-bent tanker truck. It was enough for Jennings to support Steven's 1974 feature debut for Universal Pictures, *The Sugarland Express*, a Texas-set crime drama starring Goldie Hawn.

Jennings backed Steven again when *Sugarland*'s producers, Richard D. Zanuck and David Brown, were preparing to film *Jaws*, Peter Benchley's best-selling 1974 novel about a human-hunting Great White shark, for Universal. My husband performed a similar function in

In action and at rest with Charlton Heston. Jennings and I knew Chuck since before he made *Ben-Hur* (1959). He was very much a gentlemen and always professional. And he obviously loved doffing his shirt in every movie, as he did at the beginning of *Earthquake*.

Being the wife of a big producer has its benefits—and its risks. With Jennings having hired me for a supporting role in his mega-magnitude opus *Earthquake*, I knew I had to be one of the troops and not "Mrs. Lang." As a show business veteran who never demanded a dressing room or much of anything except a spotlight, I knew it couldn't be that difficult. And besides, if Shelley Winters could hold her breath and make like a mermaid all the way to an Academy Award nomination in *The Poseidon Adventure*, I could hang from a fire hose—strapped into an office chair—three stories above the floor of Stage 12 at Universal Studios.

The scene: A catastrophic temblor has struck Los Angeles, and the workers in a high-rise office building are trapped on the upper floors of the damaged edifice because the emergency stairwell has collapsed. Charlton Heston, in the film's lead role as architect Stewart Graff, decides that the best way to get the survivors past the gap in the structure is to hook a fire hose to an office chair and lower them one by one.

Remember—this was years before digital special effects were introduced. My co-star, Lorne Greene, thought we should use doubles for the slow-speed stunt. But our ace cinematographer Philip Lathrop (*Don't Make Waves; They Shoot Horses, Don't They?*) wanted to have the camera tight on the principal actors' faces and then pull back to show the full extent of their jeopardy as the rescue unfolds. So I turned to Lorne and said, "Honey, I think *you* want to use a stunt double. Everybody should do what they want."

As it turned out, Lorne and everyone else followed my lead and got into that swinging chair.

While I dangled precariously several dozen feet off the floor thinking *What the hell did I get myself into?*, effects technicians were paying tribute to me elsewhere on the lot—collapsing the stacked-platter-shaped Hollywood headquarters of Capitol Records, my former recording label. But I got the last laugh when, in a scripted would-be nod to my Burlington Mills hosiery-shilling days, I eagerly stripped off my pantyhose to create a makeshift restraint for the dangling office chair.

The Stuntmen's Association of Motion Pictures made me an honorary captain for my cinematic derring-do. Audiences loved it. And so did my producer-husband.

promoting George Roy Hill to helm Zanuck/Brown Productions' *The Sting* at Universal two years earlier; the film was not only was a major hit, but the studio's first Best Picture Academy Award winner since *All Quiet on the Western Front* in 1930.

That Jennings never got, or sought, credit for helping to package two of Universal's biggest hits was very frustrating for me. It was particularly tough in the case of *Jaws*. Before the novel was published, Peter Saphier, a young vice president in Jennings' production wing, brought the galleys to my husband. We took the pages with us on a trip to the south of France, read them—and knew immediately that the story had mass appeal. But the higher-ups in the Black Tower weren't as enthused and missed the chance to buy the book for a song. Jennings then slipped it to Zanuck/Brown, but by the time they moved on it, *Jaws* was a bestseller and commanded a royal sum.

In return for working in the studio's best interests, Jennings enjoyed the leeway to brainstorm ideas and develop concepts, which he freely shared. Other producers viewed him the go-to guy at Universal for suggestions and solutions because they knew he wasn't after their jobs. The lack of internal competition within his sphere made his position more fun and the lot more habitable.

With *Earthquake*, Jennings got a sweet, long-overdue taste of having his name prominently displayed in the credits—and in the promotional materials—for one of his projects.

Recognizing the brand value of the original *Airport*, my husband planned several in-name-only sequels ranging in scenario from a mid-air collision to a crash in the Bermuda Triangle to a Concorde jet chased by heat-seeking missiles fired by a traitorous U.S. businessman. The running thread in the series was a character named Joe Patroni—a good-natured airline troubleshooter played by George Kennedy, who first appeared in the 1970 film.

The sequel, *Airport 1975*, filmed quickly and released a month ahead of *Earthquake* as a genre appetite-whetter, concerned a 747 flying with serious instrument damage and a giant hole in the cockpit after a smaller plane crosses its path. It's up to the head flight attendant (Karen Black) to keep the jet aloft until her pilot boyfriend (Charlton Heston) can attempt a mid-air pilot transfer from a military aircraft. Meanwhile, back in the cabin, Gloria Swanson

My husband was so proud of my stuntwork in *Earthquake* that he commissioned this special mock one-sheet poster giving me top billing.

My husband and I (left) promoted *Airport 1975*, *Earthquake*, and Jennings's other pictures heavily overseas. Jennings recognized the value of international sales and marketing in the film industry a couple decades before anyone else—and made sure his larger-budget "event" movies had wide appeal in concept and casting. Three hundred European film distributors attending this particular screening of *Earthquake* in Rome were doubly impressed when they learned that the movie's powerful Sensurround effect had knocked glasses off shelves at a bar next to the theater. (We were detained by the irate bar owner until we promised to pay for the breakage.)

(as herself) applies makeup while a nun with a guitar (Helen Reddy) serenades a kidney transplant patient (Linda Blair).

Leasing an actual 747 and using his vast negotiating powers, Jennings received permission from the Air Force, the Federal Aviation Administration, and the U.S. Department of Defense to shoot the exterior flight scenes. *Airport 1975* earned back its $4 million cost many times over.

And so the multi-character, multi-star formula continued in *Airport '77*, with Jack Lemmon at the controls of a hijacked jetliner that crash-lands in the ocean and sinks, trapping its passengers in the watertight cabin until a daring military-driven rescue can be attempted from the ocean's surface. (We figured Irwin Allen would dig this one.) I had small role as a flight attendant and, being the executive producer's wife, I survived.

After surviving the old Hollywood studio system at MGM and our respective personal travails, my pal Ava Gardner and I wore our battle scars proudly (courtesy of Universal's makeup team) on the set of *Earthquake*.

AVA GARDNER

Ava Gardner was unquestionably the most beautiful woman I ever met. Even without makeup, she was just gorgeous. Her face was made for the silver screen; no still photo could do it justice. You already know why if you've seen her work in movies like *Mogambo* (1953) and *The Sun Also Rises* (1957). Of all the great moments

When principal photography on *Earthquake* wrapped in May 1974, Ava autographed her never-worn film crew shirt—a denim blouse, extravagantly embroidered across the shoulders—and presented it to me as a fun gift.

in *Show Boat* (1951), the film's iconic image is one of Ava throwing a kiss goodbye. She was the personification of the close-up.

Back in our days on the MGM lot, Ava and I often lunched together in the commissary. All of the newer contract players were instructed to wear waist cinchers that discouraged eating (and breathing!) while adhering to a diet of unsweetened Jell-O and watermelon. One day, Ava sat down across from me, took one distasteful look at my plate, and let her Southern drawl slip in admonishment: "Monica, what are you doing? If you can't have all you want in life, at least have a bite of something you like!" She promptly ordered one piece of key lime pie and a glass of iced coffee.

Arriving in Hollywood an insecure girl who had been raised on a North Carolina tobacco farm, Ava learned to take chances, educate herself, and savor the day. It was just too bad that, as was the case with me and so many others at MGM, the studio didn't know what to do with her—attempting to mold her into the next Rita Hayworth instead of letting her flourish as herself. Which she eventually did.

Ava wanted a steadfast love, but after several failed marriages—including, most infamously, to Frank Sinatra—that didn't happen. She was mercurial and a bit of a wanderer. But she was also earthy and fun. At home, Ava was a bandanna-wearing, barefoot-in-torn-jeans kind of gal, and she hated what she considered the bullshit of Hollywood. She valued the freedom and privacy she eventually found in London; there, she could be herself.

In 1973, when Ava signed on to play Remy Royce-Graff, the long-suffering wife of philandering architect Stewart Graff (Charlton Heston) in *Earthquake*, it was evident that time had taken its toll. But she still had that ravishing face and carriage. And she was sharp on the set. When the director called for her, she was ready—unlike others who never had what she had and thought they were hot-shit divas.

Ava avoided the press and spent most of her time in her trailer when she wasn't needed in a scene. We had plenty in common, including our birth year, similarly strong sibling relationships, and a love of music. She often invited me in to chat and listen to Sinatra tunes. It was great to have Ava on that movie, and to have her hang out in my kitchen at home.

It was even better to have her as my friend.

My husband's powers of persuasion landed some very big stars in *Airport '77*, including Jack Lemmon, Olivia de Havilland (right), and James Stewart. Almost all of us did our own stunts (that's me as a flight attendant splashing free of the submerged 747), but at least legendary costume designer Edith Head—with an assist from my friend Burt Miller—made sure we were well-dressed for distress. Jack, who took flight *and* diving lessons to prepare for his role, later sent Jennings a hilarious photo of himself sopping wet on the movie set, signed thusly: "What the hell do you mean it's a glamorous role? Screw you!"

In taking a story credit on *The Concorde…Airport'79*, my husband harbored Cold War narrative ambitions that outdistanced their execution by screenwriter Eric Roth (who went on to write *Forrest Gump*, for which he won the Academy Award in 1994, and many other brilliant scripts). But we obtained the permission of the Concorde's Toulouse, France-based manufacturer, Aerospatiale, to use one of its fleet. I had fun essentially playing my own singing self as a passenger. And the European actors among the cast, including Alain Delon, Sylvia Kristel, and Bibi Andersson improved the picture's foreign distribution prospects.

Despite new challenges to the film industry in the form of home video and pay cable,

© UNIVERSAL CITY STUDIOS, Inc.

I had a walk-on part as a bakery owner in Jennings's 1978 production *Nunzio*, a sweet little drama set in New York City about a mentally-challenged grocery deliveryman who aspires to be a superhero. My son Rocky was an assistant on the production.

Jennings was proud to have launched a coach-class franchise that stayed profitably aloft at Universal for years. In 1979, when we heard about an air crisis movie spoof in the works at Paramount Studios, we almost considered it a tribute. My reputation as a good sport was strong around town, so I wasn't surprised when I received word that I was possibly up for a part in it. Unfortunately, the opportunity got lost in inter-studio politics.

When *Airplane!* landed in theaters the following summer, Jennings and I were there in the audience with our buckets of popcorn—busting a gut to the point of tears like everyone else.

Jennings and I continued to soar right into 1980 on the wings of *The Concorde*. After the film's stateside release, we invited George Kennedy and his wife Joan to join us on a whirl-wind worldwide publicity junket for the film—hitting major cities such as Rio de Janiero, Buenos Aires, Cape Town in South Africa, Paris, and Washington, D.C. In Mexico City, Jennings and I did a live talk show and fielded questions from the audience in fractured Spanish with the help of a translator. The air travel we put in during this exhausting, month-long international push must have set some kind of record. But it was a grand time.

That spring, we flew to London for a special charity screening of Jennings's latest pro-duction, *Little Miss Marker*, with Walter Matthau, Julie Andrews, and a child actress named Sara Stimson in a remake of the 1934 Shirley Temple film based on a Damon Runyon story. At a reception afterward, we were graced by the presence of the Prince of Wales—also known as Prince Charles. We were his guests of honor; he was very charming and grateful for our participation in the event.

Jennings and I enjoyed the attention of Prince Charles at a 1980 London charity screening of Universal Pictures' *Little Miss Marker*, which was produced by my husband.

After a twenty-year absence from recording, I returned with the album *Never Let Me Go* (last released by Equinox). Its high-tech digital creation was all new to me, but my son Mike Lang guided me through the project as producer. Beautifully orchestrated, the album contained two of my favorite songs: "The Hungry Years," written by Neil Sedaka, and "The World of Slow," which I wrote for my son Rocky when he graduated high school.

Monica Lewis

NEVER LET ME GO

Jimmie Walker and I were relatively mellow seatmates among the largely outlandish passengers on *The Concorde...Airport '79*. Between scenes, my friend and Concorde "pilot" George Kennedy—his character, Joe Patroni, helped solve the crises in all of my husband's *Airport* sequels—swapped old show business stories.

We stayed pretty close to home for several months afterward. In November 1980, seeing my former paramour Ronald Reagan—who Jennings, working for MCA's Revue Productions, championed for the TV hosting role of *General Electric Theater* a quarter century earlier—win his bid to become the country's fortieth president was quite a spectacle, if not the ideological outcome we wanted. And the hostage crisis in Iran, with fifty-two U.S. citizens still remaining captive a year after militants seized our embassy in Tehran, kept us on edge, hoping it would end with their safe release. (It did, in January 1981.)

Everything was fine as we crossed into the New Year. Jennings had a number of movies in development, while Rocky was busy pursuing his own youthful filmmaking ambitions. And then, I got terrifying message one afternoon in January: My husband had taken seriously ill at the office.

According to his assistant, Jennings was on the phone at his desk when he began rambling and passed out, slumping to the floor. She called paramedics, who administered treatment and rushed him, unconscious, to a hospital not far from the studio.

With my good friend Donna Schifrin by my side at home for support, I contacted my husband's personal physician. We had Jennings transferred to Cedars-Sinai Hospital, near Beverly Hills. I said to Donna: "I'm not ready for anything to happen to Jennings." We went immediately to Cedars-Sinai, where the doctor was waiting for us with a top neurologist.

My husband had suffered a major seizure. He was disoriented as he gradually came out of it that evening and—unusual for him—he didn't want to speak. He jotted a few things on paper with a pencil, including my name and Donna's. The next day, he was totally with it but extremely fatigued and very concerned about me. I couldn't hide my fear.

Jennings had no prior history of epilepsy. But through x-rays, the doctors discovered that an old head injury he sustained playing lacrosse in college had calcified and moved, causing a neural disorder in his brain. The doctors prescribed a medication called Dilantin, which suppresses abnormal electrical activity and does not work with excess alcohol in the blood. When they asked Jennings how much he drank, he said, "A lot!" They told him he could get away with one glass of wine at dinner. We knew the old Jennings was back when he joked, "Doctor, I rinse my mouth with a glass of wine. Either I drink or I don't—so I won't." Jennings never touched another alcoholic beverage.

As my husband's health normalized over the next few months, there was an edginess creeping into the executive suites in MCA/Universal's Black Tower. After the gold-rush early part of the 1970s culminated with *Earthquake* and *Jaws*, a number of Jennings's pictures were considered underperformers. His efforts later in the decade—beginning in 1975 with the Clint Eastwood espionage thriller *The Eiger Sanction* and including the pirate adventure *Swashbuckler*, *Nunzio*, *Little Miss Marker*, and the feature debut of Don Adams's popular *Get Smart* TV character, *The Nude Bomb*—had not met studio expectations. And it was evident that the younger, and now higher up, executives Jennings had mentored were jostling for power.

After more than three decades of faithful service to Lew Wasserman and MCA/Universal, Jennings Lang—the "most colorful company man in town," as he was labeled by the *Los Angeles Times*—was transitioned from vice president of production for Universal Pictures to Universal Studios-based independent producer. My husband assured the trade press that he remained a part of the MCA/Universal family and valued the freedom the new arrangement afforded him, like shopping his projects to other studios if Universal passed on them. In late 1981, his development slate included *The Sting II*, with our buddies Jackie Gleason and singer Mac Davis set to star; a fourth, made-for-cable-TV *Airport* sequel; and a sequel to *Earthquake*.

In the Black Tower, from the mailroom to the secretarial pool, Jennings was adored; when he vacated the building that fall, they said the sun went out. But for my husband, it was a new dawn all around. He was back where he always felt most comfortable—ensconced in a bungalow on the studio backlot amid the writers and other creative staff. Nearly a year after the seizure, he had lost weight and was in great shape, and he could out-walk everyone.

Our inner social circle was dealt two sharp blows during this period of change. Tragedy befell our dear friends Robert Wagner and Natalie Wood in November 1981, when Natalie drowned during a boating excursion to Santa Catalina Island, off the coast of Southern California. We went to be with Robert right away. And then in March 1982, my best buddy Burt Miller, who did the costume work on virtually all of my husband's shows from *Wagon Train* in 1957 through *The Sting II*, died suddenly at just fifty-six. There was much sadness and reflection for the Langs.

The year 1982 brightened. With Jennings now the boss of his own company, he was able to take time off to take care of himself—and me. It turned out to be the last best year of our lives.

Rocky and Dustin Hoffman hamming it up with my military issue helmet from Korea at our home in 1983. My son was working with Dustin on a documentary about the enormously popular feature comedy *Tootsie*, for which the actor won critical raves in the title role. Rocky's sixty-eight-minute work, *A Better Man: The Making of Tootsie*, can be seen on the movie's twenty-fifth anniversary DVD.

In February 1983, Jennings was entering the elegant Scandia Restaurant on Sunset Boulevard for a business lunch when he felt a sharp pain in his chest. He returned to his car and drove to his doctor, who gave him a stress test. The results were not good: My husband was diagnosed with a faulty heart valve, which needed to be replaced. He required single-bypass surgery as well.

I was a wreck. Rocky was in New York creating a documentary about the cross-dressing comedy *Tootsie*, starring Dustin Hoffman, which had been released in December and was a monster hit for Columbia Pictures. Sydney Pollack, the feature's director and an informal supervisor on the documentary, told Rocky to return home and continue editing the project in Los Angeles so that he could be close to us.

Meanwhile, ShoWest, the top international convention of film distributors and theater operators, had named Jennings "Showman of the Year." He was still recovering from his operation at Cedars-Sinai when the award was presented in Las Vegas, so Rocky attended the event and accepted it in his father's stead. Sprung from the hospital a month later, Jennings started exercising again and followed all health guidelines. He was back on his feet and well enough for us to attend the Cannes Film Festival in April.

Jennings anticipated the production start-up on *Stick*, an adaptation of the 1982 crime novel by best-selling author and screenwriter Elmore Leonard, with whom he had last worked on the John Sturges-directed Clint Eastwood Western *Joe Kidd*. They both saw *Stick* as a taut, film noir-type picture with Roy Scheider as Ernest "Stick" Stickley, an ex-convict who winds up on the run after witnessing an illegal drug deal ending in murder.

Universal Pictures had first right of refusal on the project, and it also had an unfulfilled commitment to Burt Reynolds for him to act in and direct a film. Burt loved the script for *Stick*. Although he didn't quite fit Jennings's conception, my husband liked Burt and—with more prodding from Universal—the project went forward with Burt attached as star and director. The cast also included Candice Bergen, George Segal, and Charles Durning.

Production began in Fort Lauderdale, Florida, in November 1983. I was to appear in the film as a singer, performing a tune called "Harbor Lights," so I met Jennings in Miami with the intent to spend some quality time with him on location. Additionally, I was worried about Jennings having developed a heart flutter, for which his doctors had given him a new prescription. They had recommended he wear a Holter monitor—a portable device worn on the chest to monitor heart and central nervous system activity—for a few days before leaving for Florida, but he felt there wasn't time.

My first night with Jennings in the Sunshine State, all hell broke loose at MCA/Universal. There was a shakeup in the Black Tower, and although Jennings was no longer in the hierarchy, all his former protégés and colleagues called him seeking solace or advice. The next morning, I got my hair dyed, and when I returned to our hotel suite, Jennings was in his jogging suit exercising in front of the TV. I went into another room and settled in with a Rita Hayworth movie. Within minutes, I sensed someone behind me.

Jennings was clutching the doorway. His eyes were wide.

I jumped up. "What's the matter, honey?"

He didn't answer.

I asked him again. No answer. I told him to sit down. He moved unsteadily over to a chair and sat heavily. I asked him to give me his hand, and he gave me his left hand. I asked him to give me his other hand. He could not lift it.

I called the lobby receptionist, and two security guys were at the door within minutes. They called the paramedics, who arrived almost as quickly and tested Jennings. They placed him on a stretcher and transported him to Broward General Hospital.

We had planned to have dinner with George Segal and his wife that evening. George very generously spent the night in the hospital with us instead.

Our doctor in L.A. gave me explicit instructions to relay to the physician at Broward. The Southern doctor was very sweet. He listened to me patiently and said, "Darlin', I'll do everything he wants me to do, but it's like pissin' in the wind. Your husband has had a complete stroke."

The statement's ring of finality was a shock.

I called the boys, and Rocky rounded up his brothers. They all got to Fort Lauderdale quickly, as did some of my own family from New York. Rocky stayed with us for the next ten days. My husband was unable to speak, and I was scared, but at least I was surrounded by love. When the doctors gave the okay to move Jennings, Lew Wasserman sent his private jet to retrieve us.

Back home, our neurologist kept Jennings hospitalized for three months. We learned that his heart valve had misfired, forming a clot that tore into his brain.

Everyone was devastated. This was not the idyllic concluding act I had envisioned for our home movie.

APPLYING THE FACE OF TELEVISION

Although the material needs of World War II halted the production of civilian broadcasting equipment in America between 1942 and 1945, fine-tuning of the all-electronic technology behind the country's existing 5,000 or so television screens continued. In 1944, the technical staff of David Sarnoff—owner of NBC and founder of RCA—asked me to participate in a test to determine how different shades of facial makeup appeared when broadcast in black and white. My first "TV role" was not, as evidenced by my *very* casual attire, for public viewing. But as soon as TV became more widely available later in the decade, I was ready for show time.

COLORS USED FOR TELEVISION FACIAL MAKEUP

FLESH TONE   EYE SHADOW   LIPSTICK

MacDonald

Monica Lewis

sings...

IF I LOVED YOU
ALWAYS

BUT NOT FOR ME
I'LL SEE YOU IN MY DREAMS

SOMEONE TO WATCH OVER ME
THEY DIDN'T BELIEVE ME

SPEAK TO ME OF LOVE
I'LL SEE YOU AGAIN

Signature records
ALBUM S-6

My hit 1946 jazz compilation album for Signature Records, *Monica Lewis Sings*, helped give the independent label solid footing among the majors. That summer, I posed for top fashion photographer Andre de Dienes—famous for his work and love affair with Marilyn Monroe—at Jones Beach on Long Island, New York (below). Images from this shoot appeared nationally in *Holiday* magazine and others.

When Lana Turner's personal life prevented the box-office star from fulfilling her obligations to MGM, the studio made me over into her mirror image after I joined the roster in 1950.

D

GETTING ANIMATED AS
MISS CHIQUITA

In early 1947, I secured my largest-ever endorsement deal when United Fruit Company hired me to promote its Chiquita Banana brand. Following the vocal talents of Patti Clayton and Elsa Miranda, I provided the new musical voice of Miss Chiquita—a singing, dancing cartoon banana created by artist Dik Browne (of eventual "Hägar the Horrible" comic strip fame). My main duty was to teach housewives how to ripen bananas properly and then bake them in a "pie-yi."

In addition to doing radio spots, I spent an all-expense-paid week in Los Angeles performing voiceovers for a series of one-minute theatrical shorts that combined live action and animation. The banana character was also used in print ads and on promotional holiday greeting cards containing chirpy lyrics.

During my lucrative fourteen-year reign as Miss Chiquita, United Fruit (now known as Chiquita Brands International, Inc.) saw an unprecedented jump in sales—with demand for the company's product running twenty percent ahead of supply. And that wasn't "pie-yi" in the sky!

The publicity department at Metro-Goldwyn-Mayer spoofed my Chiquita ad work with this ripe 1950 setup. (Yes, that's a giant banana stem jutting from my hat.)

Look

15¢ JULY 17, 1951

BARUCH
Answers 13
Questions
WAR · RUSSIA
KOREA · DRAFT
INFLATION

That's me (lower right) twirling with MGM's other "dancing daughters" (at center, then clockwise from lower left): Cyd Charisse, Leslie Caron, Debbie Reynolds, and Sally Forrest. Like other stars promoting movies for their studios, I appeared regularly in *Look*'s "Photocrime" features, which introduced and solved a mystery through sexy, dramatically staged photos.

F

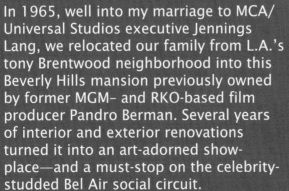

In 1965, well into my marriage to MCA/ Universal Studios executive Jennings Lang, we relocated our family from L.A.'s tony Brentwood neighborhood into this Beverly Hills mansion previously owned by former MGM– and RKO-based film producer Pandro Berman. Several years of interior and exterior renovations turned it into an art-adorned show-place—and a must-stop on the celebrity-studded Bel Air social circuit.

Our beautiful backyard, which included a pool, pool house, tennis court, and extensive brick-work deck, was the scene of lavish Hollywood parties attended by the likes of Barbra Streisand and The Beatles, as well as high-powered political fundraisers for the Kennedys and others. It was one of my favorite places to steal a kiss with Jennings.

H

You know you've arrived when some-one endeavors to make paper dolls in your image. (A set in the likeness of my friend Debbie Reynolds also circulated.) They created a fun, and promotional, fashion statement.

At the piano in the late 1980s with my stepson Michael Lang. Mike is an extraordinarily talented musician, composer, and live performer, and he has contributed to the sound-tracks of dozens of film and TV productions including 1990s big-screen hits such as *Noises Off*, *The Bridges of Madison County*, and *As Good as it Gets*.

Ronald Reagan's most special gift to me during our two-year romance was this gold medallion depicting St. Genesius, the patron saint of actors. It was designed by Beverly Hills jeweler-to-the-stars William Ruser.

J

My nephew, Marlo Lewis Jr., a highly placed political analyst (and by the way, a hot blue-grass singer and guitarist).

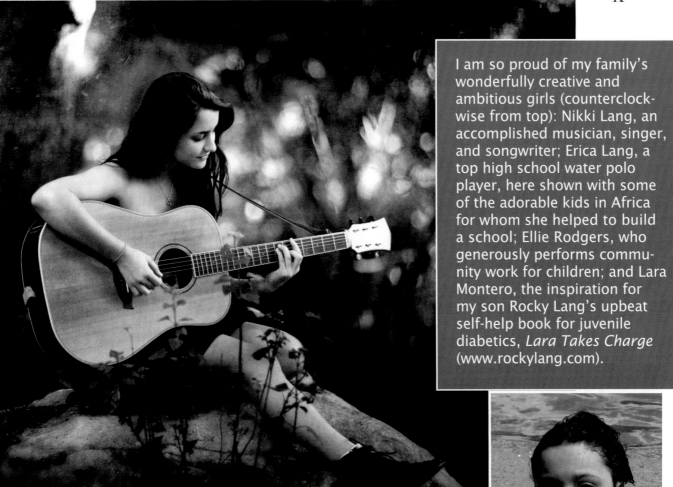

I am so proud of my family's wonderfully creative and ambitious girls (counterclockwise from top): Nikki Lang, an accomplished musician, singer, and songwriter; Erica Lang, a top high school water polo player, here shown with some of the adorable kids in Africa for whom she helped to build a school; Ellie Rodgers, who generously performs community work for children; and Lara Montero, the inspiration for my son Rocky Lang's upbeat self-help book for juvenile diabetics, *Lara Takes Charge* (www.rockylang.com).

I attended the 2008 American Diabetes Foundation "Father of the Year" presentation with the honoree—my son Rocky Lang, who is also a film producer and published author. Rocky savored the moment with the other special women in his life (below, from left): daughters Erica and Nikki, wife Heather, and daughter Ellie.

Posing for the cover of my 1990 album *My Favorite Things* (DRG Records), featuring the music of George Gershwin and Richard Rodgers.

6 AUTUMN LEAVES

Seeing Jennings Lang, the bold, brilliant, ebullient businessman and beloved husband and father, robbed by a stroke of his speech and much of his movement was an emotionally debilitating blow to all who knew him. But knowing Jennings also meant accepting that he would never want anyone to wallow in pity or sorrow. Although his abrupt change had immediate repercussions on our household and social circle, we were grateful he was alive. And we knew the only way to grace would be in continuing to conduct life as normally as possible.

Collective family trauma quickly turned to action.

While Jennings was still in the hospital, where he received wonderful care and therapy, I researched every piece of assistive medical equipment known to man. To prepare for my husband's return home, I had ramps constructed for the exterior doorways and an electric stair lift installed in the foyer. I also had two lifts installed in the backyard: one between the back patio and the pool area, and another designed to raise and lower an individual into the pool itself. I spared no effort or expense to make the property livable for a disabled person.

The first six months after Jennings returned were the most terrifyingly uncertain of my life. The prognosis was that he would improve physically but not be able to speak. I defied that notion with the help of a marvelous speech pathologist, Vivian Sheehan, who helped actress Patricia Neal regain her speech after a stroke. I had physical therapists of every stripe coming through the house. Our Mountain Drive residence went from being Party Central to the best-run rehabilitation center on the west side of Los Angeles.

Thankfully, Jennings could still read. And it was a relief to all of us that my husband never lost his ability to think or process information or make decisions. I viewed the stroke's impact on his verbal function as especially cruel because he was a man defined by expression. But Jennings kept up with everything in politics and current events through the newspaper and television, and he responded with easily comprehended sounds and gestures to news that in some way moved him. But Jennings remained a giant receiver—keeping up with everything in politics and current events through television and responding with easily comprehended sounds and gestures to news that in some way moved him.

Long the baby of the family, Rocky became the man of the house. Our son attended all the doctor's meetings and lined up even more therapy for Jennings than I ordered. He helped his father bathe and spent many hours just talking to him and keeping him engaged. Rocky took Jennings in his wheelchair to many local sporting events, including the Los Angeles

George Segal with Jennings, celebrating my husband's seventieth birthday at our home in Beverly Hills in 1985. George starred in Jennings's productions *Roller-coaster* (1977) and *Stick* (1985).

Clint Eastwood, who remained one of our most steadfast friends and visitors following Jennings's stroke, attended my husband's birthday party with then-partner and frequent film co-star Sondra Locke.

Dodgers baseball games, and often cajoled people into exchanging seats to make these experiences more comfortable for his dad. Rocky's old school chums were constant visitors and understood the importance of keeping the atmosphere upbeat; they even had a sweatshirt made for Jennings that said, "OUR CHAMP: From the Class of '77."

I taught Jennings to write with his left hand so he could sign checks. (The side of his brain governing his ability to work with numbers was unharmed.) And we got him to swim in the pool every day with the aid of floats affixed to his paralyzed right arm and leg. Jennings still had enormous, bull-like strength—he would swim for an hour with his left arm and left leg only. He didn't want to get out of the pool.

Clearly, Jennings thought he was going to get back up to speed, or he wouldn't have worked so hard. Finally, I decided that he was well enough to walk down the whole flight of stairs in the front hall—holding on to both the railing and to me.

Many of our friends remained steadfast and supportive as the months wore on, while others—evidently disturbed to the point of discomfort by my husband's condition—simply stopped calling. I was too focused on holding my family together to

Grammy-winning composer Lalo Schifrin, close friends, John and Maggy Martino, and I fete my husband's seventieth year. Lalo scored Jennings's productions *Coogan's Bluff* (1969), *The Beguiled* (1971), *Nunzio* (1978), and many others.

waste a second or an ounce of energy fretting over the latter. Clint Eastwood, Steven Spielberg, Robert Wagner, and Billy Wilder were among our closest friends who continued to visit regularly, and Lalo and Donna Schifrin were always there for us. Robert brought Jennings silk ascot ties, and Clint provided a holistic doctor to monitor my husband's overall health.

In 1986, after she herself had suffered a pair of strokes, Ava Gardner contacted me to recommend a specialist she had found helpful. Reconnecting with Ava conversationally filled me with the actual sense of ease I was routinely just pretending to convey. "And by the way, honey," she slurred jokingly, "if you hear of a job or anyone who's looking for an over-the-hill Southern broad with a corrected drawl, a useless arm, a dragging leg, and a lip droop, tell them to give me call."

Ava died from pneumonia not long after that. But her ability to stay good-humored through her last days was inspirational. It redoubled my determination to maintain my husband's quality of life as long as I humanly could.

As Jennings made relative progress in recovery during his early post-stroke years, I gradually resumed a modest social

Director Billy Wilder, who directed the Jack Lemmon-Walter Matthau comedy *The Front Page* (1974) for Jennings, was one of several high-caliber filmmakers my husband attracted to Universal Studios. He was a very bright, incredibly funny friend.

MARCH 27, 1995 $2.95

THE PLAYERS

How the men who gave you *Jurassic Park*, *The Lion King* and Nirvana are creating a media colossus overnight
PLUS: How to win an Oscar

To Jennings, Thanks for helping to get me here. All my love, Steven

From top: Steven Spielberg, David Geffen and Jeffrey Katzenberg of DreamWorks

GRACE NOTE FROM A WUNDERKIND

Steven Spielberg always treated the Jennings Lang clan like family. This very powerful yet very kind and loyal individual remained appreciative of my husband and the opportunities Jennings extended to him at Universal Studios early in his career. And Jennings was so proud of Steven and his accomplishments.

All of the world knows the Spielberg film canon, and everyone has their favorites. For me, the way Steven has conducted his life, raised his children, expressed his philanthropy, and realized himself as a cinematic artist crystallized with his masterpiece *Schindler's List* (1993). The film represented his emergence into adulthood—the evolution of a kid we knew who did nice things, who loved fantasy and happy endings, and who finally arrived as an important force not just onscreen, but in his community and in culture.

When Steven formed DreamWorks SKG studios along with entertainment industry moguls Jeffrey Katzenberg and David Geffen in late 1994, he signed the *Time* magazine cover that recorded this historic moment in his life and career, framed it, and presented it to Jennings personally. The accompanying message: "To Jennings, Thanks for helping to get me here. All my love, Steven."

I know my husband, who was ill at the time, treasured that moment—and it surely deepened his sense of peace and satisfaction during his final days.

I will always respect Steven Spielberg for this generous gesture, for the love he has consistently shown my family, and for the wonderful human being he is.

At the urging of family, I returned to live performing at a club called Nucleus Nuance in Los Angeles in 1987. It was just plain great to be back.

schedule at home. We reinstated our Saturday night movie event, and once again my husband was "hosting" dinner parties at the head of the table. Chatter and laughter returned to our environs, and the positive energy flow made such a difference in Jennings's day-to-day demeanor that we also occasionally dined out at some of our old haunts, like Chasen's and Spago. His mood exuded improving health.

Once Jennings achieved a level of steady subsistence in his recovery, Rocky—my biggest helper and morale booster—insisted that I practice my singing and consider some limited public performances. "You should do *something* besides run this hospital camp," he cracked.

My older son Mike, who had gotten married, had a son, and become a truly great musician both in live performance and in scoring for film and television, linked me with a young accompanist, Michael Asher, who arrived at my door not knowing what to expect. I greeted him in a tennis warm-up suit and introduced him to a man in a wheelchair. Then, we ran through some songs.

In early 1987, my dear friend Steve Gethers, a talented TV writer and director (*A Circle of Children*, *Jacqueline Bouvier Kennedy*), convinced the owner of an L.A. nightclub called Nucleus Nuance to come to my house and hear me sing. The proprietor was delighted by my performance and gave me two club dates.

With that, I ended thirty years of retirement as a vocalist—opening at the club with a one-hour set. Rocky introduced me. It was a total love-in, as the crowd consisted mostly of family and friends, and Jennings was right in front in his wheelchair. I was really nervous, but my old professionalism kicked in.

Closing the show with "Make Someone Happy," I stepped down from the stage, took my husband's good hand, and sang directly to him. There wasn't a dry eye in the house.

Jennings, with me and actors Marjoe Gortner and Charlton Heston, was like an excited kid at the 1988 debut of *Earthquake: The Big One* on the Universal Studios Hollywood Studio Tour. The elaborate backlot attraction, which simulated an 8.3 Richter scale temblor, was inspired by my husband's hit 1974 film *Earthquake*.

Following Nucleus Nuance, I played five dates at the Vine Street Bar & Grill, a hot jazz club in town, and then the Cinegrill at the Hollywood Roosevelt Hotel. I kicked around some songs with my old friend Mel Tormé—we were fans of each other's work going back to my early twenties in New York—and he helped assemble a terrific arrangement for my appearance at the Cinegrill.

Next, I took my act east and appeared at Danny's Skylight Room in midtown Manhattan, where I received terrific reviews. The thrill of performing again was personally gratifying, but the best reward was seeing Jennings sitting ringside with a huge grin— so proud and happy—and showing the rest of my family that courage under fire pays off.

Even in his challenged physical state, my husband's lust for travel and new experiences never abated. It was an enormous amount of work for me—particularly when dealing with air travel. But with research and careful pre-planning, I became a first-rate expert on flying with a stroke patient. I checked the wheelchair in the hold, removed the leg pieces, stowed them under my seat, and alerted everyone except the Pope on how everything should be handled. When there was a jet bridge to the plane door, we were in great shape. When there wasn't, I needed extra muscle to hoist Jennings up and down the stairs. The airline personnel were never less than understanding and helpful.

In 1989, we traveled to Egypt for the first time. We brought our live-in nurse along with us, and I had arranged for an air-conditioned van with a hydraulic wheelchair lift for sightseeing. When we got there, there was a no-frills van with no air and no lift. Jennings, with two big guys on both sides holding him steady, was a great sport as the vehicle rattled and rocked over the rutted desert roads. For both of us, the happiness that registered on his face

Everything in recording had gone digital by 1990, but I found my old promotional groove for this publicity pose.

236

Monica Lewis

Why did I choose you?

I created this spousal tribute album to Jennings in 1997, a year after his passing. Its eighteen songs trace the history our four-decade love affair through lyrics.

Monica Lewis
Why did I choose you?

EQUINOX

EQCD 7003

upon seeing the Great Sphinx of Giza and the rest of the country's historic wonders was a joy to behold and was worth the lack of comfort.

I was relieved when we departed Cairo for Israel, where—due to the large numbers of war injuries suffered by Israeli soldiers and civilians—there are more accommodations for the disabled. Our old friend Teddy Kollek, then the mayor of Jerusalem, had done a phenomenal job cleaning up, modernizing, and restoring the beauty of the city; from the limestone to the nighttime lighting, it was like all the brilliance of the technicians at Universal Studios and Disneyland rolled into one.

Teddy arranged for a helicopter to carry Jennings over the Judean Desert and the Dead Sea to the top of Masada—a plateau holding ancient fortifications and palaces. There, an army transport took us for a flight over the Golan Heights. Teddy added a climactic flourish to our visit by conducting a day of tribute to Jennings and his movies at the Israeli Cinematheque in Jerusalem.

It made me feel great that my husband was living and loving every moment of his life.

Jennings showed no signs of flagging energy for eleven years after his stroke. But by the start of 1995, fatigue became evident. He was sleeping longer and more often. When my husband indicated in his limited speech that he no longer wanted to go to Dodger Stadium to watch the games—his favorite activity in the world—I knew something was happening. Others noticed, too, and increased the frequency of their visits to raise his spirits.

I began to fear the worst.

Jennings always loved Palm Springs. We talked about it every year and dreamed that someday we would get a house there. After considerable research and doctor consultations, I told my husband about a rehab center near Palm Springs that cared for professional athletes and asked him if he wanted to check it out. With a huge smile, he said, "Yes!"

We drove out to the desert and toured the facility. It had a fully equipped weight room, beautiful sunny terraces, hot tubs, and a gorgeous dining room. The staff was young, attentive, and extremely professional. I had butterflies in my stomach, but Jennings loved it.

Deep down, I believe my husband had reached a point where he just wanted to be left alone. He was seventy-nine years old, and although he and the rest of us tried to spin this move as another shot at improvement, physically, he was beginning to quit.

After we relocated Jennings to the facility, I commuted between Los Angeles and the Coachella Valley and spent four days a week with him. It helped immensely that my brother Marlo and his wife Mina Bess had retired to nearby Rancho Mirage; I was able to stay with them, and they often joined us for meals and outings.

Clint Eastwood, Steven Spielberg, and several other high-profile friends of ours continued to make the drive to the desert to visit Jennings. It spoke volumes of their character that their respect for my husband had not diminished an iota.

The American Coaster Enthusiasts
honor
JENNINGS LANG
for producing
ROLLERCOASTER.
and inspiring the formation of ACE.
on the film's 25th anniversary.
Six Flags Magic Mountain
Valencia, California
June 2002

In 2002, my husband's 1977 film *Roller-coaster* was honored with a twenty-fifth anniversary screening at Six Flags Magic Mountain theme park outside L.A. by a national group called the American Coaster Enthusiasts. Jennings would have loved knowing this film had achieved cult status and that a stunt he cooked up to promote its release—a roller coaster marathon—led to the formation of this 7,000-member organization. I had only a cameo in the film, but I attended the event to accept a commemorative plaque on my husband's behalf and join a panel discussion with (flanking me onstage) screenwriter William Link and veteran production designer Henry Bumstead.

Rocky was the last of my sons to marry and leave the nest. And when he did, I knew that it would not be feasible for me financially or physically to live alone in our Beverly Hills mansion. Action always worked best for me, so I swung into it. I sold the house, found a great condominium in West Hollywood, and generally downsized—selling, donating, or giving away most of our less-practical possessions. I sold the bulk of our artwork to pay for the mounting debts incurred by Jennings's care.

Three months before his eighty-first birthday, in the year of our fortieth anniversary, Jennings exhibited a decrease in his appetite and willingness to exercise, and he began losing weight. He did not seem unhappy, but he was more reflective than he had ever been. Healthwise, he was battling a chronic form of pneumonia, which increased his fatigue and caused him to want to just sit outside in the sun.

We celebrated my husband's birthday on May 28, 1996. Family and friends attended the party I threw at the rehab facility, and amid the plates of birthday cake, balloons, and general good cheer, Jennings was all smiles. I drove home to L.A. the next morning.

The night after his party, at around 8 p.m., I called Jennings. The private phone in his room had a simple button he could press to answer and speak. As was our new custom, he'd say, "How are you? I love you." And I would jabber on for a while and say "I love you" back. Nothing else really needed to be said.

Three hours later, I received a call from the nurse on duty at the rehab facility. She told me she had gone in to check on Jennings and he told her he wanted some juice. When she returned, Jennings had passed away. Just like that—peacefully.

There were no tubes or monitors or any other medical accoutrement connected to him that one might associate with a dying person.

I called Rocky, who came to me immediately. I spent the rest of the night with my son, his wife, and their two young daughters. The next day, operating almost on autopilot, I began making all the arrangements. Politely declining assistance from any of my children, I went back to Palm Springs and took care of everything myself—the clothes, the belongings, the thanks, the cremation arrangements, and all the other impossible things that need tending in a time of grief.

I was strong for Jennings for thirteen years. He was the only person outside of my own family who offered me safe haven, who was more protective of me than anyone I had known. I tried to be that for my husband through the end.

I had promised Jennings two things: that I would never let him be in pain, and we would have a good time. I kept my promises. And now, I wanted to say the final farewell by myself.

Jennings had hung on long enough to attend Rocky's wedding in our beautiful Beverly Hills backyard and welcome two granddaughters by our son—Nicole and Erica—into the world. Long accustomed to buying sports equipment for his three boys, my husband relished every second with the girls and insisted that we shop almost daily for frilly little clothes for them. They brought him so much joy, so many laughs.

There was no funeral service for Jennings; instead, we threw a big party in his memory a month after he died. It was what he wanted. So much about him was about creating fun and maintaining a sense humor that it's almost hard to imagine how he applied himself as a top executive—producing thirty-three films and participating in the creation of umpteen TV shows and dozens of other movies.

I never knew anyone more alive or courageous than Jennings Lang. For me, no party has been the same without him. I would happily give back all the Hollywood glitz, baubles, perks, and privileges we enjoyed if I could have my husband back, and healthy, again. I miss his love and laughter.

A year after my husband's passing, I made a tribute album to Jennings and our relationship called *Why Did I Choose You?* While certainly an expression of loss, it also represented continuation with tunes like "Two for the Road" and "Live for Life" in addition to the title track. I completed the recording in only three days with a very small group of musicians and technicians. There was no redubbing; I was so prepared. It was incredibly cathartic.

My West Hollywood condo, which was my base of operations for that project, was just beautiful: a penthouse in a secure building with all the amenities and a view of the Sunset Strip, where my life in L.A. began. The lovely Suzanne Pleshette and her husband Tom Poston, both veterans of *The Bob Newhart Show*, were among my celebrity neighbors. I enjoyed the space and the central location, but the nights I spent there seemed endless. Still grappling with widowhood, I was incredibly lonely.

Spending quality time with my wonderfully supportive longtime friends, Donna and Lalo Schifrin, in 2003.

I only saw Rocky and my granddaughters on Sundays, when I drove over the Hollywood Hills to their home in the San Fernando Valley. In 2001, after several years of this routine, Rocky suggested, "Mom, why don't you build yourself a small guest house in my backyard? Then you can see the girls across the pool all the time instead of across a mountain."

I jumped at the idea. I signed with a realtor, unloaded the apartment, drew up my own floor plans, and hired a contractor. My brand-new country cottage was up and running on Rocky's property within four months.

Through the frame-like panes of the windows in my bedroom, which is filled with family photos and antique dolls from my youth, I have watched my granddaughters grow up splashing in the pool, bouncing on the trampoline, and running through the grass between fruit trees laden with promise. I could not have dreamed of a more glorious burnish on my Golden Years. I know I am blessed.

I'm often asked how I have kept the music playing.

At this point in my life, I practice vocal exercises for two hours twice a week with Mike Asher, who has become a great friend as well as my musical conductor. Each session, split by a single five-minute break, is about as good a vascular exercise as jogging. It's strictly for technique and preservation—merely keeping in shape, extending the range, and making my voice more supported from the diaphragm.

£2.90 (UK)

IN TUNE
INTERNATIONAL

THE ONLY MONTHLY MAGAZINE IN THE WORLD FOR LOVERS OF THE GOLDEN AGE OF POPULAR MUSIC

MONICA LEWIS - INTERVIEW WITH OUR COVER STAR
RAY ELLINGTON - JOE DANIELS - EVELYN KNIGHT
STATESIDE NEWS - CD and BOOK REVIEWS and much more

No 164

OCTOBER 2005

Hard to believe, but...still a covergirl in 2005.

Everyone used to say I told a great story through song. The music was never a problem for me; now, at age eighty-nine, range is an issue. I no longer have my top notes—they're gone.

I still do dance exercises every week. I took a fall recently, so my lessons are pretty funny: I hang onto a chair while doing ballet moves and tap routines in place.

When not exercising, I enjoy listening to music, reading, and keeping up with current events. Sticking around this long inevitably increases one's opportunities for déjà vu. At the time of this writing, the controversy over WikiLeaks brings to mind Daniel Ellsberg and the Pentagon Papers from forty years ago. And I'm not thrilled that ominous rumblings are emanating from North Korea again after half a century.

Meanwhile, I'm pleased to hear old tunes of mine like "A Kiss to Build a Dream On" and "The Song is You" finding a new audience on Sirius XM Satellite Radio's *Siriusly Sinatra* channel. More and more old footage of my film and TV performances, and Chiquita Banana promotional work, have been unearthed by fans and posted on YouTube and Facebook as well. I owe debt of gratitude to the music clubs and historical societies, including The Society to Preserve and Encourage Radio, Drama, Variety and Comedy (SPERDVAC), who have graciously requested interviews and invited me to speak at their events in recent years.

As a veteran of television, I'm also happy to have witnessed women doing so well in that medium. We now have Katie Couric and Diane Sawyer as news anchors. And so many former film stars of mature age are doing great work on series TV. Then, of course, there is our leader, Oprah Winfrey—what a magnificent gift she has been to the world.

Socially, I remain active through occasional outings with good friends like Donna Schifrin and Maggy Martino, who is now re-married to a wonderful man named Jack Simon, and my family. My son Mike calls me daily; his wife Karen and son David are very dear to me. Rocky's daughter, Nikki Lang, is an accomplished musician, singer, and songwriter—and well on her way to big success. Nikki's sister, Erica, went to Africa during the summer of 2010 and spent several weeks building a school for the adorable children there who need so much. And Ellie, the daughter of Rocky's wife Heather, is also involved in community work for kids. All are terrific, gorgeous people.

In addition to writing and producing for film and television, Rocky was named by the American Diabetes Association "Father of the Year" in 2008 for his contributions to the understanding of the disease through his children's diabetes book, *Lara Takes Charge*, and his founding of the Joe Toucan Diabetes Project. (His "Oscar" is sitting atop my piano.) And Rocky's first novel, *The Big Nasty*, has won rave reviews.

Hanging out at home with my gorgeous granddaughters, Nikki and Erica.

My son Mike's family continues the tradition of talented Langs: his wife Karen is a respected psychologist, and their son Dave is a superb musician.

I have learned as a parent and grandparent that listening is crucial not only in music, but in life. My own parents always asked, "What was your trick with Rocky that he turned out so well?" I said, "I listened." Too many parents don't know what their kids are doing. It's the same thing Jennings said about my mother: "She'll rattle on, but you better listen, because in the middle of it will be the one thing you should have known all your life."

To all parents: *Listen*—and teach your kids to do the same. A good relationship with our children is worth everything.

244

Rocky in Mill Valley, California, in 2010 with tennis great Billie Jean King and Joe Toucan—a training tool for children with diabetes that also serves as the mascot for the nonprofit Joe Toucan Diabetes Project (www.joetoucandiabetesproject.org). Rocky created the doll, which has been embraced by certified diabetes educators, physicians, and school nurses nationwide, and is the founder and president of the organization.

I was a popular artist in my time. I sang extremely well and gave it my all. I made plenty of mistakes, too. But whatever I lacked in smarts, I made up for in heart—and a dogged drive to entertain. Not everyone can be a genius, or may want to be one, but nothing can keep us from strutting our stuff, making existence fun, and trying to be a catalyst for good.

If the key to my survival lies in seizing, and squeezing, my earthly moment, doing what I can for others keeps the song in my heart. I know that I have been a positive force in the lives of many. I've also brought people together in ways that have led to greater things. Getting credit for any of this is much less important than the satisfaction of knowing that something I did in some way *worked*.

In life as in show business, it's just as noble to be a contributor as a leader, and to be the best supporting player you can be. Give of yourself while pursuing your dreams. And you may find that the view through *your* eyes—no matter what you have seen, experienced, or endured—will be framed in gold forever.

ACKNOWLEDGMENTS

I owe much love and gratitude to…

Dean Lamanna, my close friend and co-author, who believed in me, recognized the value of my contributions, and embraced my story from the beginning. He helped me relive it all with great good humor and attention to detail, and I could not have wanted more in a committed creative partner—or a pal.

Nan Wisherd, Flint Whitlock, Debbie Zime, and Norm Dodge at Cable Publishing, for their friendship, respect for history, and passion for putting it all together.

Maggy Martino Simon, my best friend and business manager, for running the show.

Alan Eichler, my longtime champion and music history muse, who assisted with research and kept the faith.

Theresa Eastman, for her technical support.

All of my wonderful friends, songwriters, arrangers, musicians, costumers, choreographers, photographers, fellow actors, and supporting players, bridging two incredible centuries.

Alan and Marilyn Bergman, Elmore Leonard, Ginny Mancini, Rex Reed, Debbie Reynolds, Liz Smith, and Robert Wagner, for their praise and enduring friendship.

Mike Asher, my musical director, who helped me keep the music playing.

Donna and Lalo Schifrin, for sticking by my family and reaffirming their friendship when times were tough.

My niece Joan Golub and nephew Marlo Lewis, Jr., for their infinite love.

My son Mike Lang, a consummate pianist and composer with whom I have made beautiful music, and his wife Karen and son Dave.

The undying memories of my parents Jessie and Leon, my older siblings Bobbe and Marlo, my brother-in-law William Golub, and my sister-in-law Mina Bess Lewis.

And finally and most deeply, to my son Rocky Lang and his family—wife Heather and daughters Nikki, Erica, and Ellie—for their constant encouragement, and for giving my life meaning.

It has been a great run and a lot of fun. And all of you were a part of it.

Enjoying a laugh as Frank Sinatra shows my pal Elaine Vito, our in-house harpist, how it's done during my co-hosting of the hit radio program *Music that Satisfies* in 1945.

SELECTED APPEARANCES AND WORKS

Researched by Alan Eichler

RADIO PROGRAMS

1940s

Beat the Band (as summer stand-in host)
Bob Crosby and His All-Stars (produced and syndicated by the Marine Corps)
The Bob Hope Show (several appearances continuing into the 1950s)
The Buddy Clark Show
Candlelight Revue (co-hosted with Roger Dann and featuring pianist/parodist Stan Freeman)
Eyes on the Ball (hosted by sportscaster Bill Stern)
The Ford Sunday Evening Hour
Ford Theater ("Girl Crazy," with Larry Douglas, Marilyn Daye, Ted de Corsia)
The Gloom Dodgers (intro jingle singer; WHN, New York)
Hollywood's Open House (dramatic anthology series, several episodes)
Jack Bundy's Carnival
The Jack Smith Show
The Jan August Show (as co-host; sponsored by Revere Camera)
Let Yourself Go (hosted by Milton Berle)
Make Believe Ballroom (hosted by Martin Block)
Meet Me at the Copa (as stand-in host; WMGM, New York)
Milkman's Matinee (intro jingle singer; WNEW, New York)
The Monica Lewis and Frank Farrell Show (signature music and gossip series)
Monica Makes Music (signature weekly program)
Music that Satisfies (as co-host; part of *The Chesterfield Hour*)
Musical Autographs (with Guy Lombardo and His Royal Canadians)
Scout About Town (singing guest and celebrity interviewee)
Texaco Star Theater (hosted by Milton Berle)
This is Broadway
Your Hit Parade on Parade

1950s

Guest Star (public service program produced by the U.S. Treasury Department)
The Gulf Screen Guild Theater ("Easter Parade," with Judy Garland, Fred Astaire, Peter Lawford)
MGM Musical Comedy Theater of the Air ("No Leave, No Love," with Barry Sullivan, Keenan Wynn)
The Bing Crosby Show (including skits with William "Hopalong Cassidy" Boyd, Bob Hope)
Voice of the Army

At the *Music that Satisfies* microphone in 1944.

Me with the *Music that Satisfies* crew (from left): co-host Johnnie Johnston, conductor Paul Baron, and emcee Martin Block.

RECORDINGS

1940s

Victory Disc
(a.k.a. V-Disc; U.S. military distribution)
"My Heart Stood Still" / "I'm an Old Cow-hand"
   (December 1945; reissued 2010 by Sounds of Yesteryear)
"Melancholy Mood" / "Put the Blame on Mame" (August 1946)

Signature Records
"Ain't Misbehavin'" / "Embraceable You"
"But Not for Me" / "I'll See You in My Dreams"
"Day By Day" / "Stop! I Love It"
"The Christmas Song" / "White Christmas"
"For You, For Me, Forevermore" / "Au Revoir"
"Guilty" / "Exactly Like You"
"Heartaches" / "What Am I Gonna Do About You?"
"The House I Live In" / "The Whiffenpoof Song"
"The Howlin'est, Hootin'est Gal in Town" / "Lover, Come Back to Me"
"I Got the Sun in the Morning" / "Blue and Melancholy Mood"
"I Have But One Heart"
"If I Loved You" / "Always"
"I'm Gonna Be a Bad Girl" / "We Could Make Such Beautiful Music Together"
"I'm in the Mood for Love"
"In Love in Vain"
"It Had to Be You" / "How Deep is the Ocean?"
"It's So Nice to Be Nice (to Your Neighbor)"
"Makin' Whoopee" / "By the Light of the Silv'ry Moon"
"Midnight Masquerade" / "A Thousand and One Nights"
"Put the Blame on Mame" / "Should I Tell You I Love You"
"Someone to Watch Over Me"
"Speak to Me of Love" / "I'll See You Again"
"Sweet and Low" / "The Cradle Song"
"They Didn't Believe Me"
"Thrill Me" / "Made for Each Other"
"Tony Spumoni (the Ice Cream Man)" / "The Gentleman Wouldn't Say Goodnight"
"Two Sleepy People" / "Why Does It Get Late So Early?"
"Uncle Remus Said" / "A Rainy Night in Rio"
"Waitin' for the Train to Come In"
"Walkin' with My Shadow"
"Why Do I Love You?"
"Without You" / "South America, Take It Away"

Little Stories for Little People (two-record set)
Monica Sings (first big compilation album)

Decca Records

"Don't Call It Love" / "Let's Be Sweethearts Again" (with Guy Lombardo)
"If I Live to Be a Hundred" / "When the Apple Blossoms Fall" (with The Ames Brothers)
"I'll Hold You in My Heart (Till I Can Hold You in My Arms)" / "I'll Never Say I Love You"
"It's the Bluest Kind of Blues" / "The Gentleman is a Dope"
"Just Imagine" / "Lucky in Love" (with Bob Eberly)
"An Old Magnolia Tree" / "The Market Place of Old Monterey" (with Bob Eberly)
"The One Who Gets You" / "My Own, My Only, My All"
"A Tree in the Meadow" (with The Ames Brothers)
"The Tree with the Red, Red Leaves" / "Don't Hang Around" (with The Stardusters)
"True" / "Crying for Joy" (with Bob Eberly)
"When Your Hair Has Turned to Silver" / "While We Danced at the Mardi Gras (with Bob Eberly)

My singing role in MGM's musical *Everything I Have is Yours* also landed me on its soundtrack album.

1950s

MGM Records

"La Bota" / "A Kiss to Build a Dream On"
"Let's Do It Again" / "Nevertheless (I'm in Love with You)"
"Lucky People" / "You Are the One"
"My Heart is Out of Town" / "Life is So Peculiar"
"My Lost Melody" / "I Only Have Eyes for You"
"Out o' Breath" / "I'm Glad I Gave It Up for You" (with Johnny Desmond)
"Plaything (to You)" / "I Never Knew I Loved You (Till I Lost You)"

Easy Come, Easy Go (album; reissued by Japanese Verve)
Everything I Have is Yours (film soundtrack album; title tune and "17,000 Telephone Poles")

Jubilee Records

Fools Rush In (album; reissued under various titles by Japanese Roulette, Fresh Sound, Equinox, others)

King Records

"I Wish You Love" / "Stay After School"

Capitol Records

"Autumn Leaves" / "Don't Say Goodbye When You Go"
"I Have One Gift" / "Don't Make Me Love You"
"I Don't Wanna Be Loved" / "Look What Followed Me Home Tonight"
"If I Give My Heart to You" / "When You're Near"

Columbia Records

"(If'n You Don't) Somebody Else Will" / "Met My Match"

Verve Records

Sing It to the Marines (album; reissued by Japanese Verve, Equinox)

World Transcription Service

(all with the Mack Stewart Quartet)

Disc 105
"Because of You"
"Chimney Corner Dream"
"I'll Never Know Why"
"Make the Man Love Me"
"Something Wonderful"
"Unless"

Disc 117
"Darling, How Could You?"
"Hanging Around without You"
"Hold Me, Hold Me, Hold Me"
"A Kiss to Build a Dream On"
"Never"
"Solitaire"

Disc 129
"Between the Devil and the Deep Blue Sea"
"I Still Get a Thrill"
"Taking a Chance on Love"

Disc 134
"Everything I Have is Yours"
"I Cried for You"
"Say It isn't So"

Disc 164
"I Only Have Eyes for You"
"Sometimes I'm Happy"
"A Touch of the Blues"

Disc 171
"June in January"
"Papa, Won't You Dance with Me?"
"*Zing*, Went the Strings of My Heart"

Disc 211
"Blue"
"I'm Just Wild About Harry"
"Take It Easy"

Disc 223
"I Could Write a Book"
"Dream Awhile"
"Honey"

Disc 229
"I'll Never Smile Again"
"Ma, He's Making Eyes at Me"
"She's Funny that Way"

Disc 237
"Fascinatin' Rhythm"
"I Know that You Know"
"Stars Fell on Alabama"

Disc 240
"Brother, Can You Spare a Dime?"
"Hands Across the Table"
"What a Difference a Day Made"

Disc 250
"I Love Paris"
"Sweethearts on Parade"
"Who Cares?"

Disc 261
"C'est Magnifique"
"Shoo Fly Pie and Apple Pan Dowdy"
"Street of Dreams"

Monica Lewis
but
beautiful

Monica (album, World Transcription Service
compilation; Candlelite; reissued 1999 by
Japanese Norma)

1970s

Never Let Me Go (album, new renditions;
produced by Mike Lang; Applause;
reissued 2004 by Equinox)

1980s

Monica Lewis Sings
(album, 1950s renditions; Japanese Verve)

1990s

Monica Lewis Sings Song Book Collection 1945-49 (album, 1940s renditions;
Fresh Sound)
Monica Lewis—The Song is You (album, reissue of *Sing It to the Marines*; Equinox)
My Favorite Things (album, new renditions; produced by Mike Lang; DRG)
Swings Jule Styne (album, new renditions; produced by Mike Lang; DRG)
Why Did I Choose You? (album, new renditions; produced by Michael Asher, Alan Eichler; Equinox)

2000s

Monica Lewis—But Beautiful (album, reissue of *Fools Rush In*; Blue Moon)
Monica Lewis Sings Songs of Love (album, 1950s renditions; Sepia)
Monica Lewis Swings (two-album set; reissue of *My Favorite Things* and *Swings Jule Styne*; Equinox)

Performing "La Bota" in
MGM's *The Strip* (1951).

TELEVISION PROGRAMS

1940s

Cavalcade of Stars
Texaco Star Theater (a.k.a. *The Milton Berle Show*)
Toast of the Town (a.k.a. *The Ed Sullivan Show*; debut
broadcast and several appearances into the 1950s)

1950s

The Alan Young Show
Appointment with Adventure ("Honeymoon in Spain,"
with Paul Newman)
Chelsea at Eight (a.k.a., *Chelsea at Nine*; Granada Television,
Great Britain)
The Danny Thomas Show (a.k.a. *Make Room for Daddy*)
Dress Blues (weekly program produced by the Marine Corps)
General Electric Theater ("The Day He Got Fired,"
with Richard Kiley)

Stepping out with Red Skelton in
MGM's *Excuse My Dust* (1951).

The George Jessel Show
The Jackie Gleason Show
Little Mother (unaired sitcom pilot, with Richard Irving)
M Squad
Masquerade Party
Monica Makes Music (signature program, five nights a week; WABC-TV, New York)
Peter Gunn
The Phil Silvers Show
The Red Buttons Show
Red Cross Fund Program (hosted by Ed Sullivan; with Bing Crosby, Judy Garland, Bob Hope; 2/27/1951)
Riverboat
Studio 57 ("Man on the Outside," with Lloyd Bridges)
Tales of Wells Fargo
Wagon Train

Meeting Victor Mature in RKO's
Affair With a Stranger (1953).

1960s

Arrest and Trial
Convoy
The Deputy
Ironside
Johnny Staccato
Kraft Suspense Theatre
  ("The Name of the Game," with Pat
  Hingle, Jack Kelly, Nancy Kovack)
Laramie
Laredo
Overland Trail
Shotgun Slade
The Tall Man
The Virginian

Looking my brassy best for *The Tall Man*, a 1960 TV Western.

1970s

Actor (musical play based on the early
  years of actor Paul Muni)
Barbary Coast
Emergency!
Good Morning Amercia
The Immigrants (miniseries)
Marcus Welby, M.D.
The Merv Griffin Show
The Mike Douglas Show
Night Gallery
Quincy
The Today Show

1980s

Falcon Crest
Remington Steele
Rituals
Santa Barbara

2000s

Jimmy Kimmel Live!

FILMS

1940s

Chiquita Banana (Miss Chiquita vocals for promotional animated shorts shown theatrically)
Make Mine Monica (Paramount, biographical short)

1950s

Affair With a Stranger
The D.I.
Excuse My Dust
Inside Straight
Everything I Have is Yours
The Strip

Being shoved from an ill-fated elevator in Universal's *Earthquake* (1974).

1970s

Airport '77
Charley Varrick
The Concorde...Airport '79
Earthquake
Nunzio
Rollercoaster

1980s

Stick
The Sting II

Getting tips on playing a thrill ride-averse tourist from director James Goldstone on the Six Flags Magic Mountain set of Universal's *Rollercoaster* (1977).

Attending the 1978 premiere of Universal's drama *Nunzio* with its producer, my husband Jennings Lang.

SPECIAL SIDEBARS FOUND IN HOLLYWOOD THROUGH MY EYES

Page 20 | **Pressing Discs for Victory**

Page 24 | Making *Music that Satisfies*

Page 27 | **Frank Sinatra**

Page 30 | **The Monica Lewis Fan Club**

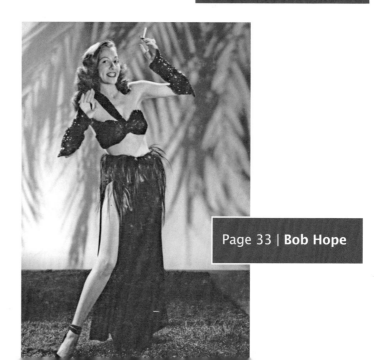

Page 33 | **Bob Hope**

Page 34 | **Generating Buzz for General Electric**

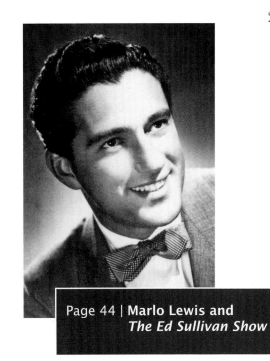

Page 44 | **Marlo Lewis and** *The Ed Sullivan Show*

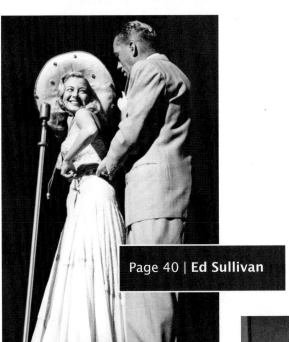

Page 40 | **Ed Sullivan**

Page 46 | **Meeting Dean (Martin) and Jerry (Lewis) at the Copa**

Page 54 | **Kirk Douglas**

260

Page 72 | **Ronald Reagan**

Page 66 | **Vic Damone**

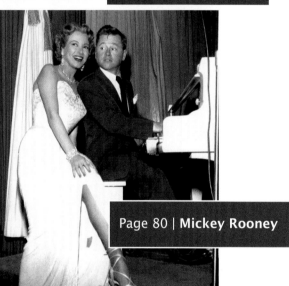

Page 80 | **Mickey Rooney**

Page 83 | *Excuse My Dust*

LOEW'S INCORPORATED
ARS · GRATIA · ARTIS

METRO-GOLDWYN-MAYER PICTURES

C U L V E R ~ C I T Y
CALIFORNIA

October 17th
1 9 5 0

Page 84 | **Growlings in
the Lion's Den
(MGM)**

Monica dear:

　　　　May this be the beginning
of many good ones for you.

　　　　Good luck and a happy picture.

　　　　　　Love

Page 93 | **Life as a
"Lana"-like**

Page 104 | **Stomping for Burlington Mills Hosiery**

Page 96 | *Everything I Have is Yours*

Page 126 | **Welcome Home, USS *Manchester***

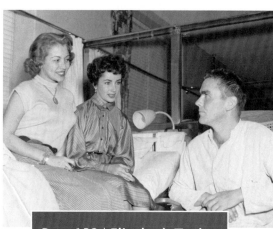

Page 132 | **Elizabeth Taylor**

Page 138 | **Danny Kaye**

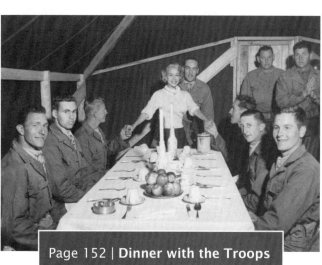

Page 152 | **Dinner with the Troops**

262

264

BACK COVER CELEBRITIES

Page 132 | **Elizabeth Taylor**

Page 110 | **Dean Martin**

Page 199 | **Clint Eastwood**

Page 214 | **Ava Gardner**

Page 120 | **Paul Newman**

Page 54 | **Kirk Douglas**

Page 72 | **Ronald Reagan**

Page 87 | **Judy Garland**

Page 197 | **Barbra Streisand**

Page 12 | **Lauren Bacall**

Page 26 | **Frank Sinatra**

Page 188 | **Edward (Ted) Kennedy**

INDEX

ABOUT THE CO-AUTHOR

Dean Lamanna is a Southern California-based journalist and editor whose work has appeared in *Ladies' Home Journal, Entertainment Weekly, Reader's Digest, Cinefantastique, New York Post, The Philadelphia Inquirer, The Fort Worth Star-Telegram, Amusement Today,* and numerous other national magazines and metropolitan newspapers, as well as on many Web sites. He has interviewed dozens of show business luminaries including Julie Andrews, Sandra Bullock, James Caan, Carol Channing, Joan Collins, Geena Davis, Peter Graves, Tippi Hedren, Charlton Heston, George Kennedy, Janet Leigh, Jack Lemmon, George Lopez, Shirley MacLaine, Carroll O'Connor, Lynn Redgrave, Arnold Schwarzenegger, Carly Simon, Will Smith, Dionne Warwick, Robert Wise, and James Woods.